MW00447245

The Elementary Teacher's Book of Lists

Titles in the Jossey-Bass Education Book of Lists Series

Jossey-Bass Teacher

Jossey-Bass Teacher provides educators with practical knowledge and tools to create a positive and lifelong impact on student learning. We offer classroom-tested and research-based teaching resources for a variety of grade levels and subject areas. Whether you are an aspiring, new, or veteran teacher, we want to help you make every teaching day your best.

From ready-to-use classroom activities to the latest teaching framework, our value-packed books provide insightful, practical, and comprehensive materials on the topics that matter most to K–12 teachers. We hope to become your trusted source for the best ideas from the most experienced and respected experts in the field.

The Elementary Teacher's Book of Lists

**Gary Robert Muschla,
Judith A. Muschla,
and Erin Muschla**

JOSSEY-BASS
A Wiley Imprint
www.josseybass.com

Copyright © 2010 by Gary Robert Muschla, Judith A. Muschla, and Erin Muschla. All rights reserved.

Published by Jossey-Bass
A Wiley Imprint
989 Market Street, San Francisco, CA 94103-1741—www.josseybass.com

No part of this publication may be reproduced, stored in a retrieval system, or transmitted in any form or by any means, electronic, mechanical, photocopying, recording, scanning, or otherwise, except as permitted under Section 107 or 108 of the 1976 United States Copyright Act, without either the prior written permission of the publisher, or authorization through payment of the appropriate per-copy fee to the Copyright Clearance Center, Inc., 222 Rosewood Drive, Danvers, MA 01923, 978-750-8400, fax 978-646-8600, or on the Web at www.copyright.com. Requests to the publisher for permission should be addressed to the Permissions Department, John Wiley & Sons, Inc., 111 River Street, Hoboken, NJ 07030, 201-748-6011, fax 201-748-6008, or online at www.wiley.com/go/permissions.

Permission is given for individual classroom teachers to reproduce the pages and illustrations for classroom use. Reproduction of these materials for an entire school system is strictly forbidden.

Readers should be aware that Internet Web sites offered as citations and/or sources for further information may have changed or disappeared between the time this was written and when it is read.

Limit of Liability/Disclaimer of Warranty: While the publisher and author have used their best efforts in preparing this book, they make no representations or warranties with respect to the accuracy or completeness of the contents of this book and specifically disclaim any implied warranties of merchantability or fitness for a particular purpose. No warranty may be created or extended by sales representatives or written sales materials. The advice and strategies contained herein may not be suitable for your situation. You should consult with a professional where appropriate. Neither the publisher nor author shall be liable for any loss of profit or any other commercial damages, including but not limited to special, incidental, consequential, or other damages.

Jossey-Bass books and products are available through most bookstores. To contact Jossey-Bass directly call our Customer Care Department within the U.S. at 800-956-7739, outside the U.S. at 317-572-3986, or fax 317-572-4002.

Jossey-Bass also publishes its books in a variety of electronic formats. Some content that appears in print may not be available in electronic books.

Library of Congress Cataloging-in-Publication Data

Muschla, Gary Robert.
    The elementary teacher's book of lists / Gary Robert Muschla,
Judith A. Muschla, Erin Muschla.
        p. cm. — (J-b ed: book of lists ; 65)
    ISBN 978-0-470-50198-6 (pbk.), 978-0-470-90501-2 (ebk.), 978-0-470-90502-9 (ebk.), 978-0-470-90503-6 (ebk.)
    1. Elementary school teaching—Handbooks, manuals, etc. 2. Education, Elementary—Curricula—Handbooks, manuals, etc. I. Muschla, Judith A. II. Muschla, Erin. III. Title.
    LB1555.M865 2010
    372.11—dc22

                                                                                                2010032372

Printed in the United States of America

FIRST EDITION
PB Printing 10 9 8 7 6 5 4 3 2 1

About This Book

Although teaching any grade or subject is demanding, teaching in the elementary grades is particularly challenging. If you are like most elementary teachers, you are responsible for teaching more than one subject, you teach students whose abilities and personalities vary widely, and you are held accountable for student performance on several standardized tests. Add to this your daily routines of effectively managing a classroom of energetic children as well as interacting with colleagues, administrators, and parents and guardians, and your day is full.

Written for classroom teachers of grades K–5, *The Elementary Teacher's Book of Lists* is designed to provide you with information on a wide range of topics that you can use to enhance your lessons, manage your classroom responsibilities, and create an environment in which learning flourishes. The book contains 273 lists, divided into six sections:

- Section 1: Reading (41 lists)
- Section 2: Writing (59 lists)
- Section 3: Mathematics (63 lists)
- Section 4: Science (50 lists)
- Section 5: Social Studies (35 lists)
- Section 6: General Reference for Elementary Teachers (25 lists)

The lists serve a variety of purposes. You may find many suitable to use as reproducibles to support your instruction, and you may use others for background information on specific topics or to generate supplementary materials for your students. Each list is written in clear, easy-to-read language, and may be used with students of various grades and abilities, enabling you to utilize the materials in a manner that best satisfies your students' needs. Every list concludes with a "Did you know?" that offers one last fact or observation about the information presented in the list. Finally, where applicable, the lists are cross-referenced so that you can refer to related lists to expand topics and provide additional information.

We trust the lists that follow will provide you with useful information, support you in planning and instruction, and help you to manage your school day more effectively. Our best wishes to you for a wonderful year.

Gary Robert Muschla
Judith A. Muschla
Erin Muschla

About the Authors

Gary Robert Muschla received his BA and MAT from Trenton State College and taught in Spotswood, New Jersey, for more than twenty-five years at the elementary school level. He is a successful author and a member of the Authors Guild and the National Writers Association.

In addition to math resources, Gary has written several resources for English and writing teachers, among them *Writing Workshop Survival Kit* (1993; second edition, 2005); *The Writing Teacher's Book of Lists* (1991; second edition, 2004); *Ready-to-Use Reading Proficiency Lessons and Activities, 10th Grade Level* (2003); *Ready-to-Use Reading Proficiency Lessons and Activities, 8th Grade Level* (2002); *Ready-to-Use Reading Proficiency Lessons and Activities, 4th Grade Level* (2002); *Reading Workshop Survival Kit* (1997); and *English Teacher's Great Books Activities Kit* (1994), all published by Jossey-Bass.

Judith A. Muschla received her BA in mathematics from Douglass College at Rutgers University and is certified to teach K–12. She taught mathematics in South River, New Jersey, for more than twenty-five years at various levels at both South River High School and South River Middle School. As a team leader at the middle school, she wrote several math curricula, coordinated interdisciplinary units, and conducted mathematics workshops for teachers and parents. She has also served as a member of the state Review Panel for New Jersey's Mathematics Core Curriculum Content Standards.

Together, Judith and Gary Muschla have coauthored several math books published by Jossey-Bass: *Hands-on Math Projects with Real-Life Applications, Grades 3–5* (2009); *The Math Teacher's Problem-a-Day, Grades 4–8* (2008); *Hands-on Math Projects with Real-Life Applications, Grades 6–12* (1996; second edition, 2006); *The Math Teacher's Book of Lists* (1995; second edition, 2005); *Math Games: 180 Reproducible Activities to Motivate, Excite, and Challenge Students, Grades 6–12* (2004); *Algebra Teacher's Activities Kit* (2003); *Math Smart! Over 220 Ready-to-Use Activities to Motivate and Challenge Students, Grades 6–12* (2002); *Geometry Teacher's Activities Kit* (2000); and *Math Starters! 5- to 10-Minute Activities to Make Kids Think, Grades 6–12* (1999).

Erin Muschla received her BS and MEd from The College of New Jersey. She is certified to teach grades K–8 with mathematics specialization in grades 5–8 and also social studies K–12. She currently teaches math at Applegarth Middle School in Monroe, New Jersey. She coauthored, with Judith and Gary Muschla, the *Math Teacher's Survival Guide, Grades 5–12* (2010), published by Jossey-Bass.

Acknowledgments

We thank Jeff Gorman, Assistant Superintendent of Monroe Township Public Schools, for his support of this project.

We also thank Chari Chanley, Principal of Applegarth Middle School in Monroe, for her encouragement.

Thanks to Dr. Brenda Leake, Professor of Elementary Education at The College of New Jersey, for her dedication to continuing education and the inspiration she imparts to her students.

We especially thank Kate Bradford, our editor at Jossey-Bass, for her guidance and suggestions from the initial concept of this book through its writing and publication.

Thanks also to Diane Turso for proofreading and making the final corrections to this book.

And finally, we thank the many colleagues who have supported and encouraged us over the years, and the many students whom we have had the pleasure of teaching.

Contents

Section 2 Writing

Contents

Section 3   Mathematics

Section 4   Science

Section 5   Social Studies

Section 6   General Reference for Elementary Teachers

The Elementary Teacher's Book of Lists

Reading

The ability to read predicts a student's future success not only in school but in life as well. Reading is the foundation for all other subjects and disciplines. It opens the doors to countless discoveries and opportunities.

List 1.1   Long Vowels and Spellings

Vowels are speech sounds that typically form the central sound of syllables. The letters *a, e, i, o, u,* and sometimes *y* represent the main vowels in the English alphabet. The following list contains common spellings of those sounds and example words.

The **long a** /ā/ has several spellings, including:

a: lady, basic, vacation

ai: main, claim, wait

ay: say, play, maybe

a-consonant-e: ate, name, space

ei: eight, neighbor, freight

ey: hey, prey, they

The **long e** /ē/ has several spellings, including:

e: we, me, she

ea: east, weak, flea

ee: see, keep, knee

e-consonant-e: these, complete, concrete

ie: field, brief, piece

i-consonant-e: police, routine, vaccine

y: memory, scary, very

The **long i** /ī/ has several spellings, including:

i: idea, title, lion

igh: might, sigh, highway

i-consonant-e: fire, five, wide

ey: eye, eyelid, eyesight

uy: buy, guy, buyer

y: try, cycle, reply

The **long o** /ō/ has several spellings, including:

o: go, hello, open

oa: coat, goal, oak

ow: owe, snow, bowl

o-consonant-e: hope, nose, spoke

The **long u** /ū/ has several spellings, including:

u: pupil, menu, human

ue: fuel, value, rescue

eau: beauty, beautiful, beautician

u-consonant-e: use, cube, confuse

 Did you know? Students who are well versed in phonics tend to be competent readers.

See List 1.2, Short Vowels and Spellings; List 1.3, Special Vowel Sounds and Spellings; List 1.4, Vowels and a Final E.

Copyright © 2010 by Gary Robert Muschla, Judith A. Muschla, and Erin Muschla

List 1.2   Short Vowels and Spellings

Unlike long vowel sounds that sound like the letters they represent, short vowel sounds are not as distinct. Most young students easily recognize the long /ā/ in *ate*, yet many have trouble recognizing the short /ĭ/ sound in *drink* as opposed to the short /ŭ/ sound in *cup*. The following list can add some clarity.

Short a /ă/: pass, at, after, that, man, stand

Short e /ĕ/: end, gem, held, help, went, kept
> *Note*: The short **e** sound may also be spelled **ea** as in *bread* and **ai** as in *said*.

Short i /ĭ/: will, miss, into, sip, big, thin

Short o /ŏ/: body, hot, rock, stop, clock, top

Short u /ŭ/: under, up, study, jump, sun, much
> *Note*: The short **u** may also be spelled **o** as in *mother*.

 Did you know? Most short vowel sounds are spelled with one letter.

See List 1.1, Long Vowels and Spellings; List 1.3, Special Vowel Sounds and Spellings; List 1.4, Vowels and a Final E.

Copyright © 2010 by Gary Robert Muschla, Judith A. Muschla, and Erin Muschla

Reading

List 1.3   Special Vowel Sounds and Spellings

When they think of vowel sounds, most students think of long vowel sounds and short vowel sounds. There are others. Depending on dialect, English has about twenty distinct vowel sounds. Some of the most common of these other vowel sounds are shown in the following list.

Vowels Affected by *R*

The /âr/ sound has several spellings, including:

ar: vary

are: spare

air: flair

The /är/ sound is often spelled **ar:** far

The /îr/ sound has several spellings, including:

ear: near

eer: cheer

er: serious

ier: pierce

The /ôr/ sound can be spelled:

ar: warm

or: force

The /ûr/ sound has several spellings, including:

er: herd

ear: search

ir: sir

ur: burst

or: world

Diphthongs

The /oi/ sound can be spelled:

oi: oil

oy: boy

The /ou/ sound can be spelled:

ou: out

ow: plow

Double O Sounds

The /o͞o/ sound can be spelled:

oo: soon

u: truth

Copyright © 2010 by Gary Robert Muschla, Judith A. Muschla, and Erin Muschla

List 1.3   continued

The /o͝o/ sound can be spelled:

    oo: good

    u: put

Broad O

The /ô/ sound has several spellings, including:

    o: long

    al: false

    au: author

    aw: saw

    oa: broad

    augh: caught

    ough: bought

Schwa

The /ə/ sound has several spellings, including:

    a: ago

    e: happen

    o: original

The /ə/ and l sound can be spelled:

    al: final

    el: marvel

    il: pencil

    le: table

    ul: awful

The /ə/ and r sound can be spelled:

    er: water

    or: motor

Did you know? *Y* can be both a vowel sound and a consonant sound. At the beginning of a word, *y* is a consonant as in *yes*, but in the middle or end of a word, *y* is a vowel as in *cycle* and *funny*.

See List 1.1, Long Vowels and Spellings; List 1.2, Short Vowels and Spellings; List 1.4, Vowels and a Final E.

Copyright © 2010 by Gary Robert Muschla, Judith A. Muschla, and Erin Muschla

List 1.4   Vowels and a Final *E*

When a word ends in *e*, the preceding vowel often has a long sound. Following are examples of words that demonstrate the Final *E* Rule.

A Words	I Words	O Words	U Words
tape	kite	cope	cube
hate	hide	robe	tube
came	prime	hope	cute
scrape	slide	rode	use
same	ripe	globe	fuse
fate	fine	code	mule
rage	shine	slope	dude

There are exceptions to the Final *E* Rule, including many words that end in *ce*, *le*, *re*, *se*, and *ve*.

CE Words	LE Words	RE Words	SE Words	VE Words
voice	apple	are	horse	give
office	single	before	house	shove
dance	circle	sure	else	love

There are other exceptions that do not fall into the above categories, some of which include *large, gone, ledge, fudge,* and *one.*

 Did you know? Over the centuries, English has absorbed thousands of words from many different languages. One result of this is phonics rules that are riddled with exceptions.

See List 1.1, Long Vowels and Spellings.

Copyright © 2010 by Gary Robert Muschla, Judith A. Muschla, and Erin Muschla

The Elementary Teacher's Book of Lists

Copyright © 2010 by Gary Robert Muschla, Judith A. Muschla, and Erin Muschla

List 1.5   Consonants and Consonant Sounds

The English consonants are *b, c, d, f, g, h, j, k, l, m, n, p, q, r, s, t, v, w, x, y,* and *z*. The letter *y* can also act as a vowel, long *e*, or long *i*. The following list provides consonant sounds and examples.

Single Consonant Sounds

b: big (*Exception*: In some words *b* is silent, as in *comb*.)

c: cat (*Exception*: In some words before *e, i,* or *y, c* is pronounced as *s*, as in *city*.)

d: dark

f: fish

g: go (*Exception*: In some words before *e, i,* or *y, g* is pronounced as *j*, as in *giraffe*.)

h: hat (*Exception*: In some words *h* is silent, as in *hour*.)

j: June

k: kind

l: leaf (*Exception*: In some words *l* is silent, as in *walk*.)

m: moon

n: new

p: paper

q: quiet (*Note*: The letter *q* is always used with *u*.)

r: red

s: sun (*Exception*: In some words *s* is pronounced as *z*, as in *nose*. In some, *s* is pronounced as *zh* as in *vision*. In others, *s* is pronounced as *sh,* as in *sure*.)

t: tea

v: very

w: water

x: box (*Exception*: At the beginning of a word, *x* is pronounced as *z*, as in *xylophone*. In others, *x* is pronounced as *gz* as in *exact*.)

y: yard (*Exception*: In some words, *y* is pronounced as long *e*, as in *city*; in others *y* is pronounced as long *i*, as in *fly*.)

z: zoo

Consonant Digraphs

ch: chin (*Exception*: In some words *ch* is pronounced as *k*, as in *character*. In a few words *ch* is pronounced *sh*, as in *chef*.)

gh: tough

ph: phone

sh: she

th: think (*Note*: The *th* in *think* is pronounced with a slight aspiration.)

Reading

th: this (*Note*: The *th* in *this* is not pronounced with an aspiration.)

wh: which

Common Silent Consonants (the silent letter is noted in parenthesis)

gh: high (gh)   lk: talk (l)

gn: gnat (g)   mb: climb (b)

kn: knife (k)   tle: whistle (t)

lf: half (l)   wr: write (w)

Consonant Blends That Start Words

bl: blend	sk: skunk	
br: bridge	sl: slow	
cl: clay	sm: smile	
cr: crop	sn: snail	
dr: dry	sp: spell	
dw: dwell	spl: splash	
fl: fly	spr: spring	
fr: free	squ: squirrel	
gl: glass	st: sting	
gr: great	str: strong	
pl: play	sw: sway	
pr: prize	thr: throw	
sc: scare	tr: train	
sch: school	tw: twin	
scr: scrape	wr: write	
shr: shrink		

Consonant Blends That End Words

ct: act	nd: sand
ft: lift	nk: think
ld: old	nt: hunt
lm: palm	pt: kept
lp: pulp	rd: word
lt: salt	rt: smart
mp: bump	sk: tusk
nce: since	sp: lisp
nch: bunch	st: lost

Copyright © 2010 by Gary Robert Muschla, Judith A. Muschla, and Erin Muschla

 Did you know? Vowels and consonants are the foundation of sounds of spoken language.

See List 1.1, Long Vowels and Spellings; List 1.2, Short Vowels and Spellings; List 1.3, Special Vowel Sounds and Spellings.

List 1.6   Common Phonograms

A *phonogram*, most often consisting of a vowel and a consonant sound, represents a word or a phoneme in speech. Many phonograms are one-syllable words; many appear in multisyllable words. Phonemes are useful in teaching reading and spelling. Some of the most common phonograms and example words follow.

ab: jab, crab, tab, slab, lab, nab

ack: back, pack, black, crack, track, sack

ag: rag, sag, wag, bag, nag, brag

ail: nail, snail, sail, mail, tail, pail

ain: main, brain, rain, pain, plain, train

ake: make, take, bake, cake, fake, rake

am: ram, clam, ham, slam, jam, swam

an: man, tan, ran, clan, fan, pan

ank: blank, thank, bank, sank, drank, yank

ap: cap, gap, map, slap, trap, clap

at: bat, flat, cat, mat, sat, rat

ay: day, ray, say, may, play, way

eat: neat, beat, seat, treat, feat, heat

ed: red, bed, fed, shed, sled, led

eed: seed, bleed, feed, weed, need, freed

ell: fell, tell, sell, dwell, bell, yell

est: rest, west, best, nest, test, jest

ew: chew, brew, grew, new, few, dew

ick: pick, kick, quick, chick, trick, sick

ide: side, tide, ride, wide, hide, pride

ight: light, tight, night, fight, sight, flight

ill: will, fill, spill, hill, still, thrill

im: grim, dim, him, brim, rim, slim

in: pin, fin, win, tin, chin, thin

ine: line, pine, nine, fine, spine, mine

ing: sing, ring, king, thing, wing, spring

ink: rink, think, sink, pink, link, drink

ip: tip, chip, ship, flip, rip, trip

ob: job, sob, rob, cob, knob, throb

ock: sock, stock, rock, flock, lock, knock

op: cop, drop, mop, flop, top, hop

ore: more, store, tore, score, sore, shore

ot: not, tot, pot, plot, hot, got

out: pout, scout, shout, sprout, flout, spout

ow: cow, now, plow, how, chow, vow

ow: low, grow, slow, show, flow, snow

uck: luck, duck, buck, truck, stuck, struck

ug: hug, bug, rug, shrug, tug, dug, plug

um: hum, glum, drum, plum, gum, sum

unk: bunk, junk, sunk, dunk, trunk, skunk

y: by, shy, dry, my, sky, fly

 Did you know? Phonograms are also known as "rimes."

Copyright © 2010 by Gary Robert Muschla, Judith A. Muschla, and Erin Muschla

List 1.7   Common Prefixes

A *prefix* is a word part added to the beginning of a base word or root. Prefixes change the meanings of the words to which they are added. Understanding the meanings of prefixes can help students decipher the meaning of new words. The following list contains prefixes that elementary students will encounter in reading, spelling, and writing.

Prefix	Meaning	Example Words
a-	on	atop, aboard, afire
after-	following	afternoon, aftershock, afterthought
auto-	self	autograph, autobiography, automobile
be-	make	befriend, becalm, bewitch
bi-	two, double	bicycle, biweekly, bimonthly
co-	with, together	coworker, coauthor, coexist
de-	not, opposite	deactivate, deform, defuse
dis-	not, opposite	dislike, dishonest, disobey
il-	not, without	illogical, illegal, illegible
im-	not, without	impossible, impatient, imperfect
in-	not, without	incomplete, invisible, inactive
inter-	among, between	international, interstellar, intersection
ir-	not, without	irresponsible, irregular, irreplaceable
micro-	short, small	microscope, microphone, microwave
mid-	middle	midnight, midway, midyear
mis-	not, wrong	misspell, mistreat, misbehave
multi-	many, much	multicolored, multivitamin, multimedia
non-	not	nonsense, nonstop, nonfat
over-	too much	overactive, overdo, overrun
post-	after	postscript, postwar, postdate
pre-	before	pretest, prehistoric, precaution
re-	again	review, rewrite, recheck
semi-	half	semicircle, semiconscious, semifinal
sub-	under, below	subzero, submarine, subgroup
super-	above, beyond	superpower, supernatural, superman
tele-	distant	telephone, telescope, television
trans-	across	transatlantic, transcribe, transplant
tri-	three	tricycle, triangle, trilateral
un-	not, opposite	unsafe, unpleasant, unpack
under-	below, less than	underground, underage, underarm

Did you know? The word *prefix* can be broken down into *pre* meaning "before" and *fix* meaning "attach or fasten."

See List 1.8, Common Suffixes.

Copyright © 2010 by Gary Robert Muschla, Judith A. Muschla, and Erin Muschla

List 1.8   Common Suffixes

A *suffix* is a word part added to the end of a word or root. Suffixes change the meaning of the word to which they are added. They may also change a word's part of speech, for example, *teach* (verb) and *teacher* (noun). Following are suffixes students in elementary grades will encounter often.

Suffix	Meaning	Example Words
-able	able to, is	likable, doable, knowledgeable
-ant	one who	servant, immigrant, assistant
-ation	state or quality of	desperation, starvation, realization
-dom	state or quality of	freedom, wisdom, boredom
-er	more	softer, harder, hotter
-er	one who	teacher, banker, baker
-ess	who (female)	actress, princess, waitress
-est	most	smartest, softest, warmest
-ful	full of	thoughtful, fearful, wonderful
-ic	of, like	heroic, allergic, historic
-ion	state or quality of	tension, attention, suspicion
-ious	state or quality of	ambitious, delicious, religious
-ish	relating to	childish, bookish, religious
-ist	one who does	artist, lobbyist, biologist
-ity	state or quality of	reality, civility, necessity
-ive	inclined to	active, negative, passive
-ize	to cause or become	specialize, prioritize, hypnotize
-less	without, does not	careless, useless, thoughtless
-like	resembling	childlike, lifelike, homelike
-ly	resembling	motherly, fatherly, scholarly
-ment	act of, state of	enjoyment, agreement, development
-ness	quality, state of	kindness, sadness, happiness
-or	one who	inventor, creator, actor
-ous	full of	joyous, dangerous, nervous
-ship	art or skill	penmanship, leadership, friendship
-some	inclined to	tiresome, wholesome, awesome
-ty	state or quality of	honesty, loyalty, amnesty
-ward	direction	backward, forward, onward
-wise	manner, direction	clockwise, counterclockwise, lengthwise
-y	full of, like	sunny, rainy, funny

 Did you know? Many English suffixes have their origins in Latin, Greek, and French.

See List 1.7, Common Prefixes.

Copyright © 2010 by Gary Robert Muschla, Judith A. Muschla, and Erin Muschla

Synonyms are words that are similar in meaning. A solid understanding of synonyms broadens a student's overall vocabulary. Although dictionaries often use synonyms in definitions, a thesaurus is the best place to find synonyms for words.

about—nearly

accept—approve

ache—pain

act—do

add—total

advise—suggest

after—following

aid—help

aim—goal

all—every

allow—permit

amazing—astounding

ancient—old

anger—rage

annoy—bother

answer—reply

anxiety—worry

ask—question

assist—help

astonish—surprise

attempt—try

automaton—robot

automobile—car

awkward—clumsy

back—rear

bad—naughty

baffle—puzzle

barrier—obstacle

basic—fundamental

beauty—loveliness

begin—start

bellow—roar

below—under

betray—reveal

bewilder—confuse

big—large

border—edge

bored—indifferent

boss—supervisor

boy—lad

brave—courageous

bright—brilliant

brook—creek

buddy—friend

build—construct

call—summon

calm—serene

capable—competent

capture—seize

careful—cautious

carry—lug

catastrophe—disaster

cease—stop

certain—sure

change—vary

cheap—inexpensive

cheat—deceive

child—kid

children—kids

clever—tricky

close—shut

comfort—ease

comical—funny

conceal—hide

concept—idea

conscientious—responsible

Copyright © 2010 by Gary Robert Muschla, Judith A. Muschla, and Erin Muschla

Copyright © 2010 by Gary Robert Muschla, Judith A. Muschla, and Erin Muschla

List 1.9   continued

consider — think

consume — eat

correct — right

country — nation

couple — pair

cure — heal

danger — peril

decoration — ornament

decrease — lessen

delicious — tasty

desire — want

different — unlike

difficult — hard

dim — dull

discover — find

display — show

distrust — suspicion

divide — separate

dumb — stupid

during — while

dwell — live

easy — simple

elastic — flexible

empty — vacant

end — finish

energy — power

enjoy — like

enormous — gigantic

enough — sufficient

error — mistake

essential — vital

examine — study

faith — trust

fight — battle

fix — repair

food — nourishment

foolish — unwise

forgive — pardon

form — shape

fortune — wealth

freedom — liberty

frequently — often

frighten — terrify

fury — rage

gentle — kind

gift — present

give — grant

glad — happy

glen — valley

globe — world

go — leave

goal — objective

good — suitable

grand — great

grasp — hold

grateful — thankful

grow — mature

happen — occur

hardy — tough

have — possess

hear — listen

hold — keep

huge — vast

hurry — rush

ill — sick

image — picture

immediately — now

impolite — rude

incline — slant

incredible — unbelievable

injure — wound

instruct — teach

job — occupation

join — unite

labor — work

late — tardy

learn — understand

lengthy — long

little — small

look — see

main — primary

many — numerous

may — might

melt — thaw

method — way

neat — orderly

need — require

new — recent

noise — uproar

nothing — zero

ocean — sea

ominous — threatening

one — single

open — unlock

ordinary — usual

part — portion

peak — summit

place — spot

plain — simple

power — strength

precious — valuable

provide — supply

pull — yank

push — shove

put — set

quick — fast

rash — reckless

record — write

refuse — reject

relate — tell

renew — restore

say — state

seize — take

slender — thin

story — tale

strong — sturdy

swear — vow

taut — tense

term — word

tired — weary

unclear — vague

uncommon — unusual

value — worth

Copyright © 2010 by Gary Robert Muschla, Judith A. Muschla, and Erin Muschla

 Did you know? Because synonyms are words with similar though not necessarily the same precise meanings, students should not use a thesaurus in place of a dictionary.

See List 1.10, Antonyms.

List 1.10   Antonyms

Antonyms are words that are opposite or nearly opposite in meaning. As with synonyms, a sound understanding of antonyms expands a student's vocabulary, aiding significantly in reading and writing competence.

above—below
add—subtract
adult—child
afraid—confident
after—before
alive—dead
all—none
allow—prohibit
always—never
ancient—modern
answer—question
apart—together
appear—vanish
approve—ban
arrive—leave
asleep—awake
attack—defend
away—toward
back—front
backward—forward
bad—good
barbaric—civilized
bashful—bold
beautiful—ugly
begin—end
big—little
bitter—sweet
blunt—sharp
bored—interested
bottom—top
boy—girl

break—fix
breezy—calm
bright—dull
brutal—gentle
busy—idle
careless—cautious
cause—effect
cheap—expensive
cheerful—gloomy
chilly—warm
clean—dirty
clear—obscure
close—open
cold—hot
come—go
common—exceptional
complex—simple
continue—pause
courageous—cowardly
create—destroy
crooked—straight
crowded—empty
cruel—kind
cry—laugh
curious—indifferent
dangerous—safe
dark—light
day—night
death—life
decrease—increase
deep—shallow

Copyright © 2010 by Gary Robert Muschla, Judith A. Muschla, and Erin Muschla

defeat — victory

different — same

difficult — easy

doubt — trust

down — up

downcast — happy

dry — wet

empty — full

end — start

enemy — friend

even — odd

everything — nothing

evil — good

fail — pass

false — true

fancy — plain

far — near

fast — slow

father — mother

few — many

fiction — fact

find — lose

first — last

forbid — permit

forget — remember

freeze — melt

frown — smile

generous — stingy

give — take

great — unimportant

group — individual

guilty — innocent

happy — sad

hard — soft

healthy — sick

help — hurt

hero — villain

hide — reveal

high — low

horizontal — vertical

huge — tiny

humble — proud

ignorance — knowledge

in — out

inferior — superior

inside — outside

joy — sadness

kind — mean

large — small

left — right

less — more

lie — truth

long — short

loose — tight

lose — win

loss — profit

love — hate

man — woman

move — stay

multiply — divide

nasty — nice

negative — positive

north — south

nothing — something

now — then

often — seldom

old — young

over — under

part — whole

permit — refuse

play — work

polite — rude

Copyright © 2010 by Gary Robert Muschla, Judith A. Muschla, and Erin Muschla

List 1.10   continued

poor — wealthy

powerful — weak

private — public

problem — solution

pull — push

quick — slow

quit — start

receive — send

right — wrong

rough — smooth

separate — unite

short — tall

sit — stand

sour — sweet

start — stop

strength — weakness

strong — weak

sunrise — sunset

thick — thin

thrifty — wasteful

uselessness — worth

with — without

 Did you know? Writers can sometimes find the exact word they need by first thinking of its antonyms.

See List 1.9, Synonyms.

Copyright © 2010 by Gary Robert Muschla, Judith A. Muschla, and Erin Muschla

List 1.11   Homographs

Homographs are words that are spelled alike but have different meanings and origins. Although many homographs are pronounced the same, some have different pronunciations. The following list offers a variety of homographs your students are likely to use in reading, spelling, and writing.

angle: figure formed when two lines meet at a point

angle: to fish with line and hook

ball: formal dance

ball: round object

band: a group of musicians

band: a strip of material used for binding

bank: long mound (usually of dirt or snow)

bank: edge of a pond, stream, river, or lake

bank: place where financial business is conducted

bark: outer covering of a tree

bark: sound of a dog

bat: a club

bat: a flying mammal

batter: to hit again and again

batter: mixture used in baking

batter: a baseball player

bear: a large animal

bear: to carry or support

bill: statement of money due

bill: beak of a bird

blow: a powerful hit

blow: to expel a current of air

bowl: a rounded dish

bowl: to play the game of bowling

box: a container

box: to fight with fists

buck: a dollar

buck: a male deer

can: a metal container

can: to be able to

clip: to cut

clip: to fasten or attach

close (klōs): nearby

close (klōz): to shut

content (kŏn′ tĕnt): that which is contained

content (kən tĕnt′): pleased, satisfied

count: a title of nobility

count: to list or call numbers in order

date: sweet fruit of an Eastern palm tree

date: the time of an event

desert (dĕz′ ərt): a dry wasteland

desert (dĭ zûrt′): to abandon

Copyright © 2010 by Gary Robert Muschla, Judith A. Muschla, and Erin Muschla

The Elementary Teacher's Book of Lists

dove (dŭv): a bird of the pigeon family

dove (dōv): past tense of *dive*

down: a place below another

down: soft feathers of a young bird

duck: a water bird with webbed feet and broad beak

duck: to dip or dodge quickly

fair: beautiful

fair: just

fair: a bazaar

fan: a devoted enthusiast

fan: machine used to put air into motion

fast: a high rate of speed

fast: to go without food

fine: of high quality

fine: money paid for breaking the law

firm: hard

firm: a company or business

flat: a small apartment

flat: level

fleet: a group of ships

fleet: fast, quick

fly: a small bug

fly: to move through the air

fresh: disrespectful behavior

fresh: new

grave: a place for burial

grave: of great importance

hatch: emergence of young from an egg

hatch: opening in the deck of a ship

hide: the skin of an animal

hide: to place or keep out of sight

husky: big and powerful

husky: a sled dog

invalid (ĭn′ vəl ĭd): a disabled, bedridden person

invalid (ĭn văl′ ĭd): not acceptable

kind: a type of group

kind: caring, friendly

lead (lēd): to go first or show the way

lead (lĕd): a soft, heavy metal

lean: standing in a slanted manner

lean: slim

left: direction

left: past tense of *leave*

light: not heavy

light: not dark

like: similar to

like: to enjoy or be pleased with

long: a great distance or measure

long: to wish or hope for

mean: to intend

mean: to be unkind

mean: an average of a set of numbers

Copyright © 2010 by Gary Robert Muschla, Judith A. Muschla, and Erin Muschla

minute (mī no͞ot′): very small

minute (mĭn′ ĭt): sixty seconds

miss: an unmarried woman

miss: fail to hit or strike

nag: an old horse

nag: to scold

object (əb jĕkt′): to protest

object (ŏb′ jĭkt): a thing

pen: a writing tool

pen: an enclosed area

pitcher: a baseball player

pitcher: a container for pouring
   liquid

pole: long piece of wood

pole: one of the Earth's axis

present (prĕz′ ənt): now, currently

present (prĕz′ ənt): a gift

present (prĭ zĕnt′): to introduce
   formally

prune: a fruit

prune: trim

pupil: student

pupil: part of the eye

rare: meat cooked for a short time

rare: uncommon

rash: a sore or eruption on the skin

rash: hasty

rest: sleep or relaxation

rest: the part that is left

row: a line

row: the use of oars for moving
   a boat

saw: a hand tool used for cutting

saw: past tense of the verb *see*

school: a group of fish

school: an institution for learning

sock: a short stocking

sock: to strike or hit

soil: dirt or ground

soil: to make dirty

spell: a period of time

spell: an enchantment

spell: to say or write the letters of
   a word

stick: thin piece of wood

stick: to pierce

story: a work of fiction

story: the floor of a building

swallow: to take in through
   the mouth

swallow: a small bird

tear (târ): to pull or rip apart

tear (tîr): a drop of liquid from
   the eye

tick: sound of a clock

tick: a small insect

tire: rubber placed around a wheel

tire: to become weary

Copyright © 2010 by Gary Robert Muschla, Judith A. Muschla, and Erin Muschla

Copyright © 2010 by Gary Robert Muschla, Judith A. Muschla, and Erin Muschla

List 1.11   **continued**

top: highest point

top: a spinning toy

wake: to rouse from sleep

wake: waves left by a ship passing
through water

wind (wĭnd): moving air

wind (wīnd): to turn around

yard: a length of three feet

yard: area surrounding a building

 Did you know? Homographs that have different pronunciations are also known as *heteronyms*. A good example is *object*, meaning "a thing," and *object*, meaning "to protest."

See List 1.12, Homophones.

Reading

List 1.12   Homophones

Homophones are words that have the same sound but different meanings, spellings, and origins. Because they sound the same, homophones are easy to use incorrectly. Just think of how many times you have seen *there*, *their*, and *they're* used in place of each other in your students' writing. Familiarizing your students with the words in the following list will help them to avoid mistakes with homophones.

ad: short for *advertisement*

add: to total

air: the atmosphere

heir: a successor to property or rank

allowed: permitted

aloud: speaking with a loud voice

ant: a small insect

aunt: one's father's or mother's sister

ate: past tense of *eat*

eight: the number after seven

ball: a round object

bawl: to cry

band: a musical group

banned: not allowed

base: the bottom part

bass: a very low voice

be: to exist

bee: a flying insect

blew: past tense of *blow*

blue: color of a clear daytime sky

bough: a tree limb

bow: the forward part of a ship

brake: device for stopping a vehicle

break: to crack

buy: to purchase

by: near

bye: short for *good-bye*

cell: basic unit of life

sell: to trade for money

cent: a hundredth part of a dollar

scent: a smell

sent: past tense of *send*

cereal: food made from grains

serial: story presented in parts

cite: to present as proof

sight: the ability to perceive with eyes

site: a place

close: shut

clothes: clothing

coarse: rough

course: the way traveled

creak: a grating sound

creek: a small stream

dear: highly valued

deer: an animal

Copyright © 2010 by Gary Robert Muschla, Judith A. Muschla, and Erin Muschla

die: to stop living

dye: substance used for coloring materials

fair: a bazaar

fare: fee for transportation

feat: a great deed

feet: part of body used for walking

fir: a type of evergreen tree

fur: hair covering the body of animals

flea: a tiny insect

flee: to run

flew: past tense of *fly*

flu: short form of *influenza*

flue: a duct in a chimney

flour: milled grain

flower: bloom

for: preposition

four: the number after three

hair: filament growing from skin of an animal

hare: a rabbit

heal: to bring back to health

heel: back part of the bottom of the foot

he'll: contraction for *he will*

hear: to perceive with the ear

here: in this place

heard: past tense of *hear*

herd: a group of animals

hi: a greeting

high: far up

hoarse: husky sounding

horse: a large animal

hole: an opening

whole: entire, complete

hour: sixty minutes

our: belonging to us

in: preposition

inn: a place of food and lodging

knew: past tense of *know*

new: not existing before now

knight: a warrior of feudal times

night: time between daylight and sunset

knot: an intertwining of rope

not: in no way

know: to be aware of

no: a negative answer or reply

lead: a soft, heavy metal

led: past tense of *lead*

loan: to lend, or something that is lent

lone: single

made: past tense of *make*

maid: a female servant

meat: food from an animal

meet: to come together

might: power

mite: a small insect

Copyright © 2010 by Gary Robert Muschla, Judith A. Muschla, and Erin Muschla

oar: a paddle

or: a conjunction

ore: a mineral deposit

one: the lowest cardinal number

won: past tense of *win*

pain: distress

pane: glass in a window

pair: two of a kind

pear: a fruit

peace: calmness

piece: a part

plain: simple

plane: flying vehicle

pray: to worship

prey: an animal hunted and killed for food

principal: most important in rank

principle: fundamental law or truth

rain: moisture falling from clouds

reign: period of rule of a king or queen

rein: leather strap used to control a horse

read: past tense of *read*

red: color of blood

right: proper, correct

write: to set down in words

road: a path

rode: past tense of *ride*

rowed: past tense of *row*

root: part of a plant that grows underground

route: course or way

rose: a flowering bush

rows: lines

sail: a sheet of canvas used to catch wind

sale: exchange of goods or services for money

sea: the ocean, or part of an ocean

see: to perceive with the eyes

sew: to mend

so: in such manner

sow: to plant

soar: to fly high

sore: painful

some: a part of

sum: total

son: a male child

sun: the star at the center of our solar system

steal: to rob

steel: strong metal

tail: a flexible extension of an animal's spine

tale: a story

their: possessive pronoun meaning *of them*

there: in a particular place

they're: contraction for *they are*

through: a preposition

threw: past tense of *throw*

Copyright © 2010 by Gary Robert Muschla, Judith A. Muschla, and Erin Muschla

to: in a direction toward
too: also
two: the sum of one and one

wait: to stay
weight: the amount of heaviness

way: path
weigh: to measure how heavy

weak: feeble
week: a period of seven days

weather: the state of the atmosphere
whether: if

who's: contraction for *who is*
whose: possessive form of *who*

wood: the hard material of a tree
would: past tense of *will*

your: possessive pronoun meaning *of you*
you're: contraction for *you are*

 Did you know? Homonyms are words that have the same sound and often the same spelling but different meanings.

See List 1.11, Homographs.

Copyright © 2010 by Gary Robert Muschla, Judith A. Muschla, and Erin Muschla

List 1.13   Ways to Build Vocabulary

A broad vocabulary is essential for reading comprehension, clear speaking, and interesting writing. To help your students expand their vocabularies, encourage them to do the following.

1. Read as much as possible. Read a variety of selections: novels, short stories, nonfiction books in a variety of subjects, and magazines.

2. Use context clues to decipher the meanings of new words. The way unfamiliar words are used in sentences often enables students to discover their meanings.

3. Use a dictionary to find the meanings of new words. Write down new words and their meanings in a notebook.

4. Be aware that many words have multiple meanings. Learn the different meanings of words.

5. Learn the meanings of prefixes and suffixes and use them in understanding words.

6. Make an effort to use new words in speaking and writing. Only when they use new words will students be able to incorporate those words into their vocabularies.

7. Learn the meanings of words in spelling lists.

8. When learning a new word, think of synonyms and antonyms for it. Associating the word with other words will help students remember it.

9. Break compound words apart to make their meaning clear.

10. Use a thesaurus to vary word usage in writing.

11. Learn new words in every subject, not just reading.

12. Learn new words by doing crossword puzzles and other word games.

 Did you know? English is one of the most widely spoken languages on Earth. One out of every six people around the world is able to speak English.

See List 1.14, Important Words for Primary Students to Know; List 1.15, Important Words for Elementary Students to Know; List 1.16, Compound Words; List 1.17, Idioms.

Copyright © 2010 by Gary Robert Muschla, Judith A. Muschla, and Erin Muschla

List 1.14   Important Words for Primary Students to Know

Some words in English are used much more frequently than others, especially in the primary grades. Young students who understand these words have a head start in learning how to read.

a	crayon	her	one
about	cup	hill	or
am	day	him	orange
an	desk	his	other
and	did	horse	out
are	dirt	how	pants
arm	do	I	part
as	doctor	if	pear
at	dog	in	pen
baby	doll	into	pencil
ball	down	is	people
banana	dress	it	pig
band	duck	its	plane
be	each	juice	plate
bear	eight	letter	police officer
been	elephant	like	rabbit
bicycle	farmer	lion	radio
bird	field	long	rain
boat	find	look	rock
book	first	made	said
bowl	fish	make	second
boy	five	man	see
bread	flower	many	seven
bus	for	may	she
bush	fork	meat	shirt
but	four	milk	shoes
by	from	monkey	sign
call	fruit	moon	six
can	game	more	so
cat	get	movie	soda
cereal	giraffe	my	sofa
chair	girl	nine	some
chest	go	no	soup
chicken	grape	not	spoon
cloud	grass	now	star
come	had	number	sun
computer	has	nurse	table
cook	hat	of	television
could	have	oil	ten
cow	he	on	than

Copyright © 2010 by Gary Robert Muschla, Judith A. Muschla, and Erin Muschla

List 1.14   continued

the	to	water	with
their	tomato	way	woman
them	train	we	word
then	tree	were	would
there	truck	what	write
they	two	when	you
this	up	which	your
three	use	who	
time	was	will	

 Did you know? Vocabulary is a powerful factor in reading success.

See List 1.15, Important Words for Elementary Students to Know.

Copyright © 2010 by Gary Robert Muschla, Judith A. Muschla, and Erin Muschla

From age two on, the average student learns about five new words each day. Assimilating those words into his or her vocabulary is a key to a student's overall success in school. By the time they are in fifth grade, most students have vocabularies of several thousand words. Some words, of course, appear more often in elementary curricula than do others. Many of those words are in the following list.

Copyright © 2010 by Gary Robert Muschla, Judith A. Muschla, and Erin Muschla

ability	article	brain	child
aboard	asleep	break	children
accept	assembly	breakfast	chorus
achieve	attack	bruise	chuckle
acrobat	attention	budget	church
action	attract	bureau	circle
address	audience	burn	citizen
adult	automatic	business	climate
advance	average	cabinet	coarse
adventure	avoid	calm	cocoon
advice	awake	camera	collar
afraid	aware	canal	combine
against	awhile	cancel	comedy
agent	bacon	candidate	command
agreement	badge	canoe	common
alert	balcony	canvas	company
alley	ballot	capture	complete
alligator	bare	career	concert
allow	bargain	careful	conserve
alone	barrel	carpet	contain
American	basic	carton	continent
among	basket	cartoon	correct
amuse	beagle	castle	costume
ancestor	beautiful	catcher	cough
ancient	begun	cause	country
animal	believe	caution	county
annoy	beneath	celebration	courage
answer	beware	cellar	course
antonym	bicycle	century	cousin
apartment	billion	certain	creation
apology	biography	chance	crowd
appoint	blew	character	cruel
area	blizzard	charge	culture
aren't	blunder	charm	current
argue	bother	chase	curtain
arrive	bought	cheap	cyclone
arrow	bound	chief	cylinder

damage	erosion	government	junior
danger	escape	governor	knee
darkness	essay	great	knock
decrease	estimate	grocery	knot
defeat	evening	growl	lamb
defend	event	habit	language
degree	exchange	halfway	lantern
delight	exercise	handkerchief	later
deny	expand	handsome	laughter
describe	expensive	harbor	launch
despair	explain	harmony	lawyer
destroy	explode	harvest	lazy
detail	explore	haven't	lead
didn't	extinct	hazard	league
disagree	factor	hearth	level
discover	factory	height	liberty
discuss	faint	history	lively
disgrace	famine	hockey	loaf
dishonest	fancy	honor	lonesome
divide	feast	horizontal	loyal
dodge	feather	hospital	lucky
doesn't	feature	human	luggage
dollar	fertile	humble	lumber
dolphin	festival	humid	lyrics
double	fiction	humor	machine
draw	figure	hundred	magic
drawn	flannel	illustrate	majesty
east	flesh	image	mammal
echo	flute	imagine	marvel
edge	foolish	impossible	mature
educate	forecast	include	maybe
eighth	fortune	incorrect	mayor
either	fossil	increase	measure
elbow	fraction	independent	medicine
elect	frantic	Indian	mention
element	freedom	individual	million
elevator	frontier	industry	mineral
employ	fudge	instance	minute
enemy	future	instruct	mirror
energy	garage	interest	misplace
enormous	gasoline	interview	mission
entire	general	invent	misspell
entrance	generous	invite	moist
envelope	ghost	janitor	molecule
equal	giggle	jewel	motion
eraser	glory	journey	movie

Copyright © 2010 by Gary Robert Muschla, Judith A. Muschla, and Erin Muschla

mumble	pasture	publish	scent
muscle	patch	pulley	scientist
museum	patience	pupil	scoop
music	patient	purpose	scooter
musical	perform	quick	scrape
mustn't	photograph	quit	screen
mystery	piano	quite	search
narrow	picture	raccoon	secret
nation	pillar	railroad	section
nature	pioneer	rainbow	separate
nearly	pitcher	react	sergeant
needle	pizza	realize	serious
negative	playmate	reason	settler
neighbor	pleasure	rebuilt	share
nerve	plenty	recall	shatter
never	poetry	receive	shelf
ninth	poison	recent	shiver
nonsense	polar	record	shoulder
normal	police	refuse	shovel
north	polite	region	shower
northern	population	rehearse	sickness
notebook	porch	relate	sign
notion	portion	remark	silent
number	pottery	remember	sincere
numeral	pound	remove	singer
o'clock	powder	repair	singular
office	power	reply	size
often	practice	reptile	skiing
open	praise	rescue	skillful
operation	prepare	research	skin
opposite	present	restful	skirt
orchestra	price	retail	sleet
organize	prince	return	slender
ornament	principal	reward	slipper
ounce	principle	rhyme	slumber
outfit	print	ridge	smart
outside	private	river	smash
oven	prize	roast	snowflake
overhear	produce	robot	soldier
oxygen	product	rough	solid
package	program	sailor	something
palace	project	salad	sometime
parade	promise	salute	somewhere
parcel	property	sample	south
pardon	proud	scary	spaniel
parrot	public	scene	spare

Copyright © 2010 by Gary Robert Muschla, Judith A. Muschla, and Erin Muschla

special	subject	throne	vein
spoil	succeed	throw	vertical
spoke	sugar	thrust	video
sprinkle	suggest	together	view
spruce	sunburn	tonight	voyage
square	supply	topic	wagon
squirt	suppose	torch	waist
stairway	supreme	tornado	wasn't
standard	swift	tough	weary
stare	swim	tower	weight
statue	switch	tragic	weird
steal	sword	triangle	welcome
stiff	system	truth	weren't
stingy	tailor	tundra	west
stomach	taught	twelfth	wherever
stories	teacher	twilight	window
storm	theater	typical	wonderful
straight	there's	understand	world
stranger	they'd	unhealthy	worth
strength	they're	union	would've
stretcher	thigh	unless	wouldn't
stroke	though	unusual	wrinkle
studio	thought	useful	youth
study	thousand	vacant	zebra
style	throat	value	zero

 Did you know? By the end of fifth grade most students have acquired most of the words they will use as adults in routine life.

See List 1.14, Important Words for Primary Students to Know; List 1.16, Compound Words.

Copyright © 2010 by Gary Robert Muschla, Judith A. Muschla, and Erin Muschla

Compound words are made by combining two or more words. A compound word may be joined (*baseball*), hyphenated (*up-to-date*), or left open (*ice cream*). Encourage your students to consult a dictionary if they are uncertain about the correct spelling of a compound word.

Copyright © 2010 by Gary Robert Muschla, Judith A. Muschla, and Erin Muschla

able-bodied	blueprint	drugstore	high rise
above-ground	bookcase	dry clean	highchair
afterthought	bookkeeper	earring	highway
air conditioner	bookmark	earthquake	hilltop
airline	box seat	everybody	holdup
airmail	boxcar	everyday	home run
airplane	broadcast	eyeball	homemade
airport	brokenhearted	eyelid	homework
all-American	brother-in-law	fairy tale	horseshoe
all-around	bulldog	farmland	household
all-time	buttermilk	filmstrip	housekeeper
alongside	campfire	firehouse	ice cream
anchorman	carpool	fireplace	infield
anchorwoman	classmate	fishhook	jelly bean
anybody	classroom	flagpole	jellyfish
anyhow	clipboard	flashlight	keyboard
anymore	close call	flowerpot	keypad
anyone	close-up	folklore	landlady
babysitter	clothesline	football	landlord
back door	cold shoulder	frostbite	landslide
back talk	copyright	gentleman	lawn mower
backbone	crosswalk	goldfish	leftover
backyard	cupcake	good-bye	lifeboat
badlands	cutout	grandfather	lifeguard
bad-tempered	darkroom	grandmother	lifeline
barefoot	daydream	grasshopper	life-size
baseball	daytime	haircut	lightheaded
basketball	dogcatcher	half brother	lightweight
bathroom	doghouse	half sister	light-year
battleship	door knob	halfway	locksmith
beanbag	double talk	handcuff	loudspeaker
birthday	downfall	handlebar	lukewarm
birthplace	downpour	hard-boiled	mailbox
blackout	downstairs	hardware	merry-go-round
blood pressure	downtown	haystack	midnight
bloodhound	dragonfly	headache	moonwalk
bloodshot	drive-in	headlight	motorcycle
bloodstream	driveway	headline	nearby
blood vessel	dropout	headquarters	newscast

newspaper	popcorn	skyscraper	toothbrush
newsprint	postcard	slipcover	toothpick
nightgown	pushover	snowball	touchdown
nobody	quarterback	snowdrift	trade-off
notebook	quicksand	snowfall	tryout
oatmeal	railroad	snowstorm	tugboat
old-fashioned	railway	softball	turntable
outboard	rainbow	software	turtleneck
outcome	raincoat	someone	undercover
outcry	rattlesnake	sometime	underline
outdoors	redwood	spacecraft	uproot
outfield	rip off	speedboat	upset
outfit	riptide	splashdown	up-to-date
outlaw	roadside	spotlight	videotape
outline	rowboat	stagehand	volleyball
out-of-bounds	runaway	stairway	washcloth
outside	runway	starfish	washroom
overalls	rush hour	stepfather	watchdog
overcoat	safety glass	stepmother	watercolor
overlook	sailboat	streetcar	waterfall
overpass	sandpaper	suitcase	waterfront
pancake	scarecrow	sunbeam	watermelon
paperback	school bus	sunflower	waterproof
part of speech	seafood	sweatshirt	weekday
password	seagull	sweetheart	well-to-do
payoff	seaside	tablecloth	wheelchair
peanut	seat belt	teacup	whenever
peanut butter	shipwreck	teammate	whirlpool
peppermint	shoelace	textbook	wholesale
pickup	shortstop	thumbtack	wildflower
pinball	showcase	time line	windmill
pinch hitter	showroom	time-out	wingspan
pinpoint	sidewalk	timetable	woodland
playmate	sister-in-law	tiptoe	woodpecker
playpen	skateboard	toenail	wristwatch
ponytail	skyline		zookeeper

 Did you know? The word *basketball* came into being when the game of basketball was invented.

See List 1.15, Important Words for Elementary Students to Know.

Copyright © 2010 by Gary Robert Muschla, Judith A. Muschla, and Erin Muschla

List 1.17   Idioms

Idioms are phrases that have assumed special meanings. Because the meaning of an idiom is usually quite different from the literal interpretation of the words that make it up, idioms can be troublesome for young readers as well as for ESL students. In modern usage, to "let the cat out of the bag" does not mean to open a bag and allow a cat to escape (at least not in most cases). Following are idioms you should consider sharing with your students.

a ball of fire	hungry enough to eat a horse
bark up the wrong tree	in the bag
bend over backward	in the same boat
blow off steam	jump down his (her) throat
burn the candle at both ends	keep a straight face
by the skin of your teeth	know the ropes
call it a day	let the cat out of the bag
call onto the carpet	make ends meet
cough up the money	money talks
crack a smile	off his (her) rocker
dead to the world	on thin ice
down in the dumps	out of sight, out of mind
eat your heart out	over the hill
face the music	pain in the neck
feel like a million bucks	piece of cake
feeling his (her) oats	pulling his (her) leg
get the show on the road	put on the dog
go all out	put their heads together
got a tiger by the tail	put two and two together
hang in there	raining cats and dogs
has a green thumb	red-carpet treatment
has cold feet	run rings around
hear through the grapevine	sell like hotcakes
hit the hay	shoot the breeze
hit the spot	spur of the moment
hold the fort	start the ball rolling
hold your horses	stick together

Copyright © 2010 by Gary Robert Muschla, Judith A. Muschla, and Erin Muschla

List 1.17   continued

still up in the air

turn over a new leaf

stop dead in his (her) tracks

up the creek without a paddle

sweat bullets

weigh a ton

take a rain check

wet behind the ears

throw in the towel

writing on the wall

Did you know? Many idioms have their origin in the past. "Let the cat out of the bag" dates to medieval times when sly merchants would put a cat in a bag instead of a chicken or pig. Cats were abundant and cheap; chickens and pigs were expensive. If the unsuspecting buyer paid the merchant and then opened the bag at home, he would be surprised that he was cheated. The smart buyer, of course, opened the bag and let the cat out before paying. Today, "to let the cat out of the bag" means to reveal a secret.

Copyright © 2010 by Gary Robert Muschla, Judith A. Muschla, and Erin Muschla

The Elementary Teacher's Book of Lists

List 1.18   Comprehension Strategies

There are many strategies that can help your students improve their comprehension skills. Encouraging your students to do the following can not only boost their reading skills but also enrich their reading experience.

1. Read different kinds of material: novels, nonfiction books, short stories, articles, and poetry. Also read about different subjects and topics. Reading a variety of material will broaden reading skills.

2. Before you start to read, preview the material. For articles or stories, check titles, subtitles, pictures, illustrations, and charts. For books, check the front and back covers, contents, and introductory material for information.

3. Find a quiet place to read. Interruptions weaken concentration, making it hard to become engaged with the material.

4. Visualize scenes and images. Try to see the details. This will help you understand and remember main ideas and details.

5. Pay close attention to key words and events. Try to answer the questions: Who? What? When? Where? Why? How?

6. Use context clues to help you understand the meaning of new words. (If necessary, check the definitions of new words in a dictionary.)

7. Recognize sequence. Note how one event leads to another. Look for signal words such as *first, second, third, next, now, then,* and *finally.*

8. Be aware of cause and effect. Recognize how one thing leads to another.

9. Look for connections and relationships. Ask yourself how one thing affects another. Identify differences and similarities.

10. Compare what you read to your own ideas and experiences. How is what you are reading different from what you already knew? How is it the same? Relate what you read to your own life.

11. As you read, make predictions of what will happen next. Ask yourself why you believe your predictions are valid. If your predictions prove to be wrong, try to figure out why.

12. Always examine photographs and pictures. Study graphs, charts, and tables. Such visual aids can make ideas clearer.

13. When studying or reading hard material, take notes. Write down important ideas and details.

14. Reread material if you do not understand it the first time. A second reading often results in more understanding.

15. After you finish reading, summarize what you read. This will help you remember important information.

 Did you know? The best way to become a good reader is to read.

See List 1.19, Questions to Aid Comprehension; List 1.20, Common Signal Words for Readers; List 1.21, How to Find Main Ideas and Supporting Details.

Copyright © 2010 by Gary Robert Muschla, Judith A. Muschla, and Erin Muschla

List 1.19   Questions to Aid Comprehension

Most reading teachers ask a lot of questions about the material their students read. But no matter how many questions they ask, they can always ask more. The following questions are broken down into the categories of nonfiction and fiction. They, and similar kinds of questions, can be adapted to just about any selection and will enable you to expand your reading discussions. They can also be used to provide direction for writing in reading logs.

Questions for Nonfiction Selections

- What is the author's purpose for writing this article?
- What facts does the author use to support his or her ideas?
- Do you agree or disagree with the author's ideas? Why or why not?
- Do you think the title of the selection is a good one? Why or why not?
- What does the word _____ mean in this article? What other meanings might it have?
- To what does the author compare . . . ?
- What steps are needed to . . . ?
- If you were to summarize this article in five sentences or less, what would you say?
- What advice does the author give?
- Why was the author able to write this article?
- What did you learn from this article?
- What did you find most interesting about this article? Why?
- How has this article changed your ideas about . . . ?
- If you could ask the author a question about this topic, what would it be? Why?
- Would you like to learn more about this topic? Why or why not?

Questions for Fiction Selections

- Which of the characters in this story is your favorite? Why?
- If you could pick one word to describe each character, what words would you choose? Explain.
- Describe how the character(s) changed in the story.
- If you had been in the lead character's place, what would you have done differently?
- Compare the traits of the hero and villain in this story.
- What problems do the characters face?
- How do they solve the problems?
- What is the theme, or author's message, of this story?
- If you were to tell a friend about this story, what would you say?

Copyright © 2010 by Gary Robert Muschla, Judith A. Muschla, and Erin Muschla

List 1.19   continued

- What do you think is about to happen when … ?
- Describe a situation you have been in that is similar to the story.
- How do you think the character(s) feel about what happened?
- What clues helped you solve the mystery before the lead character?
- Would you like to read other stories written by this author? Why or why not?
- If you have read another story written by this author, how was it different from this one? How was it alike?

 Did you know? Effective questioning can help students gain insight to their reading.

See List 1.18, Comprehension Strategies.

Copyright © 2010 by Gary Robert Muschla, Judith A. Muschla, and Erin Muschla

List 1.20   Common Signal Words for Readers

Signal words help readers organize and understand information. They are especially helpful to young readers because they highlight important facts. Some of the most common signal words young readers will find in their reading are included in the following list.

Words That Signal Sequence

after	finally	last
as a result	first, second, third …	last of all
at last	in conclusion	later
before	in the first place	next

Words That Signal Time

after	immediately	previously
at the same time	morning	the next day
before	night	today
currently	noon	tomorrow
during	now	when
earlier	once	yesterday

Words That Signal a Change

although	however	on the other hand
but	in spite of	rather than
despite	instead of	still
even though	on the contrary	yet

Words That Signal an Explanation

for example	just as	similar to
for instance	like	such as

Words That Signal the End

as a result	consequently	in conclusion
at last	finally	in summary

Other signals, especially for emphasis, include *italics*, <u>underlining</u>, and **bold print**.

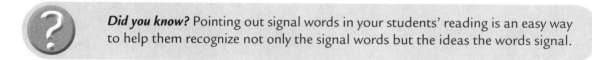

Did you know? Pointing out signal words in your students' reading is an easy way to help them recognize not only the signal words but the ideas the words signal.

See List 1.18, Comprehension Strategies.

Copyright © 2010 by Gary Robert Muschla, Judith A. Muschla, and Erin Muschla

Copyright © 2010 by Gary Robert Muschla, Judith A. Muschla, and Erin Muschla

List 1.21   How to Find Main Ideas and Supporting Details

Understanding main ideas and supporting details is essential for comprehension. To help your students identify the main ideas and details in their reading, include the following suggestions in your instruction.

- One way to find the main idea is to think of the main idea as being the topic of the paragraph. The main idea is stated in one sentence, known as the topic sentence. All other sentences give information about the topic. Consider the topic of baseball. In a paragraph in which baseball is the main idea, sentences that tell about batters, fielders, pitchers, the field, bases, and hits and runs provide details that help to describe the game of baseball.

- Another way to identify the main idea of a paragraph is to ask what all of the sentences of the paragraph are about. Each paragraph has only one main idea. All sentences in the paragraph give information to make the main idea clear. Find what all of the sentences are about and you will find the paragraph's main idea.

- A third way to find the main idea is to identify a paragraph's topic sentence. Every paragraph has a topic sentence. Because the topic sentence usually contains information about the most important person, place, or thing in the paragraph, it also contains the main idea. In many paragraphs, the topic sentence is the first sentence. But sometimes the topic sentence may be in the middle or at the end of the paragraph. To find the topic sentence, suggest that your students do the following:

  ◦ Start with the first sentence. If the rest of the sentences of the paragraph add details to the information in the first sentence, the first sentence is probably the topic sentence.

  ◦ If the first sentence is not the topic sentence, check the last sentence of the paragraph. If the other sentences add details to the idea in the last sentence, the last sentence contains the main idea.

  ◦ If the first or last sentence is not the topic sentence, check the other sentences in the paragraph. The sentence that contains the idea that all of the other sentences are about will be the topic sentence.

- After finding the main idea, check that the details in the other sentences add more information to the main idea. If they do, you have found the main idea and details of the paragraph.

Did you know? Students who can identify main ideas and details in their reading are likely to incorporate main ideas and details in their writing.

See List 1.18, Comprehension Strategies.

List 1.22   How to Use Context Clues

Context clues are words or phrases that help readers understand the meaning of a new, unfamiliar word in a sentence. The ability to decode the meaning of new words through context clues is an important reading skill. Teaching your students how to use the following types of context clues will, without question, help them become better readers.

Clues with Synonyms

The police officer <u>interrogated</u> the suspect and *asked* him many questions.

("Asked" is a synonym of "interrogated" and provides a clue to its meaning.)

Clues with Antonyms

Randy was surprised that the <u>complex</u> problem had such a *simple* solution.

(Randy's surprise at the "simple" solution is a clue to the meaning of "complex.")

Clues in Definitions

<u>Nocturnal</u> animals, *which are active at night*, have excellent eyesight.

(The words "which are active at night" define "nocturnal.")

Clues in Examples

Many people are afraid of <u>arachnids</u>, *such as spiders, scorpions, and ticks*.

(The words "such as" signal an example coming that gives meaning to "arachnids.")

Clues in Familiar Words or Phrases

Melissa's puppy was <u>energetic</u>. He *could play all day*.

(The words "could play all day" hint at the meaning of "energetic.")

 Did you know? Most good readers are adept at using context clues.

See List 1.18, Comprehension Strategies.

Copyright © 2010 by Gary Robert Muschla, Judith A. Muschla, and Erin Muschla

List 1.23   Habits of Good Readers

Good readers share many positive reading habits. Sharing the following habits with your students can encourage them to develop these habits themselves.

Most good readers do the following:

1. Read a lot. Reading is not an ability a person is born with; it is a process of many skills that are learned. The more a person reads, the better reader that person becomes.

2. Read a variety of materials, for example, novels, nonfiction books, and magazines.

3. See three, four, or more words at a time when they read. They do not focus on just one word at a time. Seeing several words at once helps them read faster.

4. Visualize ideas and scenes as they read.

5. Use context clues to help them understand the meanings of new words.

6. Choose books that interest them.

7. Have favorite authors.

8. Talk about books with their friends.

9. Become involved in what they are reading. They ask themselves questions and seek answers to their questions as they read. They try to predict what will happen next. They reflect upon the material and compare the author's ideas to their own experiences.

10. Always have a book that they look forward to reading.

 Did you know? Students who are good readers often select books that are considered to be above their grade level.

See List 1.24, Overcoming Poor Reading Habits.

Copyright © 2010 by Gary Robert Muschla, Judith A. Muschla, and Erin Muschla

List 1.24   Overcoming Poor Reading Habits

Just as important as it is for students to develop effective reading habits, they must avoid habits that undermine their ability to read. Poor reading habits sap the enjoyment from reading and make reading tiresome.

When reading, encourage your students to be mindful of the following:

1. Do not place a finger beneath words as you read. This tends to focus your eyes on one word at a time and slows your reading down.

2. Do not focus on only one word at a time. Instead focus on two, three, or more words as you read. Seeing sections of a sentence increases your speed and helps you understand ideas more quickly.

3. Do not move your lips when reading. Silently speaking the words as you read slows your reading and weakens your concentration on the material.

4. Do not stop and try to sound out or figure out the meaning of new words. Try to find the meaning of the word from context clues.

5. Do not limit your reading to only one subject or topic. Read different kinds of books and articles on different topics.

6. Do not think that good readers are born with "reading" talent. Most people become good readers through reading. They develop good reading habits and overcome poor ones.

 Did you know? Many adults who do not like to read had poor reading habits as children.

See List 1.23, Habits of Good Readers.

Copyright © 2010 by Gary Robert Muschla, Judith A. Muschla, and Erin Muschla

The Elementary Teacher's Book of Lists

List 1.25   Helping Students Select Books to Read

From an early age, many children rely on their teachers and parents or guardians to select books for them. Consequently, they may not gain much experience in selecting books for themselves. When they do choose books, they may not choose books that interest them and in time they may lose interest in reading. You have no doubt been in your school's library with your class and had students say, "I can't find a book." The tips that follow can help your students select books that they will enjoy.

When selecting books to read, suggest that your students do the following:

1. Think about things that interest you. What do you like to do? What kinds of stories do you like? What types of movies and TV shows do you like to watch? Books that satisfy your interests will be good choices for reading.

2. Think about the kinds of books you have read and enjoyed. Similar books will probably interest you.

3. If you enjoy one book of a series, you will probably like another of the same series.

4. If you like the books written by a particular author, you will probably like other books he or she has written.

5. To find books you will enjoy, browse the library, stop in bookstores with your parents or guardians when you go to the mall, and check online booksellers such as Amazon.com.

6. Ask your school librarian about books he or she might recommend for you. Many librarians have vast knowledge of books that they are quite happy to share with readers.

7. Before choosing a book, check its table of contents, read its back cover, and glance through a few pages. This can give you an idea of whether you will like the book.

8. If you are looking for books online, check its reviews. A review is the written opinion of someone who has read the book. But keep in mind that you may not agree with the reviewer's opinion. Try to read several reviews before deciding whether or not to read a book.

 Did you know? Taking your students to the library regularly, participating in classroom book clubs, and attending school book fairs gives students the opportunity to select books they will enjoy reading.

See List 1.26, Types of Fiction and Nonfiction Your Students Might Read.

Copyright © 2010 by Gary Robert Muschla, Judith A. Muschla, and Erin Muschla

List 1.26 Types of Fiction and Nonfiction Your Students Might Read

Students who read a variety of materials often develop into more competent readers than their peers who resist reading beyond a topic of special interest. Encourage all of your students to read an assortment of both fiction and nonfiction. The following list offers categories of written works from which they might choose.

action	fairy tale	poetry
adventure	fantasy	realistic fiction
animals	folk tale	reference
autobiography	historical fiction	religious
ballad	horror	romance
biography	how-to	science fiction
book review	humor	self-improvement
comedy	informational	sports
coming of age	inspirational	suspense
diary	interview	tall tale
drama	juvenile	technical
editorials	multicultural	tragedy
essay	mystery	western
ethnic	news articles	
fable	plays	

 Did you know? The word *genre* refers to distinctive categories of written material. An example of a genre is the adventure story.

See List 1.25, Helping Students Select Books to Read; List 1.27, Important Parts of a Book.

Copyright © 2010 by Gary Robert Muschla, Judith A. Muschla, and Erin Muschla

List 1.27   Important Parts of a Book

When you discuss books with your students, it is helpful to use the proper terminology. Following are terms you and your students should use when you talk about books and their parts.

- *Jacket*: The removable paper cover used to protect the binding of a book
- *Front cover*: Includes title and author
- *Back cover*: Often includes a brief summary or description designed to interest readers
- *Spine*: Usually has the title and author's name, making it easy to find books set on shelves
- *Title page*: Includes title, author, publisher
- *Copyright page*: Includes the date of publication and the International Standard Book Number (ISBN)
- *Author bio note*: Provides brief information about the author
- *Dedication*: Brief note dedicating the book to someone as a sign of affection or respect
- *Table of contents*: A listing of chapters and topics by page number
- *Preface*: Statement by the author that introduces a book and explains its scope
- *Acknowledgments*: Recognition of others who helped the author with his or her writing
- *Introduction*: The beginning or opening of a book
- *Chapters*: Main divisions of a book
- *Subheads*: Smaller divisions of a book's chapters, usually focusing on one topic
- *Illustrations*: Includes photographs, pictures, charts, tables, graphs
- *Glossary*: List of important words with their definitions, usually at the back of a book
- *Bibliography*: A list of reference books

Did you know? Johann Gutenberg is generally considered to be the inventor of the first practical printing press, which dramatically increased the availability of books. Although historians argue over the exact date of Gutenberg's invention, most agree it was between 1440 and 1450.

See List 1.26, Types of Fiction and Nonfiction Your Students Might Read.

Copyright © 2010 by Gary Robert Muschla, Judith A. Muschla, and Erin Muschla

List 1.28 Major Parts of Stories

All stories have a basic structure composed of several parts. When students understand the parts of a story, they are more likely to have a solid understanding of the whole. You should introduce the following story parts as soon as possible in your reading program.

- The *plot* of a story is the action line of the story. It consists of the events and happenings that move the story from its opening to its climax and conclusion. The plot is built around characters who face a problem. Their efforts to solve the problem are told in the story.

- The *characters* are the people who take part in the story. In some stories, especially those for young readers, characters may be animals or entirely imaginary creatures.

- The *setting* of a story is where and when the events of the story occur. Depending on a story's length and plot, a story may have just one setting, or it may have several. Settings that support the action of a story help to make a story interesting.

- The *climax* of a story is the moment when the characters solve (or fail to solve) their problem. The climax is usually the most exciting part of a story.

- The *theme* of a story is a message the author hopes to share with his or her readers. In most stories, the theme arises from the plot and becomes apparent at the story's conclusion.

Did you know? Storytelling has been a part of the human experience since its earliest times. In primitive societies, knowledge was passed on to the next generation through storytelling.

Copyright © 2010 by Gary Robert Muschla, Judith A. Muschla, and Erin Muschla

List 1.29   Reading Log Guidelines

Reading logs, also known as *reading journals, response logs,* and *literature journals,* can be important components of a reading program. They may serve as a place in which students record their reactions to reading, answer questions, or write down questions they may have about a selection. Reading logs can be useful to discussions and group activities. Following are suggestions of how you can incorporate reading logs into your reading program.

- A standard spiral notebook is a good choice for a reading log, although a log can take many forms.
- Students should write their names on their reading logs.
- Students should bring their reading logs to school each day.
- Logs should be used only for reading. They should not be used for the work in other subjects.
- You should encourage your students to record their reactions to reading done in class, and also when they read at home.
- Students should begin each entry on a new page. They should date and label their entries, for example, October 29, 2011, Chapter 6, pages 64–73.
- You should periodically collect the logs of your students and read their entries.
- You should respond to your students' entries by offering comments and suggestions. Short notes that spur critical thinking are particularly useful.
- You should encourage your students to answer questions fully and support their ideas with facts.
- You should suggest that your students periodically review their logs to see how they are growing as readers.

Did you know? While many students benefit from reading logs, some become frustrated with having to regularly complete entries after reading. For these students, logs may undermine the development of their reading skills. Consider providing such students with alternatives that foster their reading enthusiasm. For example, instead of requiring a student to write about her reactions to a scene in a story, you might ask her to draw a picture of her opinion, create a dialogue with a character about an event, or rewrite a scene and provide a different conclusion.

See List 1.19, Questions to Aid Comprehension; List 1.30, Some Suggestions for Student Entries in Reading Logs.

Copyright © 2010 by Gary Robert Muschla, Judith A. Muschla, and Erin Muschla

Reading logs can serve many purposes. At its most basic, a reading log serves as a record of what students read. Logs may also be a place in which students write responses to their reading. Responses can take various forms, examples of which follow.

- Answers to specific questions you pose
- Questions students pose to themselves or to other students for group discussions
- Completion of statements such as:
  - What I really liked about this book was . . .
  - I was really disappointed because . . .
  - What surprised me the most was . . .
  - The story made me feel . . .
  - Something new I learned was . . .
- A poem about a character, the plot, or a place in the story
- An opinion in agreement or disagreement with the material
- An imaginary interview with a character
- A diary entry from the viewpoint of a character
- An alternative ending
- A list of what students feel are the most important ideas in a book
- Possible different scenes or characters
- A letter written to a character or the author
- A list of possible different titles
- An explanation of something students learned
- Comments about how the story relates to students' lives
- A review of the book in no more than five sentences

 Did you know? Providing a wide range of ideas and options for making entries in reading logs helps to address the diverse interests of students.

See List 1.29, Reading Log Guidelines.

Copyright © 2010 by Gary Robert Muschla, Judith A. Muschla, and Erin Muschla

Copyright © 2010 by Gary Robert Muschla, Judith A. Muschla, and Erin Muschla

List 1.31   Famous Children's Authors

There are many outstanding authors of children's books. The following list contains twenty-five whom we consider to be among the best of these authors, along with an example of their work. The list can serve as an excellent starting point for building a classroom library.

Judy Blume, *Tales of a Fourth Grade Nothing*

Frances Hodgson Burnett, *The Secret Garden*

Beverly Cleary, *Freckle Juice*

Roald Dahl, *Charlie and the Chocolate Factory*

Sid Fleishman, *The Whipping Boy*

Virginia Hamilton, *M. C. Higgins, the Great*

Madeleine L'Engle, *A Wrinkle in Time*

C. S. Lewis, *The Lion, the Witch and the Wardrobe*

Lois Lowry, *Anastasia Krupnik*

Patricia MacLachlan, *Sarah, Plain and Tall*

A. A. Milne, *Winnie the Pooh*

L. M. Montgomery, *Anne of Green Gables*

Scott O'Dell, *Island of the Blue Dolphins*

Katherine Paterson, *Bridge to Terabithia*

Wilson Rawls, *Where the Red Fern Grows*

J. K. Rowling, the *Harry Potter* series

George Selden, *The Cricket in Times Square*

Maurice Sendak, *Where the Wild Things Are*

Jerry Spinelli, *Maniac Magee*

R. L. Stine, the *Goosebumps* series

Mildred Taylor, *Roll of Thunder, Hear My Cry*

Chris Van Allsburg, *Jumanji*

E. B. White, *Charlotte's Web*

Laura Ingalls Wilder, the *Little House* series

Jane Yolen, *Owl Moon*

 Did you know? Laura Ingalls Wilder published her first book when she was sixty-five years old.

See List 1.34, Great Books for Any Primary or Elementary Classroom; List 1.36, Books for Young Readers Written by African American Authors; List 1.37, Poetry Books for Children.

Most children who are introduced to the wonders and joys of reading at an early age go on to become competent readers. With wonderful art and either no print or very little print, the books below are ideal for the very young who are just beginning to learn to read.

Across the Stream by Mirra Ginsburg

All Fall Down by Brian Wildsmith

Alligator's Toothache by Diane De Groat

Animal Alphabet by Bert Kitchen

Anno's Counting Book by Anno Mitsumasa

Another Story to Tell by Dick Bruna

The Bear and the Fly by Paula Winter

Big Ones, Little Ones by Tana Hoban

Brown Bear, Brown Bear, What Do You See? by Bill Martin Jr.

Carl Goes Shopping by Alexandra Day

The Cat Sat on the Mat by Brian Wildsmith

Creepy Castle by John Goodall

The Creepy Thing by Fernando Krahn

The Chick and the Duckling by Mirra Ginsburg

Chicka Chicka Boom Boom by Bill Martin Jr. and Jon Archambault

Deep in the Forest by Brinton Turkle

Do You Want to Be My Friend? by Eric Carle

Frog Goes to Dinner by Mercer Mayer

Goodnight Baby Bat by Debi Gliori

The Great Cat Chase by Mercer Mayer

Have You Seen My Duckling? by Nancy Tafuri

Hiccup by Mercer Mayer

Hooray for Fish by Lucy Cousins

Junglewalk by Nancy Tafuri

The Little Star Who Wished by Michael Broad

Look Book by Tana Hoban

Looking Down by Steve Jenkins

The Midnight Adventures of Kelly, Dot and Esmeralda by John Goodall

Moonlight by Jan Ormerod

Not a Box by Antoinette Portis

The Odd Egg by Emily Gravett

Pancakes for Breakfast by Tomie dePaola

The Paperboy by Dav Pilkey

Copyright © 2010 by Gary Robert Muschla, Judith A. Muschla, and Erin Muschla

Copyright © 2010 by Gary Robert Muschla, Judith A. Muschla, and Erin Muschla

List 1.32   continued

Penguin by Polly Dunbar

Picnic by Emily Arnold McCully

Rosie's Walk by Pat Hutchins

Russell the Sheep by Rob Scotton

The Secret in the Dungeon by Fernando Krahn

The Silver Pony by Lynd Ward

The Snowman by Raymond Briggs

Tiger in the Snow! by Nick Butterworth

Time Flies by Eric Rohmann

What a Tale by Brian Wildsmith

Whose Nose and Toes? by John Butler

Window by Jeannie Baker

The Yellow Umbrella by Henrik Drescher

 Did you know? Very young children often memorize the words of favorite books before being able to actually read them.

See List 1.33, Books for Beginning Readers.

List 1.33   Books for Beginning Readers

Books with rhyme and repetition can help beginning readers become familiar and comfortable with the structure of written material—reading left to right, gaining understanding from words and pictures, and recognizing word and sentence patterns. Such books also foster early vocabulary development and aid comprehension. The following books serve well in any beginning reading program.

Busy Monday Morning by Janina Domanska

Can I Keep Him? by Steven Kellogg

The Chick and the Duckling by Mirra Ginsburg

Chicken Soup with Rice by Maurice Sendak

Click Clack Moo: Cows That Type by Doreen Cronin

Cookie's Week by Cindy Ward

Crocodile Beat by Gail Jorgensen

Dear Zoo by Rod Campbell

Fortunately by Remy Charlip

A Funny Fish Story by Joanne and David Wylie

The Gingerbread Boy by Paul Galdone

Good Night, Owl by Pat Hutchins

Greedy Cat by Joy Cowley

Henny Penny by Paul Galdone

Hey! Get Off Our Train by John Burningham

The House That Jack Built by Rodney Peppe

I Know an Old Lady by Rose Bonne and Alan Mills

I Went Walking by Sue Williams

If You Give a Mouse a Cookie by Laura Joffe Numeroff

In a Dark Dark Wood by June Melser and Joy Cowley

Is Your Mama a Llama? by Deborah Guarino

It Looked Like Spilt Milk by Charles G. Shaw

Joshua James Likes Trucks by Catherine Petrie

Just Like Daddy by Frank Asch

The Little Red Hen by Paul Galdone

More Spaghetti I Say! by Rita Gelman

Mrs. Wishy-Washy by Joy Cowley

Mud by Wendy Cheyette Lewison

My Bike by Craig Martin

Noisy Nora by Rosemary Wells

Oh, A-Hunting We Will Go by John Langstaff

The Old Woman and Her Pig by W. Mars

Copyright © 2010 by Gary Robert Muschla, Judith A. Muschla, and Erin Muschla

"Pardon?" Said the Giraffe by Colin West

Pumpkin Pumpkin by Jeanette Titherington

Q is for Duck, An Alphabet Guessing Game by Mary Elting and Michael Folsom

Seven Little Rabbits by John Becker

The Three Billy Goats Gruff by Marcia Brown

The Three Little Bears by Paul Galdone

The Three Little Pigs by Paul Galdone

Things I Like by Anthony Browne

Too Much Noise by Ann McGovern

A Treeful of Pigs by Arnold Lobel

The Very Busy Spider by Eric Carle

Where Are You Going, Little Mouse by Robert Kraus

Who Said Red? by Mary Serfozo

Did you know? Rhyme and repetition make books for beginning readers predictable and enjoyable.

See List 1.32, Books for Pre-Readers; List 1.34, Great Books for Any Primary or Elementary Classroom.

Copyright © 2010 by Gary Robert Muschla, Judith A. Muschla, and Erin Muschla

List 1.34   Great Books for Any Primary or Elementary Classroom

There are countless great books for children. While any list of this nature, of course, is subjective and will exhibit some overlap, the following books, broken down roughly for primary and elementary students, provide plenty of choices. You should choose those books you feel are most suitable for your students.

Primary

Across the Stream by Mirra Ginsburg

Alexander and the Terrible, Horrible, No Good, Very Bad Day by Judith Viorst

Amelia's Road by Linda Altman

Amos and Boris by William Steig

Angel Child, Dragon Child by Michele Maria Surat

Animals Should Definitely Not Wear Clothing by Judi Barrett

Annie and the Old One by Miska Miles

Anno's Counting House by Mitsumasa Anno

Anno's Mysterious Multiplying Jar by Masaichiro and Mitsumasa Anno

Araminta's Paint Box by Karen Ackerman

Bearsie Bear and the Surprise Sleepover Party by Bernard Waber

Brown Bear, Brown Bear What Do You See? by Bill Martin Jr.

Bunny Cakes by Rosemary Wells

Bunny Money by Rosemary Wells

The Bus Ride by Anne McLean

Buz by Richard Egielski

Chester's Way by Kevin Henkes

The Chick and the Duckling by Mirra Ginsburg

Chicken Soup with Rice by Maurice Sendak

Cinderella, or the Little Glass Slipper by Charles Perrault

Cookie's Week by Cindy Ward

The Courage of Sarah Noble by Alice Dalgliesh

Do Not Open by Brinton Turkle

Each Peach Pear Plum by Janet and Allan Ahlberg

Eloise by Kay Thompson

Elmer by David McKee

Emily and the Enchanted Frog by Helen V. Griffith

The Enormous Crocodile by Roald Dahl

Everybody Needs a Rock by Byrd Baylor

Feathers for Lunch by Lois Ehlert

Flossie and the Fox by Patricia McKissack

Frog and Toad Together by Arnold Lobel

Copyright © 2010 by Gary Robert Muschla, Judith A. Muschla, and Erin Muschla

Gathering the Sun: An Alphabet in Spanish and English by Alma Flor Ada

Good Driving, Amelia Bedelia by Peggy Parish

The Great Kapok Tree by Lynne Cherry

Growing Vegetable Soup by Lois Ehlert

Hailstones and Halibut Bones by Mary O'Neill

Hattie and the Fox by Mem Fox

Horace by Holly Keller

I Am Not Going to Get Up Today! by Dr. Seuss

I Hate English by Ellen Levine

I Like Books by Anthony Browne

I Want a Dog by Dayal Kaur Khalsa

If You Give a Moose a Muffin by Laura Numeroff

In a Cabin in a Wood by Darcy McNally

Is Your Mama a Llama? by Deborah Guarino

Jamaica's Find by Juanita Havill

James and the Giant Peach by Roald Dahl

The Little Red Hen by Paul Galdone

Little Red Riding Hood by Trina Schart Hyman

Lon Po Po by Ed Young

Madeline by Ludwig Bemelmans

Make Way for Ducklings by Robert McCloskey

Millions of Cats by Wanda Gag

The Mitten by Jan Brett

The Mixed-Up Chameleon by Eric Carle

Mud by Wendy Cheyette Lewison

Nana Upstairs, Nana Downstairs by Tomie dePaola

The Napping House by Audrey Wood

The New Adventures of Mother Goose by Bruce Lansky

Pat the Bunny by Dorothy Kunhardt

The Patchwork Quilt by Valerie Flournoy

Polkabats and Octopus Slacks by Calef Brown

Squirrels by Brian Wildsmith

Ten Nine Eight by Molly Bang

A Toad for Tuesday by Russell E. Erickson

There Was an Old Lady Who Swallowed a Fly by Simms Taback

Town Mouse, Country Mouse by Jan Brett

The Very Hungry Caterpillar by Eric Carle

Copyright © 2010 by Gary Robert Muschla, Judith A. Muschla, and Erin Muschla

Wagon Wheels by Barbara Brenner

What a Tale by Brian Wildsmith

Where the Wild Things Are by Maurice Sendak

Elementary

Afternoon of the Elves by Janet Taylor Lisle

Anastasia Krupnik by Lois Lowry

Anne of Green Gables by L. M. Montgomery

The Bones in the Cliff by James Stevenson

Bridge to Terabithia by Katherine Paterson

Bunnicula by Deborah and James Howe

Castle in the Attic by Elizabeth Winthrop

The Cat in the Hat by Dr. Seuss

The Cat Sat on the Mat by Alice Cameron and Carol Jones

Charlie and the Chocolate Factory by Roald Dahl

Charlotte's Web by E. B. White

Child of the Owl by Laurence Yep

The Comeback Dog by Jane Resh Thomas

Cousins in the Attic by Gary Paulsen

Coyote Dreams by Susan Nunes

The Cricket in Times Square by George Selden

Danny the Champion of the World by Roald Dahl

A Dog Called Kitty by Bill Wallace

Ella Enchanted by Gail Carson Levine

Fly Away Home by Eve Bunting

Freckle Juice by Beverly Cleary

Frindle by Andrew Clements

Goosebumps (any books of the series) by R. L. Stine

Grasshopper Summer by Ann Turner

The Green Book by Jill Paton Walsh

Harry Potter (any of the books of the series) by J. K. Rowling

How Does It Feel to Be Old? by Norma Farber

How to Eat Fried Worms by Thomas Rockwell

I'll Meet You at the Cucumbers by Lilian Moore

The Indian in the Cupboard by Lynne Reid Banks

Island of the Blue Dolphins by Scott O'Dell

Jumanji by Chris Van Allsburg

The Lion, the Witch and the Wardrobe by C. S. Lewis

Copyright © 2010 by Gary Robert Muschla, Judith A. Muschla, and Erin Muschla

Little House (any books of the series) by Laura Ingalls Wilder

Little Women by Louisa May Alcott

The Lucky Stone by Lucille Clifton

Lyddie by Katherine Paterson

M. C. Higgins, the Great by Virginia Hamilton

Maniac Magee by Jerry Spinelli

The Midwife's Apprentice by Karen Cushman

Molly's Pilgrim by Barbara Cohen

My Great-Aunt Arizona by Gloria Houston

The Night the Bells Rang Natalie Kinsey-Warnock

No Mirrors in My Nana's House by Ysaye M. Barnwell

Nothing but the Truth by Avi

Nothing Ever Happens on 90th Street by Roni Schotter

Number the Stars by Lois Lowry

Old Henry by Joan W. Blos

Once Upon a Dark November by Carol Beach York

Owl Moon by Jane Yolen

The Pinballs by Betsy Byars

The Polar Express by Chris Van Allsburg

Redwall by Brian Jacques

Roll of Thunder, Hear My Cry by Mildred Taylor

Romona Quimby, Age 8 by Beverly Cleary

Sarah, Plain and Tall by Patricia MacLachlan

The Secret Garden by Frances Hodgson Burnett

Seedfolks by Paul Fleschman

Shades of Gray by Carolyn Reeder

Shadow Spinner by Susan Fletcher

Sounder by William Armstrong

The Spell of the Sorcerer's Skull by John Bellairs

Stone Fox by John R. Gardiner

Summer of the Monkeys by Wilson Rawls

Tales of a Fourth Grade Nothing by Judy Blume

A Taste of Salt by Frances Temple

Toad Food and Measle Soup by Christine McDonnell

Tuck Everlasting by Natalie Babbit

Wan Hu Is in the Stars by Jennifer Armstrong

Water Dance by Thomas Locker

Copyright © 2010 by Gary Robert Muschla, Judith A. Muschla, and Erin Muschla

Where the Red Fern Grows by Wilson Rawls

The Whipping Boy by Sid Fleishman

Winnie the Pooh by A. A. Milne

Witch Week by Dianna Wynne Jones

A Wrinkle in Time by Madeleine L'Engle

Did you know? The Caldecott Medal is awarded each year to the artist of the most distinguished American picture book. For a list of Caldecott winners, visit the Web site of the American Library Association at http://www.ala.org/ala/mgrps/divs/alsc/awardsgrants/bookmedia/caldecottmedal/caldecottmedal.cfm. (Or you can simply search the Internet with the term "Caldecott Medal Winners" to find numerous Web sites about the award.) The Newbery Medal is awarded to the author of the most distinguished contribution to American literature for children. For a list of Newbery winners, visit the Web site of the American Library Association at http://www.ala.org/ala/mgrps/divs/alsc/awardgrants/bookmedia/newberymedal/newberymedal.cfm. (Or use the term "Newbery Award Winners" to search the Internet to find other useful Web sites.)

See List 1.31, Famous Children's Authors; List 1.33, Books for Beginning Readers; List 1.36, Books for Young Readers Written by African American Authors.

Copyright © 2010 by Gary Robert Muschla, Judith A. Muschla, and Erin Muschla

Reluctant readers are children who have little interest in reading. Many reluctant readers lack strong reading skills, which only adds to their reading reluctance. Most, if asked, will tell you that they do not like to read. Your best strategy for motivating reluctant readers is to provide them with high-interest books that have strong story lines and relatively easy language. The books in the following list are aimed at the elementary grades, where reluctant readers begin to emerge.

Beware the Mare by Jessie Haas

Cam Jansen and the Mystery of the Stolen Diamonds by David Adler

The Chalk Box Kid by Clyde R. Bulla

Chevrolet Saturdays by Candy Dawson Boyd

Crash by Jerry Spinelli

Danger Guys by Tony Abbot

December by Eve Bunting

George the Drummer Boy by Nathaniel Benchley

Ghosthunters and the Incredibly Revolting Ghost! by Cornelia Funke

The Golly Sisters Go West by Betsy Byars

Going with the Flow by Claire H. Blachford

The Good, the Bad, and the Goofy by Jon Scieszka

How to Train Your Dragon by Cressida Cowell

Jason and the Losers by Gina Willner-Pardo

Julian Rodriguez by Alexander Stadler

Kidnap Kids by Todd Strasser

Losers, Inc. by Claudia Mills

Lost and Found by Andrew Clements

Marco's Monster by Meredith Sue Willis

Maxx Comedy: The Funniest Kid in America by Gordon Kormon

Meanwhile by Jules Feiffer

Monster Manners by Beverly Collins

My Haunted House by Angie Sage

My Life as a Fifth Grade Comedian by Elizabeth Levy

My Life in Dog Years by Gary Paulsen

Oggie Cooder by Sarah Weeks

Shark in School by Patricia Reilly Giff

Shoeshine Girl by Clyde R. Bulla

Copyright © 2010 by Gary Robert Muschla, Judith A. Muschla, and Erin Muschla

List 1.35   continued

Skeleton Man by Joseph Bruchac

Skylark by Patricia MacLachlan

Star Jumper: Journal of a Cardboard Genius by Frank Asch

Wayside School Gets a Little Stranger by Louis Sachar

The Zack Files, My Son the Time Traveler by Dan Greenburg

 Did you know? Some reluctant readers may be hampered by an undiagnosed learning disability. Identifying and overcoming the effects of the disability can improve the student's reading skills and make reading pleasurable.

See List 1.34, Great Books for Any Primary or Elementary Classroom.

The Elementary Teacher's Book of Lists

Copyright © 2010 by Gary Robert Muschla, Judith A. Muschla, and Erin Muschla

List 1.36   Books for Young Readers Written by African American Authors

The list below contains an assortment of outstanding books written by African American authors for young readers. Each would be a valuable addition to your reading program.

Aunt Harriet's Underground Railroad in the Sky by Faith Ringgold

The Big Box by Toni Morrison

Black Cat by Christopher Myers

The Black Snowman by Phil Mendez

Bluish by Virginia Hamilton

Bubber Goes to Heaven by Arna Bontemps

Bud, Not Buddy by Christopher Paul Curtis

Celie and the Harvest Fiddler by Vanessa Flournoy and Valerie Flournoy

Cloudy Day Sunny Day by Donald Crews

Cornrows by Camille Yarbrough

Cousins by Virginia Hamilton

Danitra Brown Leaves Town by Nikki Grimes

An Enchanted Hair Tale by Alexis DeVeaux

Goin' Someplace Special by Patricia C. McKissack

Grandma's Purple Flowers by Adjoa J. Burrowes

Hold Fast to Dreams by Andrea Davis Pinkney

The House of Dies Drear by Virginia Hamilton

I Love My Hair by Natasha Tarpley

John Henry by Julius Lester

Just Us Women by Jeannette Caines

Justin and the Best Biscuits in the World by Mildred Pitts Walter

Kevin and His Dad by Irene Smalls

The Little Tree Growin' in the Shade by Camille Yarbrough

Martin Luther King by Rosemary L. Bray

Minnie Saves the Day by Melodye Benson Rosales

Mirandy and Brother Wind by Patricia C. McKissack

Moja Means One: Swahili Counting Book by Muriel Feelings and Tom Feelings

More Than Anything Else by Marie Bradby

Nathaniel Talking by Eloise Greenfield

No Mirrors in My Nana's House by Ysaye M. Barnwell

On the Day I Was Born by Debbi Chocolate

The Patchwork Quilt by Valerie Flournoy

Copyright © 2010 by Gary Robert Muschla, Judith A. Muschla, and Erin Muschla

List 1.36   continued

The River That Gave Gifts by Margo Humphrey

Show Way by Jacqueline Woodson

Spin a Soft Black Song by Nikki Giovanni

Stevie by John Steptoe

Sweet, Sweet Memory by Jacqueline Woodson

Tar Beach by Faith Ringgold

To Be a Drum by Evelyn Coleman

Turtle Knows Your Name by Ashley Bryan

The Watsons Go to Birmingham—1963 by Christopher Paul Curtis

The Well: David's Story by Mildred D. Taylor

When I Am Old with You by Angela Johnson

White Socks Only by Evelyn Coleman

 Did you know? Virginia Hamilton is among America's most honored authors of children's books.

See List 1.34, Great Books for Any Primary or Elementary Classroom.

Copyright © 2010 by Gary Robert Muschla, Judith A. Muschla, and Erin Muschla

List 1.37   Poetry Books for Children

The rhyme, rhythm, and imagery of poetry can excite the imaginations of children and instill in them a love for words. The following books offer poems that are particularly appealing to students.

Falling Up by Shel Silverstein

Favorite Poems Old and New selected by Helen Ferris

The Genie in the Jar by Nikki Giovanni

The Great Frog Race and Other Poems by Kristine O'Connell George

Honey I Love by Eloise Greenfield

It's Raining Laughter by Nikki Grimes

Joyful Noise: Poems for Two Voices by Paul Fleischman

Knock at a Star: A Child's Introduction to Poetry by X. J. Kennedy and
   Dorothy M. Kennedy

A Light in the Attic by Shel Silverstein

The Random House Book of Poetry for Children selected by Jack Prelutsky

Read-Aloud Poems for the Very Young selected by Jack Prelutsky

Sing a Song of Popcorn by Beatrice Shenk deRegniers

Sing to the Sun by Ashley Bryan

Sky Scrape/City Scape: Poems of City Life by Jane Yolen

The Sun Is So Quiet by Nikki Giovanni

The 20th Century Children's Poetry Treasury selected by Jack Prelutsky

Where the Sidewalk Ends by Shel Silverstein

Did you know? Without music, the lyrics of songs are poems.

Copyright © 2010 by Gary Robert Muschla, Judith A. Muschla, and Erin Muschla

List 1.38   Magazines for Children

Magazines can be sources of high-interest reading material for students. Along with fostering the development of reading skills, they can promote the habit of reading for enjoyment. The magazines that follow are easily contacted through their Web sites.

American Girl Magazine: www.americangirl.com

Boy's Life Magazine: www.boyslife.org

Children's Digest: www.cbhi.org/cbhi/magazines/childrensdigest.shtml

Cobblestone: www.cobblestonepub.com

Cricket: www.cricketmag.com

Faces: www.cobblestonepub.com

Girl's Life: www.girlslife.com

Highlights for Children: www.highlightskids.com

Humpty Dumpty's Magazine: www.humptydumptymag.org

Jack and Jill: www.jackandjillmag.org

National Geographic Kids: www.kids.nationalgeographic.com

Ranger Rick: www.nwf.org/RangerRick

Spider: www.cricketmag.com

Stone Soup: www.stonesoup.com

Your Big Backyard: www.nwf.org/YourBigBackyard

 Did you know? Many print magazines also offer original content through their Web sites.

Copyright © 2010 by Gary Robert Muschla, Judith A. Muschla, and Erin Muschla

List 1.39   Suggestions for Parents and Guardians to Help Their Children with Reading

Parents and guardians can play a major role in the development of their children's reading ability. Their support and encouragement can not only help their children master fundamental reading skills, but help them acquire an appreciation of reading. Following are some suggestions.

- Make reading an important part of your home. Have books on hand and subscribe to magazines for both you and your children.
- Be a reader. Read a variety of materials—newspapers and magazines, novels, and nonfiction books. When children see their parents or guardians reading for pleasure, they will come to view reading as important and enjoyable.
- Let your children see you reading advertisements, letters, and solicitations. All demonstrate that reading is an essential skill.
- Read to your children every day. Start when they are very young and remember that even older children enjoy being read to. Reading to your children models fluency, inflection, and familiarity with words and phrases. Encourage older children to read to their younger brothers and sisters.
- Reread favorite books to your children often. For very young children, choose picture books, books with rhyme, and books with a lot of repetition. Rereading favorite books lays the foundation for reading skills by helping children become familiar with story lines, recognize words, and gain a sense of sentence patterns.
- Talk about stories. Point out repetitive words and encourage your children to say them as you read them. This fosters word recognition and comprehension.
- Use the pictures in books to help clarify and enhance the story. Point out and explain illustrations and photographs.
- Help your children develop vocabulary by using synonyms and antonyms.
- As you read a story, periodically stop and ask your children to predict what will happen next. Encourage them to share their ideas about the story.
- Give books as gifts.
- Help your children build a library in their rooms. Include fiction and nonfiction, as well as reference books such as a dictionary, thesaurus, and a child's almanac.
- Visit your public library regularly. Help your children select books, and involve them with special library events such as story time.
- Visit book stores. Browse for books. Encourage your children to look for books that they find interesting.
- Share your favorite stories and books with your children.
- Treat books with respect. Regard them as wonderful repositories of knowledge that can excite the imagination. When your children see you value books, they will too.

 Did you know? Reading ability is a crucial factor for success in other subjects.

Copyright © 2010 by Gary Robert Muschla, Judith A. Muschla, and Erin Muschla

List 1.40   Reading Teaching Tips

A key element to a successful reading program is the use of multiple strategies and approaches for instruction. The following tips can help you make reading a productive and enjoyable part of your students' day.

- Use a variety of interesting, age-appropriate reading materials, including novels, nonfiction books, short stories, articles, and poetry.
- Incorporate reading across your curriculum. Emphasize to your students that reading is important to all subjects.
- Provide plenty of time for reading. Do not assume that students devote much time to reading at home.
- Encourage individual reading. Consider reserving time for silent reading in your classroom.
- Plan class, group, and individual reading activities.
- Use reading logs as a means to engage students in their reading, probe for deeper insight, and stimulate critical thinking.
- Teach phonics, especially for beginning readers, but also for older students if necessary.
- Be aware of the progress of your students. Address problems quickly.
- Teach vocabulary in reading and also in other subjects.
- Teach students how to use context clues to find the meaning of new words.
- Discuss reading to enhance comprehension.
- Talk about books and encourage your students to talk about books with each other.
- Display titles of your students' favorite books on the bulletin board, perhaps as "Books of the Month."
- Invite the parents and guardians of your students to support your efforts in class by encouraging their children to read at home.
- Be a cheerleader for your students and their reading. When your students know that you support their efforts at reading, they will work harder.

Did you know? Most teachers agree that a balanced approach to reading instruction, which includes phonics, word recognition skills, and the use of interesting, authentic reading materials, is most effective.

See List 1.39, Suggestions for Parents and Guardians to Help Their Children with Reading.

Copyright © 2010 by Gary Robert Muschla, Judith A. Muschla, and Erin Muschla

List 1.41 Checklist for a Successful Reading Program

Successful reading programs have several positive elements in common. Evaluating your reading program according to the following criteria can help you build a program for your students that is productive and enjoyable.

- ☑ Reading is respected as a subject and valued as a skill.
- ☑ A variety of reading materials are available to students—nonfiction books, novels, magazines, short stories, plays, and poetry.
- ☑ Students are encouraged to read a variety of selections.
- ☑ Phonics, word recognition, and comprehension are central to instruction.
- ☑ Instruction takes into account different learning styles and includes activities for the whole class, groups, and individuals.
- ☑ Reading skills are taught in context in meaningful selections.
- ☑ Students are taught helpful reading strategies such as using context clues, focusing on groups of words rather than a single word while reading, and formulating questions and seeking answers as they read.
- ☑ Reading materials are interesting and appropriate for the age and abilities of students.
- ☑ Time for reading is provided in school; reading at home is encouraged.
- ☑ Students are encouraged to select books for themselves.
- ☑ Students are encouraged to respond to their reading.
- ☑ Students are given opportunities to share their ideas about what they read with their classmates.
- ☑ The classroom is filled with books and reading materials. In addition to classroom materials, regular trips to the school library are scheduled.
- ☑ Effort and achievement in reading are supported and applauded.
- ☑ The progress of students is monitored closely. Intervention and remediation, when necessary, are quick and effective.
- ☑ Assessment is fair and practical.
- ☑ An underlying objective of the class is to help students build confidence in their ability to read.
- ☑ The class fosters an appreciation of reading, not just as a subject in school, but as an important ability to other aspects of life.

 Did you know? For many children, their teachers are the most significant factor in their learning to read.

See List 1.40, Reading Teaching Tips.

Copyright © 2010 by Gary Robert Muschla, Judith A. Muschla, and Erin Muschla

Writing

Writing is a process that is the result of various skills. To write with competence, students must be able to formulate, organize, and express ideas clearly and succinctly within the conventions of correct grammar and punctuation. By presenting your students with effective instruction and meaningful writing experiences, you will help them acquire the skills they need to become proficient young writers.

List 2.1   The Writing Process: The Way Writers Write

Writing is a process that includes five stages: prewriting, drafting, revising, editing, and publishing. Each stage is composed of several possible activities. Understanding the writing process enables students to focus their efforts on each stage, which in turn helps them produce quality work.

- *Prewriting* may include finding ideas, choosing a topic, identifying a purpose, brainstorming, researching, focusing a topic, analyzing, organizing, writing an outline, and free writing.
- *Drafting* may include writing, thinking, rearranging, reading, pausing, and elaborating.
- *Revising* may include rewriting, rethinking, clarifying, and additional researching.
- *Editing* may include proofreading, polishing, and correcting grammar and mechanics.
- *Publishing* may include displaying writing on bulletin boards or class Web sites, publishing in a class newspaper, and reading.

 Did you know? The stages of the writing process are fluid and recursive. Writers move back and forth through the stages as they work.

List 2.2   Habits of Good Student Writers

While writing is truly an individual process—each writer approaches a topic in her own way—all good writers, no matter their age, share many of the same characteristics. Good student writers acquire many of the following habits.

- Write often, at least several times each week
- Record their thoughts and musings in journals
- Find interesting ideas for writing
- Focus their topics
- Develop their ideas
- Research ideas for facts and details
- Strive to communicate their ideas clearly
- Work hard to learn and apply the rules of English grammar
- Learn and use correct mechanics
- Try different forms of writing
- Revise and edit their writing
- Enjoy reading and pay attention to how other writers construct their material
- Have favorite authors and favorite kinds of writing
- Take pride in their writing
- Work to improve as writers

 Did you know? Competent writers are usually capable readers and competent readers are usually capable writers. The two processes—reading and writing—are complementary.

Copyright © 2010 by Gary Robert Muschla, Judith A. Muschla, and Erin Muschla

List 2.3   Finding Ideas for Writing

The world is full of ideas for writers. Helping your students learn how to identify topics to write about allows them to take a major step toward the development of competent writing skills.

- *Examining personal experiences.* Things students have done, heard, or read about; their likes and dislikes; observations or questions can all be possible ideas for writing. Personal experience can be an unending stream of ideas.

- *Creating a list of associated ideas.* Starting with a broad topic—sports, for example—students write down any idea that comes to mind. One idea leads to another, which can be the idea out of which a topic springs. For instance, the beginning topic of sports might lead to a personal narrative about a time the student attended a major sports event with his family.

- *Brainstorming with others.* A small group of students chooses a general topic and offers as many ideas about it as they can. They keep generating ideas until they find some they would like to write about. They then pursue these ideas further.

- *Free writing.* Students start to write on a random topic, perhaps "I'm searching for an idea to write about." They continue to write about the topic, following wherever their ideas and writing take them. Sometimes the act of writing itself can lead to ideas to develop.

- *Discovering relationships.* Students think of a general idea and examine how it is related to or connected with other ideas. The general idea of animals, for instance, can lead to pets, which can lead to puppies, and the time the student's family brought a new puppy home.

- *What about? What if? What next?* These questions can be applied to an ordinary or general event or idea that the student then views from different perspectives. For example, a snowstorm cancels school for a day. *What about* the storm last year that caused school to be canceled for an entire week? *What if* students did not have to go to school at all? What would they do all day? After leaving his science report home, forgetting his lunch, and arriving at school late because he missed the bus, a student might ask himself, *What next?* Such examples can open the door to fresh ideas for writing.

Copyright © 2010 by Gary Robert Muschla, Judith A. Muschla, and Erin Muschla

 Did you know? Isaac Asimov, a prolific author, wrote more than 500 books. He always had ideas for writing.

See List 2.4, Writing Prompts.

The Elementary Teacher's Book of Lists

List 2.4   Writing Prompts

No matter how hard young writers may search for a topic to write about, some days good ideas remain elusive. For those days, the following prompts might help.

1. It was the best day of my life . . .
2. Who would have thought that . . . ?
3. I could not believe my ears. The cat was talking . . .
4. I really enjoy . . .
5. It was the scariest night . . .
6. I never understood the secret of the old house until . . .
7. If I could do anything I wished, I would . . .
8. I never felt so silly . . .
9. My favorite book is . . .
10. Our new neighbors were strange . . .
11. Last summer, my family and I went to the greatest . . .
12. Of all the movies I have seen . . .
13. My favorite TV show . . .
14. My favorite movie . . .
15. Animals are . . .
16. The storm was the worst . . .
17. The best holiday is . . .
18. The most important people in my life are . . .
19. I remember the time . . .
20. Every year, my family . . .
21. I really like to play . . .
22. My special talent . . .
23. I was home alone and heard . . .
24. My favorite place to be is . . .
25. I will never forget . . .

 Did you know? Prompts can be especially helpful for reluctant writers.

See List 2.3, Finding Ideas for Writing.

Copyright © 2010 by Gary Robert Muschla, Judith A. Muschla, and Erin Muschla

List 2.5 Developing Writing According to the Five *W's* and *How*

Your students will often find a good, or even great, idea to write about, but then they will struggle to build that idea into solid writing. Asking and answering questions about the idea can lead them to details that will enable them to develop a fine story or article. Encourage your students to build their ideas around the five *W*'s and *How*.

- *Who?* Who is the story about? What are the character's names? What are they like?

- *What?* What happens in the story? What events take place? What details describe the events?

- *When?* When does the story or event happen? Did it happen in the past? Might it happen in the future? Is it happening now? Did it happen during the night or during the day?

- *Where?* Where does the story or event happen? Does it take place at home? In school? In the mall? At a park? What details describe the setting?

- *Why?* Why do the events happen? What causes them? What do the events lead to?

- *How?* How do the events occur? What details can tell the reader exactly what is going on?

 Did you know? The facts in most newspaper articles answer the five *W*'s and *How*.

See List 2.3, Finding Ideas for Writing; List 2.6, Basic Structure for Composition.

Copyright © 2010 by Gary Robert Muschla, Judith A. Muschla, and Erin Muschla

List 2.6   Basic Structure for Composition

As the writing skills of your students develop, you should introduce them to the fundamental structure that underlies most forms of writing. Understanding that both nonfiction and fiction are organized according to a plan enables students to assume command of their writing. They learn that writing is a process controlled by the author. This can be a powerful realization that boosts confidence and leads to better composition.

The Introduction (Also Referred to as the Opening or Lead)

- Introduces the subject
- States the main idea of the piece
- Leads into the body

The Body

- Develops the main idea
- Adds details, facts, and examples that help to explain the main idea

The Conclusion (Also Referred to as the Closing)

- Ends the piece
- May offer a brief summary or a final idea

Did you know? Identifying the introduction, body, and conclusion of reading selections with your students can help them understand the basic structure of articles and stories.

See List 2.5, Developing Writing According to the Five W's and How.

Copyright © 2010 by Gary Robert Muschla, Judith A. Muschla, and Erin Muschla

Some words appear more than others in the writing of students. Awareness of these words provides a foundation of vocabulary that students can use to express their thoughts with clarity and details.

a	balloons	call	didn't
about	baseball	called	died
across	basketball	came	different
afraid	be	can	dinner
after	bear	can't	does
again	beautiful	candy	doesn't
against	because	car	dog
air	become	care	dogs
all	bed	cars	doing
almost	been	cat	don't
along	before	catch	done
also	begin	caught	door
always	being	change	down
am	believe	charge	dream
America	best	children	each
an	better	circus	earth
and	big	city	eat
animal	bike	class	else
another	black	clean	end
any	boat	clothes	enough
anything	book	cold	even
are	books	come	every
around	both	comes	everybody
as	boy	coming	everyone
ask	boys	could	everything
asked	bring	couldn't	except
at	broke	country	eyes
ate	brother	cut	family
away	build	dad	fast
baby	bus	day	father
back	but	days	favorite
bad	buy	decided	feel
ball	by	did	feet

Copyright © 2010 by Gary Robert Muschla, Judith A. Muschla, and Erin Muschla

The Elementary Teacher's Book of Lists

Copyright © 2010 by Gary Robert Muschla, Judith A. Muschla, and Erin Muschla

fell	God	hour	liked
few	goes	house	likes
field	going	how	little
fight	good	hurt	live
fill	got	I	lived
finally	grade	I'd	lives
find	grand	I'm	long
fire	great	if	look
first	ground	important	looked
fish	grow	in	looking
five	had	into	lost
fix	hair	is	lot
follow	half	it	lots
food	happened	it's	love
football	happy	its	lunch
for	hard	job	mad
found	has	jump	made
four	have	just	make
free	having	keep	making
Friday	he	kept	man
friend	he's	kids	many
friends	head	killed	mark
from	heard	kind	math
front	help	knew	may
fun	her	know	maybe
funny	here	lady	me
future	high	land	mean
game	hill	last	men
games	him	later	might
gas	his	learn	minute
gave	hit	leave	miss
get	home	left	mom
getting	homework	let	money
girl	hope	let's	more
girls	horse	life	morning
give	horses	light	most
go	hot	like	mother

mountain	park	saw	stop
mouse	part	say	stopped
move	party	scared	store
much	people	school	story
music	person	schools	street
must	pick	sea	stuff
my	picture	second	such
myself	place	see	sudden
name	planet	seen	suddenly
named	plant	set	summer
need	play	seventh	sure
never	played	she	swimming
new	playing	ship	take
next	police	shot	talk
nice	president	should	talking
night	pretty	show	teach
no	probably	sick	teacher
not	problem	since	teachers
nothing	put	sister	team
notice	ran	sit	tell
now	read	sleep	than
number	ready	small	that
off	real	snow	that's
oh	really	so	the
old	reason	some	their
on	red	someone	them
once	rest	something	then
one	ride	sometimes	there
only	riding	soon	these
or	right	space	they
other	river	sport	they're
our	room	sports	thing
out	rules	start	things
outside	run	started	think
over	running	states	this
own	said	stay	thought
parents	same	still	three

Copyright © 2010 by Gary Robert Muschla, Judith A. Muschla, and Erin Muschla

through	TV	way	winter
throw	two	we	wish
time	united	week	with
times	until	weeks	without
to	up	well	woke
today	upon	went	won
together	us	were	won't
told	use	what	work
too	used	when	world
took	very	where	would
top	walk	which	wouldn't
tree	walked	while	write
trees	walking	white	yard
tried	want	who	year
trip	wanted	who's	years
trouble	war	whole	yes
try	was	whose	you
trying	wasn't	why	you're
turn	watch	will	your
turned	water	win	

Did you know? The words in this list make up the bulk of all written material.

Copyright © 2010 by Gary Robert Muschla, Judith A. Muschla, and Erin Muschla

List 2.8   Kinds of Sentences

There are four kinds of sentences. Each has a different purpose.

1. Declarative sentence
   - Makes a statement
   - Ends with a period
     Example: The puppy is playful.
2. Interrogative sentence
   - Asks a question
   - Ends with a question mark
     Example: Is it raining?
3. Imperative sentence
   - Tells or asks someone to do something
   - Ends with a period
     Example: Please open the window.
4. Exclamatory sentence
   - Shows strong feelings
   - Ends with an exclamation point
     Example: Look out for the ice!

 Did you know? The declarative sentence is the most used sentence in English.

See List 2.9, Sentence Forms.

List 2.9   Sentence Forms

Sentences have different forms. Two of the most common are the simple sentence and the compound sentence.

1. Simple sentence: Has one complete subject and one complete predicate
   Example: Brianne finished her homework. (Brianne is the complete subject and finished her homework is the complete predicate.)
   Example: Did you finish your homework? (You is the complete subject and did finish your homework is the complete predicate.)
2. Compound sentence: Contains two or more simple sentences, joined by a comma and *and*, *but*, or *or*
   Example: Peter plays the drum, and his sister plays the flute.

 Did you know? *And*, *or*, and *but* are known as conjunctions.

See List 2.8, Kinds of Sentences; List 2.10, Subjects and Predicates.

Copyright © 2010 by Gary Robert Muschla, Judith A. Muschla, and Erin Muschla

List 2.10   Subjects and Predicates

Every sentence has two main parts: the *subject* and the *predicate*. Every subject may be broken down into a complete subject and a simple subject. Every predicate may be broken down into a complete predicate and a simple predicate.

Complete subject

- Includes all the words of a sentence that tell who the subject is or what the subject is about

    Examples:

    <u>Jonathan</u> is a fourth-grade student.

    <u>The students</u> will learn about dinosaurs today.

    <u>The gigantic whale</u> swam close to the boat.

Simple subject

- Is the main word or words of the complete subject

    Examples:

    <u>Jonathan</u> is a fourth-grade student.

    The <u>students</u> will learn about dinosaurs today.

    The gigantic <u>whale</u> swam close to the boat.

Complete predicate

- Includes all the words of a sentence that tell what the subject is or does

    Examples:

    Jonathan <u>is a fourth-grade student</u>.

    The students <u>will learn about dinosaurs today</u>.

    The gigantic whale <u>swam close to the boat</u>.

Simple predicate

- Is the main word or words in the complete predicate

    Examples:

    Jonathan <u>is</u> a fourth-grade student.

    The students <u>will learn</u> about dinosaurs today.

    The gigantic whale <u>swam</u> close to the boat.

 Did you know? Students can find the subject of a sentence by asking themselves whom or what the sentence is about. Finding who the subject is or what the subject does can help them identify the predicate.

See List 2.11, Compound Subjects and Predicates.

Copyright © 2010 by Gary Robert Muschla, Judith A. Muschla, and Erin Muschla

List 2.11   Compound Subjects and Predicates

When a sentence has more than one subject, it is said to have a *compound subject*. When it has more than one predicate, it has a *compound predicate*. Some sentences have compound subjects and compound predicates.

A sentence with a compound subject

- Has two or more simple subjects joined by *and* or *or*

    Example: <u>Students</u> and <u>teachers</u> enjoyed the class picnic.

A sentence with a compound predicate

- Has two or more simple predicates joined by *and* or *or*

    Example: The rabbit <u>hopped</u> and <u>ran</u> across the yard.

A sentence with a compound subject and a compound predicate

- Has two or more simple subjects
- Has two or more simple predicates

    Example: <u>Kerri</u> and her <u>mom</u> <u>baked</u> cookies and <u>made</u> punch for the party. (*Kerri* and *mom* are the compound subject, and *baked* and *made* are the compound predicate.)

Did you know? Three or more subjects or predicates should be separated by commas, with *and* or *or* between the last two subjects or predicates.

See List 2.10, Subjects and Predicates.

Copyright © 2010 by Gary Robert Muschla, Judith A. Muschla, and Erin Muschla

The Elementary Teacher's Book of Lists

List 2.12   Fragments and Run-Ons

Every sentence has a subject and predicate and expresses a complete thought. Sentence fragments and run-on sentences are examples of incorrectly written sentences.

Sentence Fragment

- Is a group of words that are only a part of a sentence
- Does not express a complete thought
- Lacks a subject or predicate or both

    Examples of fragments:

    Watched TV after dinner. (Missing a subject)

    After school Adam. (Missing a predicate)

    To a restaurant for dinner. (Missing a subject and a predicate)

- To correct a fragment, rewrite it to complete a thought by adding the missing subject or predicate:

    Marci watched TV after dinner.

    After school Adam finished his homework.

    James and his parents went to a restaurant for dinner.

Run-On Sentence

- Contains two or more sentences that are joined incorrectly

    Examples of run-ons:

    The boys watched a movie they played video games.

    The boys watched a movie, they played video games.

- To correct a run-on sentence, do one of the following:
    ◦ Rewrite it as a compound sentence.
      The boys watched a movie, and they played video games.
    ◦ Rewrite it as two separate sentences.
      The boys watched a movie. They played video games.
    ◦ Combine the two separate ideas.
      The boys watched a movie and played video games.

 Did you know? To avoid fragments, students should make certain that each simple sentence they write has a complete thought. To avoid run-ons, they should make sure that the separate sentences of a compound sentence are joined by *and*, *but*, or *or*.

See List 2.9, Sentence Forms; List 2.10, Subjects and Predicates.

Copyright © 2010 by Gary Robert Muschla, Judith A. Muschla, and Erin Muschla

List 2.13   Point of View

Point of view (POV) refers to the narrator of a story. There are two basic forms of point of view: first person and third person. The point of view of a story must be consistent. A common mistake of young writers is to switch points of view within the same piece. Understanding point of view can prevent this error.

The First-Person Point of View

- The first-person POV refers to the pronoun *I*.

- In stories or nonfiction (personal narratives, for example) that are written in the first-person POV, the author is the narrator as well as a participant in the action. The author tells the story and refers to himself or herself as *I*.

- Because it is natural to write in the first person, the first-person POV is easy for students to use.

- The first-person POV is limited. The author can only write about what he or she knows to be fact. In a story written in the first-person POV, the author/narrator can not, for example, know the thoughts of another character (unless she is a mind reader).

  Example: I did my homework right after school.

The Third-Person Point of View

- The third-person POV refers to the pronouns *he*, *she*, *it*, and *they*.

- The author is not a participant in the action but is assumed to be outside the piece.

- Characters are referred to as *he*, *she*, *it*, or *they*.

- The third-person POV is less personal, but it gives the author more latitude in writing. Depending on the story, the author can write from the POVs of different characters.

  Example: Terri [She] did her homework right after school.

 Did you know? Most writing is done in the third-person POV. Multiple POV refers to an author's use of several viewpoint characters in a story. Novelists often use multiple POVs to tell long, complicated stories.

Copyright © 2010 by Gary Robert Muschla, Judith A. Muschla, and Erin Muschla

List 2.14 Figurative Language: Similes, Metaphors, and Personification

Figures of speech add visual imagery to writing. By the time they reach the elementary grades, many students are already using similes, metaphors, and personification in writing. Providing them with instruction in the use of these figures of speech can significantly enhance their development as fledgling authors.

Similes

- Use *like* or *as* to make comparisons

    Examples:

    The baby's eyes were blue like the sky.

    The storm clouds were dark as night.

Metaphors

- Make comparisons without using *like* or *as*

    Examples:

    The wrestler was a giant.

    The field was a carpet of wild flowers.

Personification

- Gives human qualities to nonhuman things or ideas

    Examples:

    The birds sing outside my window every morning.

    The mountains guarded the valley.

 Did you know? Encouraging your students to identify figures of speech in their reading will help them gain a clear understanding of the use and power of similes, metaphors, and personification.

Copyright © 2010 by Gary Robert Muschla, Judith A. Muschla, and Erin Muschla

List 2.15   Guidelines for Revision

Revision is a time that writers "re-see" their work. During revision, they may add and delete information, reshape ideas, and polish expression. It is a critical stage of the writing process. Yet, for many students revision is also the most troublesome part of writing. Revision is hard work, compounded by the fact that most students are not sure how to revise. The following questions can provide direction. When revising their work, your students should ask themselves:

1. Did I focus my topic?
2. Does my writing have three parts: introduction, body, and conclusion?
3. Does my introduction present my topic to readers clearly?
4. Did I include main ideas and details in the body?
5. Do all the main ideas relate to my topic?
6. Do all details support the main ideas?
7. Did I end with a conclusion?
8. Did I use correct sentence structure?
9. Do the subjects and predicates of my sentences agree?
10. Did I use a consistent point of view?
11. Are the tenses of my verbs correct?
12. Is my writing clear? Did I say exactly what I wanted to say?

 Did you know? Many authors find revision to be the most demanding stage of the writing process. Ernest Hemingway rewrote the last page of the ending of his *A Farewell to Arms* thirty-nine times before he was satisfied with it.

Copyright © 2010 by Gary Robert Muschla, Judith A. Muschla, and Erin Muschla

See List 2.1, The Writing Process: The Way Writers Write; List 2.16, Guidelines for Proofreading; List 2.17, Words That Are Easy to Confuse.

The Elementary Teacher's Book of Lists

List 2.16   Guidelines for Proofreading

Proofreading is a step of the writing process in which a writer makes any remaining corrections to punctuation, grammar, and spelling. The following questions can help focus the proofreading efforts of your students. When your students proofread their work, they should ask themselves:

1. Do all sentences begin with a capital letter?
2. Are all proper nouns and proper adjectives capitalized?
3. Do all sentences end with correct punctuation?
4. Are paragraphs indented?
5. Are pronouns used correctly?
6. Are commas used correctly?
   - To separate items in a list
   - To connect compound sentences
   - After introductory words and phrases
7. Are apostrophes used correctly?
   - With possessive nouns
   - With contractions
8. Are quotation marks used correctly?
   - For the titles of stories, articles, poems, and songs
   - For dialogue
9. Are italics or underlining used correctly?
   - For the titles of books
   - For the titles of newspapers and magazines
   - For the titles of movies and TV shows
10. Are all words used and spelled correctly?

 Did you know? Allowing students to work in pairs to proofread each other's work can sharpen the proofreader's skills as well as help the writer to make final corrections to his or her work.

See 2.1, The Writing Process: The Way Writers Write; List 2.15, Guidelines for Revision; List 2.17, Words That Are Easy to Confuse.

Copyright © 2010 by Gary Robert Muschla, Judith A. Muschla, and Erin Muschla

List 2.17   Words That Are Easy to Confuse

English is a rich language, but in some instances a very confusing language. Words that have similar sounds, similar meanings, or similar spellings result in mistakes for writers of all ages. Sharing the following list with your students can ease some of the muddle for them.

accept: to receive
except: to leave out

advice: an offered suggestion
advise: to give advice

affect: to act upon
effect: a result

all ready: prepared
already: before this time

all together: all in one place
altogether: entirely

among: mixed with
between: in the middle of two

assistance: help
assistants: helpers

beside: at the side of
besides: in addition

breath: air taken into the lungs
breathe: to inhale and exhale

close: to shut
clothes: clothing

command: order
commend: to praise

conscience: knowing right or wrong
conscious: awareness of surroundings

costume: special clothing
custom: habits of doing things

country: a nation
county: a part of a state

desert: dry wasteland
dessert: treat served after a meal

device: something built
devise: to invent or scheme

envelop: to surround
envelope: the cover of a letter

farther: to a greater distance
further: in addition to

fewer: smaller in number
less: not as much

finale: the end
finally: at the end

foreword: introduction of a book
forward: toward the front

human: a person
humane: kind

later: coming afterward
latter: the second of two

lay: to place or put down
lie: to be in a reclined position

Copyright © 2010 by Gary Robert Muschla, Judith A. Muschla, and Erin Muschla

List 2.17   continued

lightening: to make less heavy

lightning: static electrical discharge
in air

loose: not tight

lose: to be deprived of

of: belong to

off: away

past: of a former time

passed: having gone beyond

picture: a drawing

pitcher: a baseball player

quiet: without noise

quit: to give up

quite: completely

recent: not long ago

resent: to feel offended

than: a conjunction

then: at that time

thorough: complete

through: going from end to end

 Did you know? Understanding the meanings and spellings of the words in this list, along with careful proofreading, can reduce errors in usage.

See List 1.12, Homophones; List 2.15, Guidelines for Revision; List 2.16, Guidelines for Proofreading.

Copyright © 2010 by Gary Robert Muschla, Judith A. Muschla, and Erin Muschla

The words of English can be divided into eight parts of speech. Some words, depending on how they are used, can be classified in more than one category.

Noun

- A word that names a person, place, thing, or idea
- May be a common noun, naming any person, place, thing, or idea
- May be a proper noun, naming a particular person, place, thing, or idea (Proper nouns must be capitalized.)

    Examples: girl, boy, Amanda, tree, Chicago, water, Rio Grande River, bird, sky, street, mountain, truth, North America

Verb

- A word that shows action or state of being

    Examples: play, walked, read, ran, talk, study, start, stop, am, is, was, were

Pronoun

- A word used in place of a noun

    Examples: I, you, he, she, it, we, you, they, him, her, them, our, their, who, whom, whose

Adjective

- A word used to describe a noun or pronoun
- May be a proper adjective, formed from a proper noun (Proper adjectives must be capitalized.)

    Examples: tall, little, English, long, Mexican, short, narrow, German, cold, Chinese

Adverb

- A word used to describe a verb, adjective, or another adverb

    Examples: quietly, quickly, always, very, swiftly, often

Conjunction

- A word used to join words or groups of words

    Examples: and, or, but, because, since, however, either

Copyright © 2010 by Gary Robert Muschla, Judith A. Muschla, and Erin Muschla

List 2.18   continued

Preposition

- A word used to show the relationship of a noun or pronoun to another word

  Examples: at, below, for, to, during, after, toward, into, from

Interjection

- A word or group of words used to express strong emotion

  Examples: oh my goodness, ah, gee (Some interjections are followed by exclamation points.) Look out! Oh no! Aha!

 Did you know? Different languages classify words differently. German, for instance, has eleven major parts of speech.

Copyright © 2010 by Gary Robert Muschla, Judith A. Muschla, and Erin Muschla

A *noun* is a word that names a person, place, thing, or idea. Nouns can be single words or two or more words used together. There are different kinds of nouns.

- Common nouns name any person, place, thing, or idea. Some examples follow:
  - *Persons*: student, teacher, man, woman, singer, carpenter, police officer
  - *Places*: town, city, state, country, valley, park, island
  - *Things*: pencil, book, bicycle, cat, flower, river
  - *Ideas*: goodness, freedom, happiness, truth, courage
- Proper nouns name a particular person, place, thing, or idea. Proper nouns are always capitalized. Some examples follow:
  - *People*: George Washington, Barack Obama, J. K. Rowling
  - *Days*: Monday, Wednesday, Saturday, Sunday
  - *Months*: January, April, July, October
  - *Continents*: North America, South America, Asia, Australia
  - *Countries*: United States of America, Canada, Mexico, China
  - *States*: New Jersey, Kansas, California, Alaska
  - *Cities*: New York, Chicago, Dallas, Los Angeles
  - *Buildings*: the White House, Sears Tower, Taj Mahal
  - *Bridges and tunnels*: Golden Gate Bridge, Lincoln Tunnel
  - *Oceans, rivers, and lakes*: Atlantic Ocean, Mississippi River, Lake Superior
  - *Mountains, plains, and valleys*: Mt. McKinley, the Great Plains, the San Fernando Valley
  - *Holidays*: Fourth of July, Memorial Day, Veterans Day
- Singular nouns name one person, place, thing, or idea.

  Examples: student, boy, girl, teacher, town, car, horse, puppy, computer, liberty
- Plural nouns name more than one person, place, thing, or idea.

  Examples: students, boys, girls, teachers, towns, cars, horses, puppies, computers, freedoms

Copyright © 2010 by Gary Robert Muschla, Judith A. Muschla, and Erin Muschla

List 2.19   continued

- Possessive nouns show ownership. They may be singular or plural. They always require an apostrophe.

  Examples: Jenna's bike, Charles's coat, the man's briefcase, the boys' soccer team, the puppies' mother, the children's tree house

 Did you know? The word *noun* comes from the Latin *nomen,* which means "name."

See List 2.20, Rules for Forming Plural Nouns; List 2.21, Special Irregular Plural Nouns; List 2.22, Possessive Nouns.

Copyright © 2010 by Gary Robert Muschla, Judith A. Muschla, and Erin Muschla

List 2.20   Rules for Forming Plural Nouns

The plural forms of most nouns are made by adding -s or -es. The spelling of some singular nouns changes when they become plural. There are special rules for forming the plurals of these nouns.

Rule	Examples
1. To form the plural of most nouns, add -s.	girl—girls; flower—flowers; lake—lakes
2. To form the plural of nouns that end in -s, -x, -ch, -sh, or -zz, add -es.	guess—guesses; box—boxes; branch—branches; bush—bushes; buzz—buzzes
3. To form the plural of nouns that end with a vowel and -y, add -s.	boy—boys; day—days; monkey—monkeys
4. To form the plural of nouns that end with a consonant and -y, change the -y to -i and add -es.	body—bodies; country—countries; puppy—puppies
5. To form the plural of some nouns that end in -f or -fe, change the -f to -v and add -s.	wife—wives; knife—knives
For some others, change the -f to -v and add -es	wolf—wolves; thief—thieves; calf—calves
For some, make no change and add -s.	chief—chiefs; cliff—cliffs
6. To form the plural of nouns that end with a vowel and -o, add -s.	stereo—stereos; radio—radios; patio—patios
7. To form the plural of most nouns that end with a consonant and -o, add -es.	potato—potatoes; hero—heroes
For some, only add -s.	silo—silos

 Did you know? Paying close attention to the spelling of plural nouns when reading and writing can help students remember the correct forms.

See List 2.21, Special Irregular Plural Nouns.

Copyright © 2010 by Gary Robert Muschla, Judith A. Muschla, and Erin Muschla

List 2.21   Special Irregular Plural Nouns

The nouns below do not follow any rules for forming their plurals. Their plural forms must be learned and remembered.

Different Singular and Plural Forms

child: children	mouse: mice
foot: feet	ox: oxen
goose: geese	tooth: teeth
man: men	woman: women

Same Singular and Plural Forms

deer: deer	series: series
moose: moose	species: species
offspring: offspring	trout: trout
salmon: salmon	wheat: wheat

Did you know? *Fish* has two acceptable plural forms: *fish* and *fishes*.

See List 2.20, Rules for Forming Plural Nouns.

List 2.22   Possessive Nouns

Possessive nouns show ownership—that a person or something owns a thing. There are three rules for forming possessive nouns.

Rules	Examples
1. To form the possessive of a singular noun, add an apostrophe and *-s* to the noun.	the cage of the lion: the lion's cage the pen belonging to James: James's pen
2. To form the possessive of a plural noun that ends in *-s*, add an apostrophe after the *-s*.	the toys of the kittens: the kittens' toys the coats of the girls: the girls' coats
3. To form the possessive of a plural noun that does not end in *-s*, add an apostrophe and *-s* to the noun.	the desks of the children: the children's desks the nest of the mice: the mice's nest

Did you know? Students often have difficulty remembering to use apostrophes with possessive nouns. Consistent reinforcement with examples can clarify confusion.

See List 2.20, Rules for Forming Plural Nouns; List 2.21, Special Irregular Plural Nouns.

Copyright © 2010 by Gary Robert Muschla, Judith A. Muschla, and Erin Muschla

Writing

List 2.23   Action Verbs

Action verbs are words that show action. They tell what the subject of the sentence does or did. They are often the main word in the predicate of a sentence. Use the following list to help your students become familiar with action verbs.

bake	draw	keep	rub	teach
bark	drive	know	run	tell
believe	earn	laugh	rush	thank
break	eat	leave	save	think
bring	enjoy	like	scream	throw
build	enter	listen	see	toss
buy	fall	lose	shake	treat
call	fight	make	shout	trip
can	fill	miss	show	type
carry	finish	mow	shrink	use
catch	fly	open	sing	visit
chase	forget	pass	sip	wait
choose	forgive	pick	sit	walk
clap	free	pitch	slide	want
clean	give	play	slip	wash
climb	go	print	snore	watch
close	guess	prove	soar	wear
come	hear	pull	speak	win
cough	hike	rake	start	wish
count	hit	read	stop	wonder
cry	hope	receive	study	work
dance	hurry	remember	swim	write
dig	invite	ride	take	yell
dive	jump	roar	talk	

 Did you know? A direct object is a noun or pronoun that follows a verb and receives the action of the verb. It answers the questions *What?* or *Whom?*

See List 2.24, Linking Verbs; 2.26, Rules for Forming Verb Tenses; List 2.27, Irregular Verbs.

Copyright © 2010 by Gary Robert Muschla, Judith A. Muschla, and Erin Muschla

The Elementary Teacher's Book of Lists

List 2.24   Linking Verbs

A *linking verb* links the subject of a sentence to a noun or adjective in the predicate. The word that follows the linking verb names or describes the subject.

- Many linking verbs are forms of the verb *to be*: be, am, is, are, was, were, being, been. *Examples*:

  I <u>am</u> happy.

  Mr. Collins <u>is</u> a carpenter.

  The children <u>were</u> noisy.

- Some verbs can be linking or action verbs. To be a linking verb, these verbs must be able to take the place of a form of the verb *be* in a sentence. Examples of linking verbs (other than forms of the verb *to be*) include: appear, become, feel, grow, sound, seem, look, taste. *Examples*:

  The candy <u>tastes</u> sweet.   The candy <u>is</u> sweet.
  Jared <u>seemed</u> surprised.   Jared <u>was</u> surprised.
  The pies and cakes <u>were</u>   The pies and cakes <u>looked</u>
     delicious.   delicious.

 Did you know? When a noun follows a linking verb, it is called a *predicate noun*. When an adjective follows a linking verb, it is called a *predicate adjective*.

See List 2.23, Action Verbs; List 2.26, Rules for Forming Verb Tenses.

Copyright © 2010 by Gary Robert Muschla, Judith A. Muschla, and Erin Muschla

List 2.25   The Tenses of Verbs

The *tense* of a verb shows the time a sentence happens. There are three main verb tenses: present, past, and future.

- Verbs in the present tense show that something is happening now. *Examples:*
  Lindsey <u>dances</u> in the school play today.
  Her mother <u>watches</u> the play.
  Kaitlin and Stephanie <u>dance</u> in the school play.
- Verbs in the past tense show that something has happened. *Examples:*
  Lindsey <u>danced</u> in the school play yesterday.
  Her mother <u>watched</u> the play.
  Kaitlin and Stephanie <u>danced</u> in the school play.
- Verbs in the future tense show that something will happen. *Examples:*
  Lindsey <u>will dance</u> in the school play tomorrow.
  Her mother <u>will watch</u> the play.
  Kaitlin and Stephanie <u>will dance</u> in the school play.

 Did you know? Other verb tenses are present perfect tense, past perfect tense, and future perfect tense.

See List 2.26, Rules for Forming Verb Tenses; List 2.27, Irregular Verbs.

Copyright © 2010 by Gary Robert Muschla, Judith A. Muschla, and Erin Muschla

List 2.26   Rules for Forming Verb Tenses

When their tenses change, the forms of most verbs change, too. The following rules can provide your students with guidance when changing the tenses of verbs.

- To form the present tense when the subject of the sentence is singular, do the following:
  - For most verbs, add -s. *Examples*:

    start: starts   run: runs   talk: talks

  - For verbs that end in -s, -ch, -sh, -x, or -z, add -es. *Examples*:

    guess: guesses   catch: catches   rush: rushes   fix: fixes   buzz: buzzes

  - For verbs that end with a consonant and -y, change the -y to -i and add -es. *Examples*:

    hurry: hurries   fry: fries   try: tries

- To form the past tense in any sentence, do the following:
  - For most verbs, add -ed. *Examples*:

    walk: walked   jump: jumped   climb: climbed

  - For verbs that end in -e, add -d. *Examples*:

    skate: skated   free: freed   dance: danced

  - For verbs that end with a consonant and -y, change the -y to -i and add -ed. *Examples*:

    try: tried   carry: carried   bury: buried

  - For verbs that end with a single vowel and a consonant, double the final consonant and add -ed. *Examples*:

    trip: tripped   slip: slipped   fan: fanned

- To form the future tense in any sentence, use *will* or *shall* with the verb. *Example*:

  Sara and her father <u>will walk</u> to the park.

 Did you know? Young writers sometimes shift back and forth between past and present tenses in their writing. Such inconsistency makes writing unclear. Encourage your students to focus on their use of tenses during writing, and especially during editing and proofreading.

See List 2.25, The Tenses of Verbs; List 2.27, Irregular Verbs.

Copyright © 2010 by Gary Robert Muschla, Judith A. Muschla, and Erin Muschla

Writing

List 2.27   Irregular Verbs

Most verbs form their past tense by adding -d or -ed. Such verbs are called *regular verbs*. *Irregular verbs* do not form their past tense by adding -d or -ed. They have various forms, which can cause much confusion. When helping verbs such as *has*, *had*, or *have* are used with verbs in the past tense, they form a phrase called a past participle. Learning the forms of irregular verbs is the best way to avoid making mistakes with them.

Present Tense	Past Tense	Past Participle
begin	began	has, have, had begun
bet	bet	has, have, had bet
blow	blew	has, have, had blown
break	broke	has, have, had broken
bring	brought	has, have, had brought
build	built	has, have, had built
catch	caught	has, have, had caught
choose	chose	has, have, had chosen
come	came	has, have, had come
cut	cut	has, have, had cut
dig	dug	has, have, had dug
dive	dived or dove	has, have, had dived or dove
do	did	has, have, had done
draw	drew	has, have, had drawn
drink	drank	has, have, had drunk
drive	drove	has, have, had driven
eat	ate	has, have, had eaten
fall	fell	has, have, had fallen
feed	fed	has, have, had fed
fight	fought	has, have, had fought
fly	flew	has, have, had flown
freeze	froze	has, have, had frozen
get	got	has, have, had gotten
give	gave	has, have, had given
go	went	has, have, had gone
grow	grew	has, have, had grown
hide	hid	has, have, had hidden
hurt	hurt	has, have, had hurt
keep	kept	has, have, had kept
know	knew	has, have, had known
lay	laid	has, have, had laid
leave	left	has, have, had left
lie	lay	has, have, had lain
lose	lost	has, have, had lost
make	made	has, have, had made
put	put	has, have, had put
read	read	has, have, had read

Copyright © 2010 by Gary Robert Muschla, Judith A. Muschla, and Erin Muschla

Copyright © 2010 by Gary Robert Muschla, Judith A. Muschla, and Erin Muschla

Present Tense	Past Tense	Past Participle
ride	rode	has, have, had ridden
ring	rang	has, have, had rung
run	ran	has, have, had run
say	said	has, have, had said
see	saw	has, have, had seen
set	set	has, have, had set
shake	shook	has, have, had shaken
shine	shined or shone	has, have, had shined or shone
shrink	shrank or shrunk	has, have, had shrank or shrunk
sing	sang	has, have, had sung
sit	sat	has, have, had sat
sleep	slept	has, have, had slept
speak	spoke	has, have, had spoken
spring	sprang or sprung	has, have, had sprang or sprung
stand	stood	has, have, had stood
steal	stole	has, have, had stolen
stick	stuck	has, have, had stuck
strike	struck	has, have, had struck
sweep	swept	has, have, had swept
swim	swam or swum	has, have, had swam or swum
swing	swung	has, have, had swung
take	took	has, have, had taken
teach	taught	has, have, had taught
tear	tore	has, have, had torn
tell	told	has, have, had told
think	thought	has, have, had thought
throw	threw	has, have, had thrown
wake	waked	has, have, had waked
wear	wore	has, have, had worn
wet	wet	has, have, had wet
win	won	has, have, had won
write	wrote	has, have, had written

Did you know? The number of irregular verbs in English varies, depending on whether words like *shine*, which has two acceptable forms for the past and past participle are included. In general, there are slightly more than 600 irregular verbs, with none beginning with the letters *x* or *y*.

See List 2.25, The Tenses of Verbs; List 2.26, Rules for Forming Verb Tenses.

List 2.28   Verb Contractions with *Not*

When followed by the word *not*, some verbs and *not* are written as contractions. Sharing the following examples with your students can help them to learn these words.

Verb/Not	Contraction
are not	aren't
can not	can't
could not	couldn't
did not	didn't
do not	don't
does not	doesn't
had not	hadn't
has not	hasn't
have not	haven't
is not	isn't
must not	mustn't
should not	shouldn't
was not	wasn't
were not	weren't
will not	won't
would not	wouldn't

 Did you know? Emphasizing that apostrophes used in contractions indicate missing letters can help your students avoid confusing contractions with possessive nouns.

See List 2.34, Pronoun Contractions.

Copyright © 2010 by Gary Robert Muschla, Judith A. Muschla, and Erin Muschla

List 2.29   Rules for Subject-Verb Agreement

A verb must agree in number with the subject of a sentence. If the subject of a sentence is a singular noun or pronoun, the verb must be singular. If the subject of a sentence is a plural noun or pronoun, the verb must be plural. To help your students understand subject-verb agreement, share the following rules with them.

Present Tense

- When the subject of a sentence is singular, add *-s* or *-es* to the verb. *Examples*: Vanessa plays the flute. Jonathan finishes his homework before dinner.
- When the subject of a sentence is plural, do not add *-s* or *-es* to the verb. *Examples*: Vanessa and Hannah play the flute. Jonathan and his brother finish their homework before dinner.
- The pronouns *I* and *you* require the plural forms of verbs. *Examples*: I play the flute. You finish your homework before dinner.

Past Tense

- Singular and plural subjects agree with the same forms of verbs. *Examples*:

   Jonathan finished his homework before dinner. Jonathan and his brother finished their homework.

Future Tense

- Singular and plural subjects agree with the same forms of verbs. *Examples*:

   Vanessa will play the flute tomorrow. Vanessa and Hannah will play the flute tomorrow.

The Verbs *Be* and *Have*

- The verbs *be* and *have* have special forms to agree with subjects.

Subjects and Be	Present Tense	Past Tense
I	am	was
you	are	were
he, she, it	is	was
we, they	are	were

Subjects and Have	Present Tense	Past Tense
I	have	had
you	have	had
he, she, it	has	had
we, they	have	had

 Did you know? Students have the most trouble with the agreement of subjects and verbs in the present tense.

See List 2.25, The Tenses of Verbs; List 2.27, Irregular Verbs.

Copyright © 2010 by Gary Robert Muschla, Judith A. Muschla, and Erin Muschla

List 2.30   Pronouns

Pronouns are words that take the place of nouns. Many of the most commonly used pronouns are shown in the list below.

I	we	us	its	hers
you	they	them	our	ours
he	me	my	their	theirs
she	him	your	mine	who
it	her	his	yours	whom
				whose

 Did you know? Pronouns that refer to persons are often known as *personal pronouns*.

See List 2.31, Subject Pronouns; List 2.32, Object Pronouns; List 2.33, Possessive Pronouns.

List 2.31   Subject Pronouns

Subject pronouns take the place of nouns that are the subject of a sentence. Subject pronouns may be singular or plural.

Singular	*Examples:*	**Plural**	*Examples:*
I	Tom studied for the math test.	we	I studied for the math test.
you	Susan studied for the math test.	you	She studied for the math test.
he, she, it	Susan and Tom studied for the math test.	they	They studied for the math test.

 Did you know? Subject pronouns can also be used after forms of the linking verb *be*. Here is an example: The students of the month were Carlos and I.

See List 2.30, Pronouns; List 2.32, Object Pronouns; List 2.33, Possessive Pronouns.

Copyright © 2010 by Gary Robert Muschla, Judith A. Muschla, and Erin Muschla

The Elementary Teacher's Book of Lists

List 2.32   Object Pronouns

Object pronouns take the place of nouns that are the object of a verb. They can also take the place of a noun after a preposition. Object pronouns may be singular or plural.

Singular	**Plural**
me	us
you	you
her, him, it	them

Examples:

Tom told <u>Mandy</u> about the storm.
Tom told <u>her</u> about the storm.

Dad will drive <u>Gabriella</u> and <u>Angela</u> to school.
Dad will drive <u>you</u> and <u>me</u> to school.

The package was addressed to <u>Jacob</u>.
The package was addressed to <u>him</u>.

 Did you know? *You* and *it* may be subject pronouns or object pronouns.

See List 2.30, Pronouns; List 2.31, Subject Pronouns; List 2.33, Possessive Pronouns.

Copyright © 2010 by Gary Robert Muschla, Judith A. Muschla, and Erin Muschla

List 2.33   Possessive Pronouns

Possessive pronouns are pronouns that show who or what owns something. Some possessive pronouns come before a noun. Others can stand by themselves and replace a noun in a sentence. Two, *his* and *its*, can do both.

Possessive Pronouns That Come Before a Noun

Singular	Plural
my	our
your	your
his, her, its	their

Examples:
My house is the first one on the street.
Her house is next to my house.
Where is their house?

Possessive Pronouns That Stand Alone

Singular	Plural
mine	ours
yours	yours
his, hers, its	theirs

Examples:
That seat is mine.
That seat is yours.
Hers is by the window.

 Did you know? Students often confuse the possessive pronoun *your* with the contraction *you're*. They confuse the possessive pronoun *its* with the contraction *it's*. They also confuse *their* with *they're* and *there*. Clear explanations and consistent reinforcement can help your students remember the distinctions.

See List 2.30, Pronouns; List 2.31, Subject Pronouns; List 2.32, Object Pronouns.

Copyright © 2010 by Gary Robert Muschla, Judith A. Muschla, and Erin Muschla

List 2.34   Pronoun Contractions

Pronoun contractions are common in reading, writing, and speaking. They are formed from the combination of subject pronouns with some verbs. Be sure to remind your students that they must use an apostrophe to indicate the missing letters of a contraction.

Pronoun/Verb	Contraction	Pronoun/Verb	Contraction
I am	I'm	I had	I'd
you are	you're	you had	you'd
she is	she's	he had	he'd
he is	he's	she had	she'd
it is	it's	it had	it'd
we are	we're	we had	we'd
they are	they're	they had	they'd
I have	I've	I will	I'll
you have	you've	you will	you'll
she has	she's	he will	he'll
he has	he's	she will	she'll
it has	it's	it will	it'll
we have	we've	we will	we'll
they have	they've	they will	they'll

Did you know? A simple strategy to avoid misusing *you're*, *it's*, and *they're* as possessive pronouns is to rewrite each contraction into the words that form it. For example, when students rewrite *you're* to *you are*, they can easily see that it is not the possessive pronoun *your*.

See List 2.28, Verb Contractions with Not; *List 2.31, Subject Pronouns.*

Copyright © 2010 by Gary Robert Muschla, Judith A. Muschla, and Erin Muschla

List 2.35   Adjectives

Adjectives are words that describe nouns and pronouns. They tell *what kind* or *how many*. Following are examples of adjectives your students are likely to encounter in their reading and may use to add rich details to their writing.

aching	easy	humorous	rare
active	energetic	impossible	reckless
airy	enjoyable	joyful	restful
American	enormous	kind	restless
amusing	fair	large	rocky
ancient	faithful	little	rough
arid	famous	lively	royal
awful	fearful	lone	sad
beautiful	fearless	loyal	safe
bold	few	main	serious
brave	final	major	shy
brief	firm	merry	sickly
bright	foolish	Mexican	silly
broad	friendly	mighty	simple
calm	funny	minor	single
Canadian	fussy	miserable	skillful
careful	generous	moist	slender
careless	gentle	narrow	slight
certain	gigantic	nice	smart
charming	glad	noisy	soft
cheerful	gloomy	old	solar
clear	handmade	painful	sore
cloudless	happy	peaceful	sorrowful
coastal	hard	perfect	spectacular
comical	heavy	playful	speedy
cool	helpful	pleasant	steady
courageous	helpless	polar	stiff
cute	high	polite	strange
delighted	honest	powerful	strong
dense	hopeful	powerless	sunny
difficult	hopeless	pretty	swift
discouraged	huge	quick	swollen
eager	humble	quiet	tall

Copyright © 2010 by Gary Robert Muschla, Judith A. Muschla, and Erin Muschla

List 2.35   continued

terrible	tiny	useful	wonderful
thankful	tremendous	useless	worthy
thankless	tricky	wasteful	young
thin	uneasy	weak	
thoughtful	unfair	wide	
thoughtless	unhappy	witty	

 Did you know? Although adjectives usually come before the nouns they describe, they can also follow linking verbs. These adjectives are called *predicate adjectives*.

See List 2.36, Comparing with Adjectives; List 2.37, Some Special Adjectives; List 2.38, Adverbs.

Copyright © 2010 by Gary Robert Muschla, Judith A. Muschla, and Erin Muschla

List 2.36   Comparing with Adjectives

Many adjectives can be used to compare nouns and pronouns. These adjectives have three forms. The rules below can help your students use adjectives for comparing correctly.

Rules	Examples
1. For most adjectives, add *-er* to compare two things. Add *-est* to compare three or more things.	short, shorter, shortest old, older, oldest
2. For adjectives ending with *-e*, drop the *-e* and add *-er* or *-est*.	wide, wider, widest true, truer, truest
3. For adjectives ending with a consonant and *-y*, change the *-y* to *-i* and add *-er* or *-est*.	funny, funnier, funniest pretty, prettier, prettiest
4. For adjectives ending with a single vowel and a consonant, double the final consonant and add *-er* or *-est*.	thin, thinner, thinnest hot, hotter, hottest
5. For some adjectives that have two or more syllables, use *more* with the adjective to compare two things and *most* to compare three.	enjoyable, more enjoyable, most enjoyable careful, more careful, most careful
6. The words *good* and *bad* are adjectives that have special forms for comparing. They do not use *-er* or *-est*, or *more* or *most*. *Better* and *worse* compare two things. *Best* and *worst* compare three or more things.	good, better, best bad, worse, worst

 Did you know? Some students will mistakenly use *more* or *most* with the *-er* or *-est* form of an adjective, for example, "more bigger." To help them avoid this error, explain that only one form of comparison is correct for each adjective.

See List 2.35, Adjectives; List 2.37, Some Special Adjectives.

Copyright © 2010 by Gary Robert Muschla, Judith A. Muschla, and Erin Muschla

List 2.37   Some Special Adjectives

Most adjectives tell *what kind* or *how many*. Some have special functions.

Articles: *A, An,* and *The*

- Use *a* before a word that begins with a consonant sound. *Examples*: a car, a book, a house
- Use *an* before a word that begins with a vowel sound. *Examples*: an apple, an egg, an idea
- Use *the* before a specific person, place, or thing. *Examples*: the teacher, the train, the beavers

Demonstrative Adjectives: *This, That, These,* and *Those*

- When they are used before nouns, the words *this, that, these,* and *those* are demonstrative adjectives. *This* and *these* usually refer to something close by. *That* and *those* usually refer to something farther away.
- *This* and *that* are used before singular nouns. *Examples*: this pen, that pencil
- *These* and *those* are used before plural nouns. *Examples*: these pens, those pencils

Proper Adjectives

- Proper adjectives are adjectives formed from proper names. *Examples*: America: American; Mexico: Mexican; Germany: German
- They are always capitalized. *Examples*: American history, Chinese food, Greek art

 Did you know? Teaching history and geography provide great opportunities to review proper adjectives derived from the names of countries.

See List 2.35, Adjectives.

Copyright © 2010 by Gary Robert Muschla, Judith A. Muschla, and Erin Muschla

List 2.38   Adverbs

Adverbs are words that usually describe verbs, but they may also describe adjectives or other adverbs. Adverbs answer the questions *how*, *when*, *where*, or *how often* something happens. Like adjectives, adverbs can add details to the writing of your students.

almost	fearfully	playfully	softly
already	finally	pleasantly	strangely
also	firmly	powerfully	suddenly
always	forward	quickly	swiftly
anyway	frequently	recently	thankfully
brightly	gently	respectfully	then
carefully	gracefully	sadly	there
certainly	happily	safely	thoughtfully
clearly	hard	seriously	totally
cleverly	heavily	shyly	truly
closely	here	silently	unfairly
correctly	honestly	simply	very
deeply	kindly	skillfully	weakly
eagerly	loudly	slightly	when
easily	luckily	slow	where
fairly	narrowly	slowly	wildly
faithfully	often	slyly	wisely
fast	perfectly	smoothly	wishfully

 Did you know? Most adverbs end in *-ly*. Some words such as *fast*, *slow*, and *hard* may be adjectives or adverbs, depending on their use in a sentence.

See List 2.39, Comparing with Adverbs.

Copyright © 2010 by Gary Robert Muschla, Judith A. Muschla, and Erin Muschla

List 2.39   Comparing with Adverbs

Many adverbs can compare two or more actions. Like adjectives, these adverbs have three forms. The rules below can help your students use adverbs for comparing correctly.

Rules	Examples
1. For most adverbs of one syllable, and some adverbs of two syllables, add *-er* to compare two actions. Add *-est* to compare three or more actions.	hard, harder, hardest slow, slower, slowest early, earlier, earliest
2. For most adverbs of two or more syllables, use *more* to compare two actions. Use *most* to compare three or more actions.	silently, more silently, most silently easily, more easily, most easily

 Did you know? Because adverbs and adjectives are compared in the same manner, many students have difficulty seeing the difference between them. To reduce confusion, remind your students that adjectives describe nouns and pronouns.

See List 2.38, Adverbs.

List 2.40   Negative Words

Negative words mean *no* or *not*. Using two negative words in a sentence results in a double negative and makes the sentence incorrect. To avoid speaking and writing double negatives, students must be able to recognize the following negative words.

aren't	hadn't	never	none	shouldn't
can't	hasn't	no	not	wasn't
couldn't	haven't	no one	nothing	won't
don't	isn't	nobody	nowhere	wouldn't

 Did you know? The easiest way to correct a double negative is to eliminate one of the negative words in a sentence. Another way is to change one of the negative words to a positive word, for example, *no* to *any*. To avoid double negatives in their writing, encourage your students to edit and proofread their work carefully.

Copyright © 2010 by Gary Robert Muschla, Judith A. Muschla, and Erin Muschla

Writing

List 2.41   Prepositions and Prepositional Phrases

Prepositions are words that relate a noun or pronoun to another word in a sentence. A noun or pronoun that follows a preposition is called the object of the preposition. Together the preposition and its object (and any words that modify the object) form a prepositional phrase. Prepositional phrases can add details to writing. When your students write, they should carefully choose the prepositions that best express what they wish to say.

aboard	behind	in	through
about	below	inside	to
above	beneath	into	toward
across	beside	near	under
after	between	of	until
against	beyond	off	unto
along	by	on	up
alongside	down	onto	upon
around	during	out	with
at	for	over	within
before	from	past	without

Examples of prepositional phrases:

to the store	during the storm	through the tunnel	in the garage
after school	for me	on the bookcase	with Tommy and Sam

 Did you know? Of pronouns, only object pronouns can serve as the object of a preposition.

See List 2.32, Object Pronouns.

Copyright © 2010 by Gary Robert Muschla, Judith A. Muschla, and Erin Muschla

List 2.42   Conjunctions

Conjunctions are connecting words. They join words or groups of words in a sentence. They may also join two simple sentences to form a compound sentence. Three of the most commonly used conjunctions are *and*, *but*, and *or*. The following facts will help guide your students in their usage.

- The conjunction *and* adds information. It is often used to join subjects, predicates, words, and sentences. *Examples*:

  Subjects: Julia and Grace are sisters.

  Predicates: The puppy ran and played all day.

  Words: Ben finished his math, spelling, and history homework.

  Sentences: Dylan caught a cold, and he was sick all weekend.

- The conjunction *but* shows contrast. It may be used to join words or sentences. *Examples*:

  Words: Adam worked quickly but carefully on his project.

  Sentences: Marta tried to watch the whole movie, but she fell asleep.

- The conjunction *or* gives a choice. It is often used to join subjects, words, or sentences. *Examples*:

  Subjects: Ricky or Nicole will be the student of the week.

  Words: Students could work alone or in groups.

  Sentences: Jordan could listen to music, or he could play a video game.

 Did you know? *And*, *but*, and *or* are also known as coordinating conjunctions.

Copyright © 2010 by Gary Robert Muschla, Judith A. Muschla, and Erin Muschla

List 2.43   Interjections

Interjections are words or groups of words that show strong feelings or emotions. A mild interjection is followed by a comma or period; a strong interjection is followed by an exclamation point. Help your students become familiar with the following common interjections, but caution them not to overuse interjections in their writing. Too many interjections make writing rough and choppy. Interjections should only be used to express powerful feelings.

ah	hey	oh my	ugh
aha	hooray	oh no	uh oh
excellent	my	oops	well
gee	my goodness	ouch	wow
good grief	oh	phew	yeah
great	oh dear	super	yikes

Examples of sentences with interjections:

Aha! I see how Tara solved the problem.
Uh oh, I think I left my lunch home.
You found the answer. Great!

 Did you know? Interjections have no grammatical relationship to the rest of the sentence. They stand alone as expressions of strong feelings.

Copyright © 2010 by Gary Robert Muschla, Judith A. Muschla, and Erin Muschla

List 2.44   Common Abbreviations

Abbreviations are shortened forms of words. They are often used in the names of months and days, addresses, titles, and lists. Many abbreviations begin with a capital letter and end with a period. Some do not have any capital letters or periods.

Months	**Days**	**Streets and Roads**
January: Jan.	Sunday: Sun.	Street: St.
February: Feb.	Monday: Mon.	Avenue: Ave.
March: Mar.	Tuesday: Tues.	Road: Rd.
April: Apr.	Wednesday: Wed.	Drive: Dr.
August: Aug.	Thursday: Thurs.	Boulevard: Blvd.
September: Sept.	Friday: Fri.	Highway: Hwy.
October: Oct.	Saturday: Sat.	
November: Nov.		
December: Dec.		

Titles

Mister: Mr.	President: Pres.	Lieutenant: Lt.
Mistress: Mrs.	Governor: Gov.	Senior: Sr.
Doctor: Dr.	Captain: Capt.	Junior: Jr.

Time

Anno Domini (in the year of our Lord): A.D.	hour: hr.
Before Christ: B.C.	minute: min.
Common Era: C.E.	second: sec.
Before Common Era: B.C.E.	month: mo.
ante meridiem (morning): A.M. or a.m.	year: yr.
post meridiem (afternoon): P.M. or p.m.	

Other Abbreviations

amount: amt	biography: biog.
answer: ans.	building: bldg.
assistant: asst.	centigrade: C
association: assn. or assoc.	chapter: chap.
bibliography: bib	company: co.

Copyright © 2010 by Gary Robert Muschla, Judith A. Muschla, and Erin Muschla

List 2.44   continued

corporation: corp.

department: dept.

division: div.

dozen: doz.

each: ea.

edition: ed.

et cetera (and others): etc.

exempli gratia (for example): e.g.

Fahrenheit: F

figure: fig.

government: govt.

height: ht.

id est (that is): i.e.

illustration: illus.

including: incl.

Incorporated: Inc.

introduction: intro

latitude: lat.

longitude: long.

magazine: mag.

miles per hour: mph

number: no.

package: pkg.

page: p.

pages: pp.

population: pop.

reference: ref.

subject: subj.

versus: vs.

volume: vol.

weight: wt.

 Did you know? The use of abbreviations can be traced back to ancient cultures. Using a shorter form of a word was quite practical when one had to laboriously scratch words into clay tablets or write on parchment.

See List 3.33, The Customary System of Measures; List 3.37, Metric System Units and Prefixes.

Copyright © 2010 by Gary Robert Muschla, Judith A. Muschla, and Erin Muschla

List 2.45   Rules for Using End Punctuation

There are three types of end punctuation: the period, question mark, and exclamation point. The following rules highlight their use.

- Use a period to end a declarative sentence (statement). *Example*: The rain started last night.
- Use a period to end an imperative sentence (command). *Example*: Close the door.
- Use a question mark to end an interrogative sentence (question). *Example*: What is for dinner?
- Use an exclamation point to end an exclamatory sentence (exclamation). *Examples*:

  Watch out for the ice!

  What a beautiful rainbow!

Additional Rules for Using Periods

- Periods are used after initials. *Examples*:

  A. A. Milne (Alan Alexander)   J. K. Rowling (Joanne Kathleen)
- Periods are used after many abbreviations. *Examples*:

  Street: St.   Mister: Mr.   Doctor: Dr.   January: Jan.

 Did you know? The earliest writing lacked any punctuation. Most ancient texts had no spaces between words and no end marks. This certainly was one of the reasons the ability to read was limited.

See List 2.44, Common Abbreviations.

Copyright © 2010 by Gary Robert Muschla, Judith A. Muschla, and Erin Muschla

List 2.46   Rules for Using Commas

Because they have so many uses, commas can cause much confusion for students. Emphasizing the following rules can help to reduce errors.

- Use a comma between the day and the year. *Examples*:
  September 1, 2011   Nov. 3, 2011
- Use a comma between the name of a city or town and its state. *Examples*:
  Portland, Oregon   Evansville, Indiana   Jackson, New Jersey
- Use a comma to separate the words in a series. *Example*:
  Olivia packed sandwiches, snacks, and punch for the picnic.
- Use a comma after an introductory word or phrase in a sentence. *Examples*:
  Yes, I finished my homework.
  Waking from his nap, the kitten stretched and yawned.
- Use a comma to set off an appositive, a group of words that gives information about a noun. *Example*:
  The king, an old man with wise eyes, looked upon his subjects.
- Use a comma in direct address. *Examples*:
  David, your science book is on the table.
  Your coat is in the closet, Madison.
  If we don't leave now, Justin, we'll be late for the game.
- Use a comma to set off a direct quotation in a sentence. *Examples*:
  "The bike is in the garage," Brian said.
  Melissa said, "It's raining."
  "As soon as I get home," said Paulo, "I'll start my homework."
- Use a comma before *and*, *but*, and *or* in a compound sentence. *Example*:
  Allison likes to dance, and her sister likes to sing.
- Use a comma after the greeting in a friendly letter. *Examples*:
  Dear Uncle John,   Dear Megan,
- Use a comma after the closing in all letters. *Examples*:
  Yours truly,   Sincerely,

Did you know? The comma is the most commonly used punctuation mark in English.

Copyright © 2010 by Gary Robert Muschla, Judith A. Muschla, and Erin Muschla

List 2.47 Rules for Using Colons

Colons have specific uses. The following address three of the most important.

- Use a colon to separate hours and minutes in time. *Examples*:

  8:15 A.M.   7:30 P.M.

- Use a colon to set off the words in a list. *Example*:

  Emmy checked off all the homework she had to do: math, social studies, and science.

- Use a colon after the greeting of a business letter. *Examples*:

  Dear Miss Williams: Dear Sir: Dear Mr. Carter:

 Did you know? Colons came into use as punctuation marks in England around 1600. At first they were used to indicate a full stop, much like a period, and were followed by a capital letter.

List 2.48 Rules for Using Apostrophes

Apostrophes are used with possessive nouns and contractions. Some students mistakenly use apostrophes with plural nouns and possessive pronouns. Careful explanation, plenty of examples, and consistent reinforcement can boost understanding and minimize mistakes.

- Use an apostrophe to show the possessive case of nouns.
  - For singular nouns, show the possessive case by adding an apostrophe and -s. *Examples*:

    the bird's nest, the baby's crib, Carlos's sister
  - For plural nouns that end in -s, show the possessive case by adding an apostrophe. *Examples*:

    the girls' cheering squad, the puppies' mother, the kids' bikes
  - For plural nouns that do not end in -s, add an apostrophe and -s. *Examples*:

    the children's book section, the men's softball league, the mice's cage
- Use an apostrophe in contractions to show that letters are missing. *Examples*:

  she is: she's, they will: they'll, is not: isn't

 Did you know? The use of the apostrophe to show possessive nouns arose from old English that showed possession by adding an -es inflection to many nouns. In time, the -e was dropped, leaving the -s. The apostrophe was eventually added to indicate the omitted -e.

See List 2.22, Possessive Nouns; List 2.28, Verb Contractions with Not*; List 2.34, Pronoun Contractions.*

Copyright © 2010 by Gary Robert Muschla, Judith A. Muschla, and Erin Muschla

List 2.49   Rules for Using Quotation Marks

Learning to use quotation marks correctly can be difficult for young students. The rules below provide direction.

- Use quotation marks before and after a speaker's exact words. Punctuation such as commas and end marks are placed inside quotation marks. *Examples*:

  "It was a great game," said Randal.

  "Do we have band practice tomorrow?" asked Jasmine.

  Caleb said, "I don't have any homework tonight."

  "Last Sunday," said Rebecca, "we visited Aunt Sarah."

  "The rain stopped," said Alex. "The sun is already coming out."

- Use quotation marks around the titles of stories, poems, songs, articles, and the chapters of books. *Examples*:

  "The Rainy Day" (story)

  "A Patch of Old Snow" (poem)

  "Happy Birthday to You" (song)

  "Polar Bears" (article)

  "How to Teach Your Puppy Tricks" (chapter)

 Did you know? Students often use italics and underlining in place of quotation marks for the titles of short stories and poems. Reteaching and consistent reinforcement can lead to understanding of the proper usage.

See List 2.50, Rules for Using Italics.

Copyright © 2010 by Gary Robert Muschla, Judith A. Muschla, and Erin Muschla

List 2.50   Rules for Using Italics

Italics, or underlining, are used to show certain titles and names. While italics are preferred for printed material, underlining is used in handwritten material. Your students should understand when to italicize or underline written material.

- Use italics or underlining for the titles of books, movies, TV shows, and plays. *Examples*:

  Charlotte's Web (book)

  Underdog (movie)

  Sesame Street (TV show)

  Oliver (play)

- Use italics or underlining for the names of newspapers and magazines. *Examples*:

  The New York Times (newspaper)

  Highlights for Children (magazine)

 Did you know? Italic type was first used in the early 1500s. It was a condensed type suitable for the small books that were being produced. It was called *italic* because it was developed in Italy.

See List 2.49, Rules for Using Quotation Marks.

List 2.51   Rules for Using Hyphens

Hyphens have limited but definite uses. Your students should understand the following uses of hyphens.

- Use a hyphen to form some compound words. *Examples*:

  drive-in   half-hour   hard-boiled   old-fashioned

- Use a hyphen to join the separated syllables of a word. *Examples*:

  flow-er   kit-ten   ta-ble   com-put-er

 Did you know? The hyphen was introduced around the eleventh century to indicate that a word was continued on the next line. Words were not necessarily broken at syllables as they are today.

Copyright © 2010 by Gary Robert Muschla, Judith A. Muschla, and Erin Muschla

List 2.52   Rules for Capitalization

Although informal e-mail, electronic messaging, texting, and tweeting exhibit little attention to the rules of capitalization, standard written English does. Your students should apply the rules for correct capitalization in their writing.

- Capitalize the pronoun I. *Example*:

  James and I worked on a history project together.

- Capitalize all proper nouns (the names of specific persons, places, or things). *Examples*:

  Abraham Lincoln   the Golden Gate Bridge   Fluffy (a cat)

- Capitalize initials. *Examples*:

  John F. Kennedy   L. M. Montgomery   L. Frank Baum

- Capitalize titles when they are a part of a specific name. *Examples*:

  President Obama   Dr. Jones   Uncle Bill   Captain Morgan

- Capitalize the days of the week. *Examples*:

  Sunday   Tuesday   Thursday   Saturday

- Capitalize the months. *Examples*:

  January   March   July   November

- Capitalize the names of cities, states, countries, continents, rivers, lakes, oceans, and other specific geographic locations. *Examples*:

  Chicago   Arizona   United States of America
  Columbia River   Pacific Ocean   Lake Superior

- Capitalize the names of streets and avenues. *Examples*:

  Main Street   Mountain Drive   Railway Avenue   Sunrise Road

- Capitalize the names of public and religious holidays. *Examples*:

  Memorial Day   Christmas   Passover   Ramadan

- Capitalize the names of companies, organizations, and clubs. *Examples*:

  Microsoft   the Red Cross   the Stargazer's Club

- Capitalize proper adjectives. *Examples*:

  American   Mexican   French   Chinese

- Capitalize the first word in a sentence. *Example*:

  The class was excited about the trip to the museum.

- Capitalize the first word in a quotation. *Example*:

  Alyssa said, "The movie starts at eight."

Copyright © 2010 by Gary Robert Muschla, Judith A. Muschla, and Erin Muschla

The Elementary Teacher's Book of Lists

Copyright © 2010 by Gary Robert Muschla, Judith A. Muschla, and Erin Muschla

List 2.52   continued

- Capitalize the first, last word, and all important words in the titles of books, poems, stories, songs, movies, TV shows and other works. *Examples*:

  The Cricket in Times Square

  "America the Beautiful"

  The Simpsons

- Capitalize the first, last, and all important words in the names of newspapers and magazines. *Examples*:

  The New York Times

  Jack and Jill

- Capitalize all words in the greeting of a letter, but only the first word of the closing. *Examples*:

  Dear Aunt Carol,

  Yours very truly,

Did you know? The use of capital letters in English has changed over time. In old English writings, proper nouns were not usually capitalized. In the writings of eighteenth-century England, however, all nouns were usually capitalized. Today we no longer capitalize common nouns, but we do capitalize proper nouns. As shown in this list, we capitalize several other things as well.

List 2.53 Rules for Spelling Words Correctly

Because English is a language that has assimilated words from so many other languages, many English words are not spelled the way they are pronounced. This results in countless misspellings on the parts of students (and adults!). Although understanding the following rules will not make every student a great speller, it can make just about every student a better speller.

Words with *ie* and *ei*

- Spell the word with *ie* when the sound is ē, except after *c*. *Examples*:

  ē sound: brief, field

  After *c*, spell the word with *ei*: ceiling, deceive
- When the sound of a word is not ē, and especially if the sound is ā, spell the word *ei*. *Examples*:

  eight, sleigh, weight
- Exceptions to these rules include: friend, either, weird.

Adding *s* and *es* to most words

- For many words *s* can be added without a spelling change. *Examples*:

  dog: dogs   flower: flowers   star: stars
- For words that end in *ch*, *s*, *sh*, *x*, or *z*, add *es*. *Examples*:

  church: churches   loss: losses   bush: bushes
  mix: mixes   buzz: buzzes

Adding *s* or *es* to most words that end in *f* or *fe*

- Change the *f* to *v* then add *s* or *es*. *Examples*:

  wife: wives   knife: knives   elf: elves
- Exceptions to this rule include: chief: chiefs, roof: roofs.

For most words that end in *o*

- When the *o* follows a vowel, add *s* to form the plural. *Examples*:

  rodeo: rodeos   radio: radios
- When the *o* follows a consonant, add *es* to form the plural. *Examples*:

  hero: heroes   tomato: tomatoes

For most words that end in a vowel and *y*

- Keep the *y* when adding an ending. *Examples*:

  stay: stayed   enjoy: enjoying

For most words that end in a consonant and *y*

- Change the *y* to *i* before any ending that does not begin with *i*. *Examples*:

  lady: ladies   try: tried

Copyright © 2010 by Gary Robert Muschla, Judith A. Muschla, and Erin Muschla

List 2.53 continued

For most one-syllable words that end in one vowel and one consonant

- When adding an ending that starts with a vowel, double the consonant. *Examples*:

  thin: thinner   grab: grabbed   hop: hopping

For most two-syllable words that end in one vowel and one consonant

- If the accent is on the second syllable, double the consonant before adding the ending. *Examples*:

  begin: beginning   refer: referred

For words that end in a silent *e*

- When adding an ending that starts with a vowel, drop the *e*. *Examples*:

  cute: cuter   raise: raised   love: loving

 Did you know? Knowing spelling rules without being able to apply them results in little improvement in spelling ability.

See List 2.20, Rules for Forming Plural Nouns; List 2.21, Special Irregular Plural Nouns; List 2.54, Strategies for Improving Spelling.

Copyright © 2010 by Gary Robert Muschla, Judith A. Muschla, and Erin Muschla

List 2.54   Strategies for Improving Spelling

While some students learn new words quickly and remember them after seeing them once or twice, most students need to work hard to spell words correctly. The following strategies can be especially helpful to these students.

1. Try to spell all words correctly.
2. Learn and apply spelling rules.
3. Learn to spell long words by syllables.
4. Use a dictionary to check the spelling of words.
5. Learn the meanings of homophones and use them correctly.
6. Keep a list of words you have trouble spelling in a notebook.
7. Practice spelling words that give you trouble.
8. Proofread your writing carefully to catch mistakes in spelling.
9. When you write on a computer, be sure to use the spelling checker.
10. Study for spelling tests. Here are some hints:
    - Study in a quiet place.
    - Look at the word and say the letters to yourself.
    - Try to see the word in your mind.
    - Think how each sound is spelled.
    - Cover the word and spell the word to yourself.
    - Write the word on a piece of paper.
    - Check to see that you spelled the word correctly.
    - Repeat the process until you are confident you can spell all of the words you will be tested on.

 Did you know? Every time that a student spells a difficult word correctly it becomes more likely he or she will spell the word correctly again.

See List 2.53, Rules for Spelling Words Correctly.

Copyright © 2010 by Gary Robert Muschla, Judith A. Muschla, and Erin Muschla

List 2.55   Tough Words to Spell

Some words consistently prove to be hard for students to spell. You probably see your students misspell many of the words contained in the list below. Regularly sprinkling a few of them in with spelling tests will give your students additional practice spelling these words correctly.

Copyright © 2010 by Gary Robert Muschla, Judith A. Muschla, and Erin Muschla

about	cough	it's	right
across	cousin	its	rough
address	cruel	knew	route
advise	cupboard	latter	said
again	dairy	lessons	Saturday
all right	decorate	library	says
along	disease	loose	sense
already	doctor	maybe	several
although	early	minute	since
always	enough	morning	sincerely
among	every	neither	skiing
arctic	favorite	o'clock	skis
aunt	February	off	some
awhile	finally	often	something
balloon	first	once	sometime
because	forty	peace	soon
belief	fourth	people	store
believe	friend	please	straight
birthday	fuel	poison	studying
bought	getting	practice	sugar
built	grateful	pretty	summer
busy	guard	principal	suppose
calendar	guess	principle	sure
captain	handker-	quarter	surely
ceiling	chief	quiet	surprise
children	hear	quit	surround
chocolate	heard	quite	swimming
choose	height	raise	teacher
close	hello	realize	tear
clothes	hospital	really	terrible
color	hour	receive	Thanks-
complete	house	remember	giving
	instead		their

List 2.55   continued

there	too	very	who's
they're	train	we're	whose
though	travel	wear	women
thought	trouble	weather	wonder
through	truly	weigh	would
tired	Tuesday	were	write
together	until	wherever	wrote
tomorrow	usually	which	you're
tonight	vacation	whole	your

Did you know? Even your best spellers will have trouble spelling some words.

See List 2.53, Rules for Spelling Words Correctly; List 2.54, Strategies for Improving Spelling.

Copyright © 2010 by Gary Robert Muschla, Judith A. Muschla, and Erin Muschla

List 2.56 Tips for Student Writing Journals

Writing journals can be an important component of your writing program. Journals are a place where students can write about topics of personal interest and explore thoughts and feelings that they might not pursue in a typical writing assignment. For many students, ideas that they first reflect on in journals eventually evolve into ideas for other writing. The following suggestions can help you make journal writing an important part of your writing program.

- Establish basic guidelines for journals. Standard spiral notebooks are good choices for writing journals. Students should put their names on their journals, date all entries, and use their journals only for writing. They should always have their journals in school, ready for writing.

- Suggest that students write in their journals as often as they like, in school and at home. (If they take journals home, emphasize that they must bring them to school the next day.) To help ensure that students write in their journals regularly, consider requiring them to write in their journals at least two times each week. While many students will write more often, twice weekly is enough to establish a habit of writing without frustrating students who are unenthusiastic journal writers.

- Encourage students to write on topics or ideas that interest them.

- Decide how often you will read the journals. To keep the workload manageable, try reading some a few days each week, making sure that you get to read everyone's at least once every two weeks. Collecting all of the journals at the end of the day and trying to read them in one night will be overwhelming.

- Respond to your students' journal entries. Write comments, suggestions, and observations. Encouraging your students to respond to your comments can make journals a place for dialogue about writing.

- Remember that even though the writing in a journal is personal, if you read something that you feel endangers the student or someone else, you must report it to the proper administrator.

- Encourage your students to develop journal entries that interest them. Some journal entries can be the starting point of an excellent story or article.

- Decide whether you will grade writing journals. When journals are graded, some students will write the types of material they believe will result in a good grade. This may undermine their willingness to explore ideas and experiment with different writing forms.

- Encourage your students to review their journals periodically. This will help them to see their development as writers.

 Did you know? Many professional authors keep journals, recording their thoughts and impressions. For many, the ideas that first take shape in journals eventually appear in articles, stories, and books.

Copyright © 2010 by Gary Robert Muschla, Judith A. Muschla, and Erin Muschla

List 2.57   Grading Student Writing

Grading the writing of your students must be based on fairness and consistency. Grading should not focus on only one or two aspects of writing, for example, just grammar, but rather on the various elements that account for the whole. The following breakdown identifies important parts of any writing. Possible point totals, based on 100 percent, are provided for teachers who are required to use percentages in grading. Feel free to use the grading suggestions or adapt them to suit the needs of your students while satisfying your curriculum requirements. (The grading plan for young writers that follows is adapted from Gary Robert Muschla's *The Writing Teacher's Book of Lists,* second edition, Jossey-Bass, 2004, p. 333.)

- *Focus*: The topic is clearly defined. (10 points)
- *Content*: The student uses clear ideas that relate to the topic; the ideas are logically developed. (25 points)
- *Organization*: The piece has a clear introduction, body, and conclusion. Main ideas are supported with details. (25 points)
- *Mechanics*: Punctuation, grammar, spelling, and word usage are generally correct. (20 points)
- *Word selection*: Precise words that provide distinctive details are used in descriptions. (10 points)
- *Style*: The writing is strong and clear. The writer's individual "voice" is emerging. (10 points)

 Did you know? Students (and parents) view grades as indicators of progress. However, grades should never be the only measure of a student's achievement.

Copyright © 2010 by Gary Robert Muschla, Judith A. Muschla, and Erin Muschla

List 2.58   Ways to Share the Writing of Your Students

Writing is a form of communication. It is to be shared. There are many ways you can share the writing of your students with others.

- Displays on bulletin boards in class
- Displays on hallway bulletin boards
- Readings from an author's chair, in which students read excerpts of their work to the class
- Postings on class or school Web sites
- Publishing in class or school magazines or newsletters
- Publishing in PTA newsletters
- Making photocopies of written work and sharing it with other students
- Creating books of class writing
- Conducting poetry readings in the school media center
- Sponsoring grade or school writing contests (judged by teachers of other grades)
- Displaying student writing in the school media center
- Submitting student writing to local newspapers
- Submitting work to Web sites that post the writing of students

 Did you know? Having their work published is great incentive for all writers.

Copyright © 2010 by Gary Robert Muschla, Judith A. Muschla, and Erin Muschla

List 2.59   Checklist for a Successful Writing Program

A successful writing program results from a combination of factors that you can control. Evaluating your program according to the following can help you develop a nurturing and productive writing environment for your students.

- ☑ Students respect writing as an important subject.
- ☑ Writing is taught as a process composed of stages: prewriting, drafting, revising, editing, and publishing.
- ☑ Students are encouraged to write about meaningful topics.
- ☑ The procedures of the class are practical, efficient, and supportive of writing.
- ☑ Students are encouraged to write in journals.
- ☑ The sharing of ideas is encouraged.
- ☑ Students are encouraged to experiment with different forms of writing.
- ☑ Punctuation, grammar, spelling, and word usage are taught as essential skills necessary for effective writing.
- ☑ References such as dictionaries and thesauruses are available and students are encouraged to use them.
- ☑ Time is provided for students to confer with each other about writing.
- ☑ Students are given the opportunity to work cooperatively on writing activities.
- ☑ Teacher-student writing conferences are a regular part of the class.
- ☑ Students are encouraged to use technology such as computers, printers, and the Internet in their writing.
- ☑ The writing of students is shared and published.
- ☑ The idea that the class is composed of ''writers'' is fostered.

Copyright © 2010 by Gary Robert Muschla, Judith A. Muschla, and Erin Muschla

Did you know? Unlike some other subjects in which progress is relatively steady, the progress of student writers is uneven, often characterized by two steps forward followed by a step back. Learning to write requires hard work, time, and patience on the parts of learners and teachers.

Mathematics

Mathematics instruction has moved far from the skills and drills of the past. While providing a strong foundation in the basics, today's math curricula are centered around problem solving and critical thinking. By planning and presenting meaningful math lessons and activities, you will help your students achieve success in math in your class and in the years to follow.

List 3.1   Math Concepts and Attributes

Some fundamental concepts must be developed before formal math education can begin. Basic ideas that are prerequisites for understanding mathematics follow.

above, below	inside, outside
big, small	many, few
equal, unequal	more than, less than
far, near	same, different
forward, backward	shaded, non-shaded
greater than, less than	straight, crooked
heavier, lighter	to the right of, to the left of
in order, out of order	up, down
increasing, decreasing	

Once basic concepts are developed, students can classify and compare numbers or shapes according to various attributes such as those in the list that follows.

area	odd or even
color	position
congruence	prime or composite
dimensions	properties
length	shading
measurement	shape
number	similarity
number of factors	size
number of sides	symmetry

 Did you know? Students classify not only in math class, but in other classes as well—for example, character traits in reading, animals in science, and parts of speech in writing. Being able to classify is an important skill.

Copyright © 2010 by Gary Robert Muschla, Judith A. Muschla, and Erin Muschla

List 3.2   Habits of Good Student Mathematicians

All good math students possess many of the same qualities. Encourage your students to practice the following.

Good student mathematicians:

- Are always prepared with all their materials and supplies
- Pay attention in class
- Take notes
- Work hard
- Make and test conjectures
- Share ideas and explain their thoughts and procedures
- Listen to their teacher and to the ideas of other students
- Work cooperatively with other students
- Ask questions
- Study and learn basic math facts
- Keep an assignment pad and an organized notebook or binder
- Try different methods to solve challenging problems
- Show their work and keep notes of the ways they try to solve problems
- Use technology
- Learn from their mistakes
- Complete homework and class work on time
- Check their work
- Review class notes and class work
- Study for tests
- Relate math to other subjects and to their lives
- Take pride in their efforts for learning math

 Did you know? Albert Einstein, creator of the general theory of relativity, once said, "Don't worry about your difficulties in mathematics. I assure you mine are still greater."

Copyright © 2010 by Gary Robert Muschla, Judith A. Muschla, and Erin Muschla

List 3.3   Cardinal and Ordinal Numbers

When we count, we use *cardinal numbers*, which represent the number of items in a group. When we place things in order, we use *ordinal numbers*, which denote the order of the items in a group. Several examples of cardinal and ordinal numbers follow.

Cardinal Number	Symbol	Ordinal Number	Shortened Form
One	1	First	1st
Two	2	Second	2nd
Three	3	Third	3rd
Four	4	Fourth	4th
Five	5	Fifth	5th
Six	6	Sixth	6th
Seven	7	Seventh	7th
Eight	8	Eighth	8th
Nine	9	Ninth	9th
Ten	10	Tenth	10th
Eleven	11	Eleventh	11th
Twelve	12	Twelfth	12th
Thirteen	13	Thirteenth	13th
Fourteen	14	Fourteenth	14th
Fifteen	15	Fifteenth	15th
Sixteen	16	Sixteenth	16th
Seventeen	17	Seventeenth	17th
Eighteen	18	Eighteenth	18th
Nineteen	19	Nineteenth	19th
Twenty	20	Twentieth	20th
Twenty-one	21	Twenty-first	21st
Twenty-two	22	Twenty-second	22nd
Twenty-three	23	Twenty-third	23rd
Twenty-four	24	Twenty-fourth	24th
Twenty-five	25	Twenty-fifth	25th
Twenty-six	26	Twenty-sixth	26th
Twenty-seven	27	Twenty-seventh	27th
Twenty-eight	28	Twenty-eighth	28th
Twenty-nine	29	Twenty-ninth	29th
Thirty	30	Thirtieth	30th

Copyright © 2010 by Gary Robert Muschla, Judith A. Muschla, and Erin Muschla

Copyright © 2010 by Gary Robert Muschla, Judith A. Muschla, and Erin Muschla

List 3.3   continued

Successive numbers appear in following manner, following the pattern:

Forty	40	Fortieth	40th
Fifty	50	Fiftieth	50th
Sixty	60	Sixtieth	60th
Seventy	70	Seventieth	70th
Eighty	80	Eightieth	80th
Ninety	90	Ninetieth	90th
One hundred	100	One hundredth	100th
One hundred one	101	One hundred first	101st
One hundred two	102	One hundred second	102nd
One hundred three	103	One hundred third	103rd
One hundred four	104	One hundred fourth	104th
One hundred five	105	One hundred fifth	105th

 Did you know? The word *cardinal* is taken from the Latin term *cardinalis* which means "principal, chief, essential."

List 3.4   Addition Table and Additional Facts

An *addition table* is a great resource. It provides the basic facts that are fundamental for quick and accurate computation, and it can also be used to generate the fact families. Following are addition facts plus an addition table on the next page:

- The answer to an addition problem is called the *sum*.
- The numbers that are to be added are called the *addends*.
- The following properties apply (*a*, *b*, and *c* represent numbers):
  - The Commutative Property of Addition, $a + b = b + a$, states that numbers can be added in any order without changing the sum.
    Example: $2 + 3 = 3 + 2$.
  - The Associative Property of Addition, $(a + b) + c = a + (b + c)$, states that the order of grouping numbers does not change the sum.
    Example: $(2 + 3) + 4 = 2 + (3 + 4)$.
  - The Addition Property of Zero, $a + 0 = 0 + a = a$, states that the sum of zero and any number is that number. Because of this property, 0 is called the Identity for Addition.
    Example: $2 + 0 = 0 + 2 = 2$.

 Did you know? The addition table contains interesting patterns. From the upper left-hand corner to the lower right-hand corner, each number on each diagonal of the addition table increases by 2. The numbers on each diagonal from the upper right-hand corner to the lower left-hand corner remain the same.

See List 3.6, Steps for Adding and Subtracting Whole Numbers; List 3.19, Steps for Adding, Subtracting, Multiplying, and Dividing Decimals; List 3.25, Steps for Adding, Subtracting, Multiplying, and Dividing Fractions; List 3.26, Steps for Adding, Subtracting, Multiplying, and Dividing Mixed Numbers.

Copyright © 2010 by Gary Robert Muschla, Judith A. Muschla, and Erin Muschla

Addition Table

+	0	1	2	3	4	5	6	7	8	9	10	11	12
0	0	1	2	3	4	5	6	7	8	9	10	11	12
1	1	2	3	4	5	6	7	8	9	10	11	12	13
2	2	3	4	5	6	7	8	9	10	11	12	13	14
3	3	4	5	6	7	8	9	10	11	12	13	14	15
4	4	5	6	7	8	9	10	11	12	13	14	15	16
5	5	6	7	8	9	10	11	12	13	14	15	16	17
6	6	7	8	9	10	11	12	13	14	15	16	17	18
7	7	8	9	10	11	12	13	14	15	16	17	18	19
8	8	9	10	11	12	13	14	15	16	17	18	19	20
9	9	10	11	12	13	14	15	16	17	18	19	20	21
10	10	11	12	13	14	15	16	17	18	19	20	21	22
11	11	12	13	14	15	16	17	18	19	20	21	22	23
12	12	13	14	15	16	17	18	19	20	21	22	23	24

Copyright © 2010 by Gary Robert Muschla, Judith A. Muschla, and Erin Muschla

List 3.5   Place Value Chart for Whole Numbers

Place value is a difficult concept for many students to master. But since the value of any digit depends on its "place," understanding place value is an essential skill. In the example below, 4 represents 4 thousands and also 4 millions. The digit is the same, but the values are quite different. The chart below shows place value for whole numbers. The numbers are placed in groups of three, with a comma separating each group.

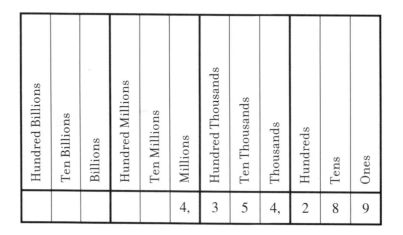

Hundred Billions	Ten Billions	Billions	Hundred Millions	Ten Millions	Millions	Hundred Thousands	Ten Thousands	Thousands	Hundreds	Tens	Ones
					4,	3	5	4,	2	8	9

Numbers can be expressed in a variety of ways. Following are four examples. The number in each example refers to the number beneath the place value chart.

- *Standard form:* The way numbers are numerically written. *Example:* 4,354,289

- *Word form:* The way numbers are expressed in words only. *Example:* four million, three hundred fifty-four thousand, two hundred eighty-nine

- *Place value form:* The way the place value of each digit is shown using words. *Example:* 4 millions, 3 hundred thousands, 5 ten thousands, 4 thousands, 2 hundreds, 8 tens, 9 ones

- *Expanded form:* The way a number is written to show the value of each digit as a power of 10. *Example:* 4,000,000 + 300,000 + 50,000 + 4,000 + 200 + 80 + 9

 Did you know? Our number system is based on ten, probably because primitive people used their 10 fingers to count. (They did not make a distinction between fingers and thumbs.)

See List 3.16, Place Value Chart for Decimal Numbers; List 3.17 Steps for Rounding Numbers.

Copyright © 2010 by Gary Robert Muschla, Judith A. Muschla, and Erin Muschla

List 3.6 Steps for Adding and Subtracting Whole Numbers

Once the basic addition facts are committed to memory, numbers can be used to find sums and differences. Following are basic steps for adding and subtracting.

Addition

Example: $382 + 54 =$

1. Line up the numbers in each place value position.

$$\begin{array}{r} 382 \\ +54 \\ \hline \end{array}$$

2. Add the numbers in the ones place, regrouping if necessary. (Since $2 + 4 = 6$, there is no need to regroup.)

$$\begin{array}{r} 382 \\ +54 \\ \hline 6 \end{array}$$

3. Add the numbers in the tens place, regrouping if necessary. (Since 8 tens + 5 tens = 13 tens, regroup 13 tens as 1 hundred + 3 tens.)

$$\begin{array}{r} 1 \\ 382 \\ +54 \\ \hline 436 \end{array}$$

4. Add the numbers in the hundreds place, regrouping if necessary. (Since 1 hundred + 3 hundreds = 4 hundreds, there is no need to regroup.)

$$\begin{array}{r} 1 \\ 382 \\ +54 \\ \hline 436 \end{array}$$

5. For larger numbers, continue in the same manner for all of the numbers in each place value position.

Subtraction

Example: $839 - 154 =$

1. Line up the numbers in each place value position.

$$\begin{array}{r} 839 \\ -154 \\ \hline \end{array}$$

2. Subtract the numbers in the ones place, regrouping if necessary. (Since 4 is less than 9, there is no need to regroup.)

$$\begin{array}{r} 839 \\ -154 \\ \hline 5 \end{array}$$

Copyright © 2010 by Gary Robert Muschla, Judith A. Muschla, and Erin Muschla

3. Subtract the numbers in the tens place, regrouping if necessary. (Since 5 tens are greater than 3 tens, you must regroup. Regroup 8 hundreds as 7 hundreds and 10 tens, rename, and subtract the numbers in the tens place.)

$$\begin{array}{r} ^{7\,13} \\ 839 \\ -\,154 \\ \hline 85 \end{array}$$

4. Subtract the numbers in the hundreds place, regrouping if necessary. (Since 1 hundred is less than 7 hundreds, there is no need to regroup.)

$$\begin{array}{r} ^{7\,13} \\ 839 \\ -\,154 \\ \hline 685 \end{array}$$

5. For larger numbers, continue in the same manner for all of the numbers in each value position.

Did you know? Addition and subtraction are opposite operations. Another word for opposite operations is *inverse* operations.

See List 3.5, Place Value Chart for Whole Numbers.

Copyright © 2010 by Gary Robert Muschla, Judith A. Muschla, and Erin Muschla

List 3.7   Multiplication Table and Multiplication Facts

Even though calculators are readily available, students should master multiplication facts. Not only will mastery enable students to compute quickly and accurately, but understanding multiplication facts is essential for working with fractions and percents. Mastery also fosters basic number sense. Below are some facts about multiplication, followed by a multiplication table on the next page.

- The answer to a multiplication problem is called the *product*.
- The number which is to be multiplied is called the *multiplicand*.
- The number which is to multiply another number is called the *multiplier*.
- The following properties apply (a, b, and c represent numbers):
  - The Commutative Property of Multiplication, $a \times b = b \times a$, states that numbers can be multiplied in any order without changing the product. *Example*: $2 \times 3 = 3 \times 2$.
  - The Associative Property of Multiplication, $(a \times b) \times c = a \times (b \times c)$, states that the order of grouping numbers does not change the product. *Example*: $(2 \times 3) \times 4 = 2 \times (3 \times 4)$.
  - The Distributive Property, $a \times (b + c) = a \times b + a \times c$, relates multiplication to addition and states that multiplying the sum of two numbers by another is the same as multiplying each number and then finding the sum. *Example*: $2 \times (3 + 4) = 2 \times 7$ or 14, which is the same as finding the sum of 2×3 and 2×4.
  - The Multiplication Property of One, $a \times 1 = 1 \times a = a$, states that the product of one and any number is that number. Because of this property, 1 is called the Identity for Multiplication. *Example*: $2 \times 1 = 1 \times 2 = 2$.
  - The Zero Product Property, $a \times 0 = 0 \times a = 0$, states that the product of 0 and any number is always 0. *Example*: $2 \times 0 = 0 \times 2 = 0$.

 Did you know? In higher mathematics, a raised dot is often used in place of the $\times$ for multiplication. For example $3 \cdot 5$ means the same as 3×5.

See List 3.13, Steps for Multiplying and Dividing Whole Numbers; List 3.19, Steps for Adding, Subtracting, Multiplying, and Dividing Decimals; List 3.25, Steps for Adding, Subtracting, Multiplying, and Dividing Fractions; List 3.26, Steps for Adding, Subtracting, Multiplying, and Dividing Mixed Numbers.

Copyright © 2010 by Gary Robert Muschla, Judith A. Muschla, and Erin Muschla

Multiplication Table

×	0	1	2	3	4	5	6	7	8	9	10	11	12
0	0	0	0	0	0	0	0	0	0	0	0	0	0
1	0	1	2	3	4	5	6	7	8	9	10	11	12
2	0	2	4	6	8	10	12	14	16	18	20	22	24
3	0	3	6	9	12	15	18	21	24	27	30	33	36
4	0	4	8	12	16	20	24	28	32	36	40	44	48
5	0	5	10	15	20	25	30	35	40	45	50	55	60
6	0	6	12	18	24	30	36	42	48	54	60	66	72
7	0	7	14	21	28	35	42	49	56	63	70	77	84
8	0	8	16	24	32	40	48	56	64	72	80	88	96
9	0	9	18	27	36	45	54	63	72	81	90	99	108
10	0	10	20	30	40	50	60	70	80	90	100	110	120
11	0	11	22	33	44	55	66	77	88	99	110	121	132
12	0	12	24	36	48	60	72	84	96	108	120	132	144

Copyright © 2010 by Gary Robert Muschla, Judith A. Muschla, and Erin Muschla

List 3.8   Prime Numbers

A *prime number* is a number greater than 1 that has only two factors, 1 and itself. For example, 2 is a prime number because its only factors are 1 and 2. The following list contains all of the prime numbers that are less than 500.

2	71	167	271	389
3	73	173	277	397
5	79	179	281	401
7	83	181	283	409
11	89	191	293	419
13	97	193	307	421
17	101	197	311	431
19	103	199	313	433
23	107	211	317	439
29	109	223	331	443
31	113	227	337	449
37	127	229	347	457
41	131	233	349	461
43	137	239	353	463
47	139	241	359	467
53	149	251	367	479
59	151	257	373	487
61	157	263	379	491
67	163	269	383	499

 Did you know? 2 is the only even prime number.

See List 3.10, Composite Numbers.

Copyright © 2010 by Gary Robert Muschla, Judith A. Muschla, and Erin Muschla

List 3.9   Prime Factorization and Factor Trees

The Fundamental Theorem of Arithmetic states that every whole number greater than 1 is either a prime number or can be expressed as the product of prime numbers. Prime factorization is a way to express composite numbers as a product of their prime factors.

Use the following steps to write the prime factorization of a number. The prime factorization of 150 is used as an example to illustrate the steps.

1. Write two factors of the number.

   Two factors of 150 are 15 and 10.

2. Write two factors of each of the factors.

   Two factors of 15 are 3 and 5.

   Two factors of 10 are 2 and 5.

3. Continue to write the factors of each of the factors until all of the factors are prime numbers.

   3, 5, 2, and 5 are prime numbers.

4. Write an expression for the product of the factors. This is the prime factorization.

   $3 \times 5 \times 2 \times 5$ is the prime factorization of 150.

5. If you wish to use exponents, count the number of times each number is a factor.

   5 is a factor 2 times. 3 and 2 are each a factor once.

6. Write the prime factorization using exponents. (The prime numbers are usually written in ascending order.)

   $2 \times 3 \times 5^2$ is the prime factorization of 150 using exponents.

Factor trees are a wonderful way to organize the factors of numbers and clarify thinking. There may be several different ways to factor the numbers and construct the trees. Two different trees for the prime factorization of 150 are provided. Note that the last set of factors of a factor tree must be prime numbers.

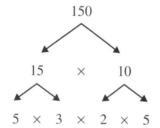   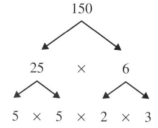

 Did you know? Except for the order of the factors, there is only one prime factorization for each composite number.

See List 3.8, Prime Numbers; List 3.10, Composite Numbers.

The Elementary Teacher's Book of Lists

Copyright © 2010 by Gary Robert Muschla, Judith A. Muschla, and Erin Muschla

A *composite number* is a number that has more than two factors. For example, the number 10 is a composite number because its factors are 1, 2, 5, and 10. The first 100 composite numbers are presented in the following list.

4	33	58	85	111
6	34	60	86	112
8	35	62	87	114
9	36	63	88	115
10	38	64	90	116
12	39	65	91	117
14	40	66	92	118
15	42	68	93	119
16	44	69	94	120
18	45	70	95	121
20	46	72	96	122
21	48	74	98	123
22	49	75	99	124
24	50	76	100	125
25	51	77	102	126
26	52	78	104	128
27	54	80	105	129
28	55	81	106	130
30	56	82	108	132
32	57	84	110	133

Copyright © 2010 by Gary Robert Muschla, Judith A. Muschla, and Erin Muschla

 Did you know? 1 is the only number that is neither prime nor composite, and every even number except 2 is composite.

See List 3.8, Prime Numbers.

Mathematics

List 3.11   Square Numbers and Cube Numbers

The *square* of a number results when a number is multiplied by itself—for example, $5 \times 5 = 25$. We say that 5 squared is equal to 25.

The *cube* of a number results when a number is multiplied by itself twice—for example, $5 \times 5 \times 5 = 125$. We say that 5 cubed is equal to 125.

The following list contains the squares and cubes of the numbers from 1 to 25.

Number	Squared	Cubed
1	1	1
2	4	8
3	9	27
4	16	64
5	25	125
6	36	216
7	49	343
8	64	512
9	81	729
10	100	1,000
11	121	1,331
12	144	1,728
13	169	2,197
14	196	2,744
15	225	3,375
16	256	4,096
17	289	4,913
18	324	5,832
19	361	6,859
20	400	8,000
21	441	9,261
22	484	10,648
23	529	12,167
24	576	13,824
25	625	15,625

Did you know? 1 and 64 are the only numbers less than 100 that are both squares and cubes.

Copyright © 2010 by Gary Robert Muschla, Judith A. Muschla, and Erin Muschla

List 3.12   Divisibility Tests

Understanding divisibility is useful in many mathematical applications. Two of the most important are simplifying fractions and finding common denominators. In more advanced mathematics, divisibility tests and common factors are essential in factoring polynomials. Following are tests for divisibility.

For a number to be divisible by:

- 2, the number must be even (ending in 0, 2, 4, 6, or 8)
- 3, the sum of the digits of the number must be divisible by 3
- 4, the number must be even and its last two digits must be divisible by 4
- 5, the number must end in 0 or 5
- 6, the number must be even and the sum of its digits must be divisible by 3
- 7, drop the units digit and subtract two times the units digit from the number that remains. If that number is divisible by 7, the original number is divisible by 7.
- 8, the number formed by the last 3 digits of the number must be divisible by 8
- 9, the sum of the digits of the number must be divisible by 9
- 10, the number must end in 0
- 11, add the alternate digits, beginning with the first digit. Next add the alternate digits, beginning with the second digit. Subtract the smaller sum from the larger. If the difference is divisible by 11, the original number is divisible by 11.
- 12, the number must be divisible by both 3 and 4

 Did you know? If a number is divisible by 9, then it is always divisible by 3. But if a number is divisible by 3, it may (or may not) be divisible by 9.

See List 3.20, Steps for Finding the Greatest Common Factor; List 3.24, Steps for Simplifying Fractions.

Copyright © 2010 by Gary Robert Muschla, Judith A. Muschla, and Erin Muschla

List 3.13 Steps for Multiplying and Dividing Whole Numbers

Think of multiplication as a short way of adding. For example, 25 times 6 is the same as adding 25 six times. Division is the same as separating a number into groups. Multiplication and division are inverse operations. The following list summarizes the steps for each.

Multiplication

Example: $76 \times 28 =$

1. Multiply by the ones digit first. ($76 \times 8 = 608$) Write the product.

$$\begin{array}{r} 76 \\ \times\ 28 \\ \hline 608 \end{array}$$

2. Multiply by the tens digits. ($76 \times 20 = 1520$) Write the product.

$$\begin{array}{r} 76 \\ \times\ 28 \\ \hline 608 \\ 1520 \end{array}$$

3. For larger numbers, repeat the process.
4. Add the partial products. ($608 + 1520 = 2{,}128$)

$$\begin{array}{r} 76 \\ \times\ 28 \\ \hline 608 \\ 1520 \\ \hline 2{,}128 \end{array}$$

Division

Example: $489 \div 23 =$

1. Estimate to determine how many groups of the divisor could be formed from the dividend. In the example, the estimate is 20. Write 2 in the tens place in the quotient.

$$23\overline{)489}\quad\overset{2}{}$$

2. Multiply the number in the quotient by the divisor. ($23 \times 2 = 46$)
3. Subtract. ($48 - 46 = 2$)

$$\begin{array}{r} 2 \\ 23\overline{)489} \\ 46 \\ \hline 2 \end{array}$$

Copyright © 2010 by Gary Robert Muschla, Judith A. Muschla, and Erin Muschla

4. Compare the difference with the divisor. The difference should be less than the divisor. If the difference is greater than or equal to the divisor, increase the estimate and redo the multiplication, subtraction, and comparison.

5. Bring down the next digit.

6. Estimate to determine how many groups of the divisor could be formed from the number formed when the new digit is brought down. In the example, the estimate is 1. Write 1 in the quotient.

$$
\begin{array}{r}
21 \\
23\overline{)489} \\
46 \\
\hline
29
\end{array}
$$

7. Multiply this number by the divisor. $(23 \times 1 = 23)$

8. Subtract. $(29 - 23 = 6)$

9. Compare the difference with the divisor. If the difference is greater than or equal to the divisor, increase the estimate and redo the multiplication, subtraction, and comparison.

10. For larger numbers, repeat the process until there are no more numbers to bring down.

11. If there is a remainder, write the remainder in the quotient.

$$
\begin{array}{r}
21 \text{ R6} \\
23\overline{)489} \\
46 \\
\hline
29 \\
23 \\
\hline
6
\end{array}
$$

Did you know? You can check multiplication by dividing the product by one of the factors. You can check division by multiplying the quotient by the divisor and adding the remainder.

See List 3.12, Divisibility Tests.

Copyright © 2010 by Gary Robert Muschla, Judith A. Muschla, and Erin Muschla

List 3.14   Big and Very Big Numbers

Big numbers are hard to imagine. Very big numbers are almost impossible to imagine. Picture one million (1,000,000) pennies stacked one on top of the other. The pile would be almost one mile high. One billion pennies (1,000,000,000) stacked one on top of the other would be almost 1,000 miles high. The following list includes some of the big and biggest numbers and their names.

Name	Numerical Form
One thousand	1,000
One million	1,000,000
One billion	1,000,000,000
One trillion	1,000,000,000,000
One quadrillion	1,000,000,000,000,000
One quintillion	1,000,000,000,000,000,000
One sextillion	1,000,000,000,000,000,000,000
One septillion	1,000,000,000,000,000,000,000,000
One octillion	1,000,000,000,000,000,000,000,000,000
One nonillion	1,000,000,000,000,000,000,000,000,000,000
One decillion	1,000,000,000,000,000,000,000,000,000,000,000

Did you know? A googol is a number equal to 10^{100}, which is the same as a 1 followed by 100 zeros. It was named in 1938 by Milton Sirotta, the then-nine-year-old nephew of Edward Kasner, a mathematician. Kasner asked his nephew what name he would give to a really large number to which the boy replied, a "googol." Kasner then coined the term a *googol* and defined it as 10^{100}. Despite its size, a googol is not the biggest number. Numbers continue forever, because no matter how big a number is, 1 can always be added to it!

See List 3.5, Place Value Chart for Whole Numbers.

Copyright © 2010 by Gary Robert Muschla, Judith A. Muschla, and Erin Muschla

List 3.15   Mathematical Signs and Symbols

Signs and symbols serve as a type of shorthand for mathematicians. The following list provides the signs and symbols used most often in mathematics.

$+$	addition or plus
$-$	subtraction or minus
$\bullet$	multiplication, multiply by, or times
$\times$	multiplication, multiply by, or times
$\div$	division, divide by
$/$	division
$\dfrac{x}{y}$	x divided by y
n^2	n squared or n to the second power
n^3	n cubed or n to the third power
$=$	equals, is equal to
$\neq$	is not equal to
$\approx$	is approximately equal to
$>$	is greater than
$<$	is less than
$\geq$	is greater than or equal to
$\leq$	is less than or equal to
$\therefore$	therefore
$\$$	dollar sign
¢	cent sign
$\#$	number or pound
$\%$	percent
$($	open parenthesis
$)$	closed parenthesis
$[$	open bracket
$]$	closed bracket
$:$	is to
$\cup$	union
$\cap$	intersection
$\in$	is an element of
$^\circ$	degree
$^\circ$F	degrees Fahrenheit
$^\circ$C	degrees Celsius
(x,y)	ordered pair

 Did you know? Understanding the signs and symbols of math is an important step toward math literacy.

Copyright © 2010 by Gary Robert Muschla, Judith A. Muschla, and Erin Muschla

List 3.16   Place Value Chart for Decimal Numbers

The place value chart for decimal numbers is an extension of the place value chart for whole numbers. The value of any digit depends on its "place." In the example below, 3 represents 3 hundreds, 3 ones, and 3 thousandths. The digits are the same, but the values are different. The chart shows place value from millions to millionths

Millions	Hundred thousands	Ten thousands	Thousands	Hundreds	Tens	Ones	.	Tenths	Hundredths	Thousandths	Ten-thousandths	Hundred-thousandths	Millionths
				3	5	3	.	2	6	3	8	9	

Decimal numbers can be expressed in a variety of ways. The number 353.26389, shown on the chart, is used in the following examples.

- *Standard form*: The way numbers are numerically written. *Example*: 353.26389
- *Word form*: The way numbers are expressed in words only. The decimal point is read as *and*. *Example*: three hundred fifty-three and twenty-six thousand, three hundred eighty-nine hundred-thousandths
- *Place value form*: The way the place value of each digit is shown using words. *Example*: 3 hundreds, 5 tens, 3 ones, 2 tenths, 6 hundredths, 3 thousandths, 8 ten-thousandths, 9 hundred-thousandths
- *Expanded form*: The way a number is written showing the value of each digit as a power of 10. *Example*: 300 + 50 + 3 + 0.2 + 0.06 + 0.003 + 0.0008 + 0.00009

Did you know? The value of each place in a decimal number is one tenth of the value of the place to the left of it.

See List 3.5, Place Value Chart for Whole Numbers.

Copyright © 2010 by Gary Robert Muschla, Judith A. Muschla, and Erin Muschla

List 3.17   Steps for Rounding Numbers

Rounding is an estimation skill used when an approximate value is needed. A rounded number tells about how many. A number can be rounded up or down, depending on the value to the right of the place rounded.

Steps for Rounding Up

1. Find the digit that is to be rounded. Draw a line under the digit.
2. If the digit to the right of the digit to be rounded is 5 or more, add one to the underlined digit.
3. Change all digits to the right of the rounded digit to zeros.
4. After rounding decimals, delete any zeros that are not placeholders.

   Examples for rounding up:

   Round 482 to the nearest hundred.   Round 73.186 to the nearest tenth.
   4 is in the hundreds place.   1 is in the tenths place.
   4̲82 ≈ 500   73.1̲86 ≈ 73.2

Steps for Rounding Down

1. Find the digit that is to be rounded. Draw a line under the digit.
2. If the digit to the right of the digit to be rounded is less than 5, the underlined digit stays the same.
3. Change all digits to the right of the rounded digit to zeros.
4. After rounding decimals, delete any zeros that are not placeholders.

   Examples for rounding down:

   Round 3,179 to the nearest thousand.   Round 194.627 to the nearest tenth.
   3 is in the thousands place.   6 is in the tenths place.
   3̲,179 ≈ 3,000   194.6̲27 ≈ 194.6

Steps for Rounding When 9 Is in the Place You Are Rounding

1. Find the digit that is to be rounded, which in this case in 9. Draw a line under the 9.
2. If the digit to the right of the 9 is 5 or more, round the 9 up by adding 1 to it. (If the digit to the right is less than 5, follow the steps for rounding down.)
3. Since $9 + 1 = 10$, write 0 in place of the 9 and add 1 to the digit to the left. Change all numbers to the right of the rounded number to zeros.

Copyright © 2010 by Gary Robert Muschla, Judith A. Muschla, and Erin Muschla

4. After rounding decimals, delete any zeros that are not placeholders.

Examples for rounding when 9 is in the place you are rounding:

Round 3,498 to the nearest ten.   Round 45.192 to the nearest hundredth.
9 is in the tens place.   9 is in the hundredths place.
3,4<u>9</u>8 ≈ 3,500   45.1 <u>9</u>2 ≈ 45.19

Did you know? Use ≈ when rounding. The symbol, which means "approximately equal to," shows that the rounded number is about the same value as the original number.

See List 3.5, Place Value Chart for Whole Numbers; List 3.16, Place Value Chart for Decimal Numbers.

Copyright © 2010 by Gary Robert Muschla, Judith A. Muschla, and Erin Muschla

List 3.18   Types of Decimals

In the broadest sense, a *decimal* is any number in the base 10 number system. Following are several types of decimals.

- *Decimal fraction*: A number that has no digits other than zeros to the left of the decimal point. *Examples*: 0.5, 0.36, 0.346

- *Mixed decimal*: A counting number and a decimal fraction. *Examples*: 9.2, 15.98, 1.06

- *Similar decimals*: Decimals that have the same number of places to the right of the decimal point. *Examples*: 4.68 and 20.87; 8.7 and 109.3

- *Decimal equivalent of a proper fraction*: A decimal fraction that equals a proper fraction. *Examples*: $0.2 = \dfrac{1}{5}$, $0.75 = \dfrac{3}{4}$

- *Finite* (or *terminating*) *decimal*: A decimal that has a finite number of digits. *Examples*: 0.1, 4.86, 15.254

- *Infinite* (or *nonterminating*) *decimal*: A decimal that has an unending number of digits to the right of the decimal point. There are two types of infinite decimals: repeating decimals and nonrepeating decimals.

  - *Repeating* (or *periodic*) *decimal*: A decimal in which the same digit or group of digits repeats. A bar is used to show that a digit or a group of digits repeats. The repeating set is called the *period* or *repetend*. *Examples*: $0.\overline{26}$, $0.\overline{7}$

  - *Nonrepeating* (or *nonperiodic*) *decimal*: A decimal that has no repeating digits. These decimals are also known as *irrational numbers*. *Examples*: $\sqrt{5}$, π

Did you know? Simon Steven (1548–1620), a Flemish mathematician, used decimal fractions in a book he published in 1585. But instead of the decimal point we use today, he used a small circle.

Copyright © 2010 by Gary Robert Muschla, Judith A. Muschla, and Erin Muschla

Mathematics

List 3.19   Steps for Adding, Subtracting, Multiplying, and Dividing Decimals

After correct placement of the decimal point, adding, subtracting, multiplying, and dividing decimals are very similar to working with whole numbers. The procedures are explained below.

Adding Decimals

Example: $8.26 + 0.519 =$

1. Line up the numbers according to place value. Keep the columns straight and the digits in their proper places. Keep the decimal points in line.

   $$\begin{array}{r} 8.26 \\ + 0.519 \\ \hline \end{array}$$

2. Add zeros for placeholders if necessary.
3. After setting the problem up, bring the decimal point straight down.
4. Add as you would with whole numbers.

   $$\begin{array}{r} 8.260 \\ + 0.519 \\ \hline 8.779 \end{array}$$

Adding Decimals and Whole Numbers

Example: $4.6 + 7 =$

1. Remember that a whole number is placed to the left of the decimal point. For example, the whole number 7 is written as 7.0.
2. Follow the steps for adding decimals.

   $$\begin{array}{r} 4.6 \\ + \ 7.0 \\ \hline 11.6 \end{array}$$

Subtracting Decimals

Example: $2.96 - 0.513 =$

1. Line up the numbers according to place value. Keep the columns straight and the digits in their proper places. Keep the decimal points in line.

   $$\begin{array}{r} 2.96 \\ - 0.513 \\ \hline \end{array}$$

2. Add zeros for placeholders if necessary.
3. After setting the problem up, bring the decimal point straight down.
4. Subtract as you would with whole numbers.

   $$\begin{array}{r} 2.960 \\ - 0.513 \\ \hline 2.447 \end{array}$$

Copyright © 2010 by Gary Robert Muschla, Judith A. Muschla, and Erin Muschla

Copyright © 2010 by Gary Robert Muschla, Judith A. Muschla, and Erin Muschla

List 3.19   continued

Subtracting Decimals and Whole Numbers

Example: $8 - 5.7 =$

1. Remember that a whole number is placed to the left of the decimal point. For example, the whole number 8 is written as 8.0.

2. Follow the steps for subtracting decimals.

$$\begin{array}{r} 8.0 \\ -\,5.7 \\ \hline 2.3 \end{array}$$

Multiplying Decimals

Example: $2.67 \times 0.4 =$

1. Line up the numbers by columns, not according to decimal points.

2. Multiply as you would with whole numbers.

3. Count the places held by the digits to the right of the decimal points in the numbers you multiplied.

4. Start at the right of your answer, and count the same number of places to the left. Place the decimal point there.

$$\begin{array}{r} 2.67 \ \ (2 \text{ places}) \\ \times\,0.4 \ \ (1 \text{ place}) \\ \hline 1.068 \ \ (3 \text{ places}) \end{array}$$

Dividing a Decimal by a Whole Number

Example: $1.47 \div 7 =$

1. Place a decimal point in the quotient above the decimal point in the dividend.

2. Divide as you would with whole numbers.

$$\begin{array}{r} .2\,1 \\ 7\overline{)\,1.4\,7} \\ 1\,4 \\ \hline 7 \\ 7 \\ \hline \end{array}$$

Dividing a Decimal by a Decimal

Example: $1.47 \div 0.7 =$

1. Move the decimal point to the right of the divisor, making the divisor a whole number. This is the same as multiplying a decimal by a power of 10. (In this case you are multiplying by 10.)

2. Move the decimal point in the dividend to the right the same number of places. (This is the same as multiplying by 10.)

$$0.7\overline{)\,1.4\,7}$$

Mathematics

3. Place a decimal point in the quotient above the dividend.

4. Divide as you would with whole numbers.

$$
\begin{array}{r}
2.1 \\
0.7\overline{)1.4\,7} \\
1\,4 \\
\hline
7 \\
7 \\
\hline
\end{array}
$$

5. If necessary, add a zero or zeros to the dividend to finish dividing.

Did you know? Using graph paper is a great way to keep columns in the proper alignment when using pencil and paper to add, subtract, multiply, and divide decimals.

See List 3.6, Steps for Adding and Subtracting Whole Numbers; List 3.13, Steps for Multiplying and Dividing Whole Numbers.

Copyright © 2010 by Gary Robert Muschla, Judith A. Muschla, and Erin Muschla

List 3.20   Steps for Finding the Greatest Common Factor

A *factor* is a number that divides into a larger number evenly. The greatest common factor (GCF) is the largest number that divides into two or more numbers evenly. Being able to find the greatest common factor is an important skill for simplifying fractions. The greatest common factor of two or more numbers can be found in two ways. Each method is explained below, using the greatest common factor of 12 and 20 as an example.

Listing the Factors

1. List the factors of the first number.

   Factors of 12 = 1, 2, 3, 4, 6, 12

2. List the factors of the second number.

   Factors of 20 = 1, 2, 4, 5, 10, and 20

3. Find the largest factor that appears in both lists. This is the greatest common factor.

   The CGF of 12 and 20 is 4.

Expressing Each Number as the Product of Prime Numbers

1. Write the first number as a product of prime numbers.

   $12 = 2 \times 2 \times 3$

2. Write the second number as a product of prime numbers.

   $20 = 2 \times 2 \times 5$

3. Find the pairs of numbers common to each.

   2×2 is common to each list.

4. Find the product of the common prime numbers.

   The GCF of 12 and 20 is 4.

   (Note: If there are no common prime factors, the GCF is 1.)

 Did you know? The greatest common factor of any two prime numbers is 1.

See List 3.8, Prime Numbers; List 3.10, Composite Numbers.

Copyright © 2010 by Gary Robert Muschla, Judith A. Muschla, and Erin Muschla

A *common multiple* is a number that two or more numbers divide into evenly. The least common multiple (LCM) is the smallest multiple of the numbers. It is most useful in finding common denominators. The least common multiple can be found in three ways. Each method is explained below, using the example of finding the least common multiple of 6 and 20.

Strategy 1

1. List the multiples of the largest number.

   Multiples of $20 = 20, 40, 60, 80, 100, 120, \ldots$

2. List the multiples of the other number (or numbers).

   Multiples of $6 = 6, 12, 18, 24, 30, 36, 42, 48, 54, 60, 66, 72, \ldots$

3. Find the smallest number that is on both lists. This number is the LCM.

   60 is the LCM of 6 and 20.

Strategy 2

1. Find the product of the numbers. $6 \times 20 = 120$

2. Find the greatest common factor (GCF) of the numbers.

   The GCF of 6 and 20 is 2.

3. Divide the product of the numbers by the GCF. $120 \div 2 = 60$

4. The quotient is the LCM. 60 is the LCM of 6 and 20.

Strategy 3

1. Write the first number as the product of primes, using exponents.

   $6 = 2 \times 3 \quad 6 = 2^1 \times 3^1$

2. Write the second number as the product of primes, using exponents.

   $20 = 2 \times 2 \times 5 \quad 20 = 2^2 \times 5^1$

3. Write each of the bases and only the largest exponent of each.

   $2^2 \times 3^1 \times 5^1$

4. Find the product. $2^2 \times 3^1 \times 5^1 = 60$

5. The product is the LCM. 60 is the LCM of 6 and 20.

Did you know? The least common multiple of any two or more prime numbers is the same as their product.

See List 3.8, Prime Numbers; List 3.20, Steps for Finding the Greatest Common Factor.

Copyright © 2010 by Gary Robert Muschla, Judith A. Muschla, and Erin Muschla

List 3.22   Types of Fractions

A *fraction* is a number that names a part of a whole or a part of a set. Each fraction has a numerator and a denominator. The *denominator* is the bottom number of a fraction and tells how many equal parts make the whole. The *numerator* is the top number and tells how many parts are being considered. There are many types of fractions. Some of the most common are explained below.

- *Proper fraction*: A fraction in which the numerator is less than the denominator. *Examples:* $\frac{1}{5}, \frac{3}{4}, \frac{2}{9}$

- *Improper fraction*: A fraction in which the numerator is equal to or greater than the denominator. Improper factions are usually changed to whole or mixed numbers. *Examples:* $\frac{3}{3}, \frac{7}{6}, \frac{9}{2}$

- *Simplified fraction*: A fraction whose numerator and denominator have no common factor greater than 1. The numerator must be less than the denominator. *Examples:* $\frac{1}{3}, \frac{4}{5}, \frac{3}{11}$

- *Mixed number:* A number that is a combination of a whole number and a fraction. Thus, it is "mixed." *Examples:* $3\frac{3}{4}, 5\frac{2}{9}, 6\frac{1}{3}$

- *Equivalent fractions*: Fractions that have the same value. *Examples:* $\frac{2}{5}, \frac{4}{10}, \frac{6}{15}$

- *Like fractions*: Fractions that have the same denominator. *Examples:* $\frac{1}{7}, \frac{6}{7}, \frac{4}{7}$

- *Unit fraction*: A fraction in which the numerator is 1. *Examples:* $\frac{1}{8}, \frac{1}{12}$

- *Reciprocal*: A fraction that results from interchanging the numerator and denominator. *Example:* The reciprocal of $\frac{5}{6}$ is $\frac{6}{5}$.

 Did you know? Zero cannot be a denominator of any fraction.

Copyright © 2010 by Gary Robert Muschla, Judith A. Muschla, and Erin Muschla

List 3.23   Renaming Mixed Numbers and Improper Fractions

All mixed numbers can be written as improper fractions. Improper fractions can be written as mixed numbers or whole numbers. The following lists summarize the steps.

Renaming Mixed Numbers as Improper Fractions

Example: Rename $2\dfrac{3}{5}$ as an improper fraction.

1. Multiply the whole number by the denominator of the fraction.

    $2 \times 5 = 10$

2. Add the numerator to the product.

    $10 + 3 = 13$

3. Write the sum over the denominator.

    $\dfrac{13}{5}$

Renaming Improper Fractions as Mixed or Whole Numbers

Example: Rename $\dfrac{15}{8}$ as a mixed number.

1. Divide the numerator by the denominator.

    $15 \div 8 = 1$, remainder 7

2. The quotient represents the whole number. The remainder represents the numerator of the fraction. The denominator stays the same.

    $1\dfrac{7}{8}$

3. If there is no remainder, the fraction can be rewritten as a whole number.

    For example, $\dfrac{16}{8} = 2$.

Did you know? All mixed numbers can be written as improper fractions, but only some improper fractions can be written as mixed numbers. The others are whole numbers.

See List 3.24, Steps for Simplifying Fractions.

Copyright © 2010 by Gary Robert Muschla, Judith A. Muschla, and Erin Muschla

List 3.24   Steps for Simplifying Fractions

A fraction is in simplest form when 1 is the only common factor of the numerator and denominator. A proper fraction can be simplified by dividing the numerator and denominator by common factors. There are two strategies you may use to simplify proper fractions.

Strategy 1: Using the Greatest Common Factor

Example: Simplify $\dfrac{18}{24}$.

1. Find the greatest common factor (GCF) of the numerator and denominator.

   6 is the GCF of 18 and 24.

2. Divide the numerator and denominator by the GCF. $\dfrac{18 \div 6}{24 \div 6} = \dfrac{3}{4}$

Strategy 2: Using Common Factors

Example: Simplify $\dfrac{18}{24}$.

1. Find a common factor of the numerator and denominator.

   3 is a common factor of 18 and 24.

2. Divide the numerator and denominator by the common factor.

   $\dfrac{18 \div 3}{24 \div 3} = \dfrac{6}{8}$

3. Continue this process until the only common factor is 1.

   2 is a common factor of 6 and 8. $\dfrac{6 \div 2}{8 \div 2} = \dfrac{3}{4}$

Improper Fractions

Use the following steps to simplify improper fractions.

Example: Simplify $\dfrac{18}{4}$.

1. Write the improper fraction as a mixed number. $\dfrac{18}{4} = 4\dfrac{2}{4}$

2. Simplify the proper fraction using either of the strategies above.

   $\dfrac{18}{4} = 4\dfrac{2}{4} = 4\dfrac{1}{2}$

 Did you know? Simplifying a fraction is also called reducing the fraction to lowest terms.

See List 3.20, Steps for Finding the Greatest Common Factor; List 3.23, Renaming Mixed Numbers and Improper Fractions.

Copyright © 2010 by Gary Robert Muschla, Judith A. Muschla, and Erin Muschla

List 3.25   Steps for Adding, Subtracting, Multiplying, and Dividing Fractions

A key to competence in math is being able to follow rules for procedures. Knowing the steps for performing the basic operations with fractions is essential to mastering the skills necessary for working with fractions.

Adding Fractions with Like Denominators

Example: $\dfrac{7}{8} + \dfrac{3}{8} =$

1. Add the numerators. (Do not add denominators.)
2. Write the sum over the denominator.
3. If the sum is an improper fraction, rename it as a mixed number or a whole number.
4. Simplify if possible.

$$\begin{array}{r} \dfrac{7}{8} \\[2mm] +\dfrac{3}{8} \\[1mm] \hline \end{array}$$

$$\frac{10}{8} = 1\frac{2}{8} = 1\frac{1}{4}$$

Adding Fractions with Unlike Denominators

Example: $\dfrac{5}{6} + \dfrac{3}{4} =$

1. Find the least common denominator (LCD). This is the same as finding the least common multiple (LCM) of the denominators. In the example, the LCM of 6 and 4 is 12.

$$\begin{array}{r} \dfrac{5}{6} = \dfrac{}{12} \\[2mm] +\dfrac{3}{4} = \dfrac{}{12} \\[1mm] \hline \end{array}$$

2. Write equivalent fractions with the common denominator.
3. Add the numerators. (Do not add denominators.)
4. Write the sum over the denominator.
5. If the sum is an improper fraction, rename it as a mixed number or a whole number.
6. Simplify if possible.

$$\begin{array}{r} \dfrac{5}{6} \times \dfrac{2}{2} = \dfrac{10}{12} \\[2mm] +\dfrac{3}{4} \times \dfrac{3}{3} = \dfrac{9}{12} \\[1mm] \hline \end{array}$$

$$\frac{19}{12} = 1\frac{7}{12}$$

Copyright © 2010 by Gary Robert Muschla, Judith A. Muschla, and Erin Muschla

Subtracting Fractions with Like Denominators

Example: $\dfrac{7}{12} - \dfrac{5}{12} =$

1. Subtract the numerator of the second fraction from the first. (Do not subtract the denominators.)
2. Write the difference over the denominator.
3. Simplify if possible.

$$\dfrac{7}{12}$$
$$-\dfrac{5}{12}$$
$$\dfrac{2}{12} = \dfrac{1}{6}$$

Subtracting Fractions with Unlike Denominators

Example: $\dfrac{4}{5} - \dfrac{2}{3} =$

1. Find the least common denominator (LCD) by finding the least common multiple (LCM) of the denominators. In the example, the LCM of 3 and 5 is 15.

$$\dfrac{4}{5} = \dfrac{}{15}$$
$$-\dfrac{2}{3} = \dfrac{}{15}$$

2. Write equivalent fractions with the common denominator.
3. Subtract the second numerator from the first. (Do not subtract the denominators.)
4. Write the difference over the denominator.
5. Simplify if possible.

$$\dfrac{4}{5} \times \dfrac{3}{3} = \dfrac{12}{15}$$
$$-\dfrac{2}{3} \times \dfrac{5}{5} = \dfrac{10}{15}$$
$$\dfrac{2}{15}$$

Multiplying Fractions

Example: $\dfrac{3}{8} \times \dfrac{2}{3} =$

1. Multiply the numerators.
2. Multiply the denominators.

Copyright © 2010 by Gary Robert Muschla, Judith A. Muschla, and Erin Muschla

Mathematics

3. Simplify if possible. (Sometimes it is possible to simplify before multiplying. Then follow the previous steps.)

$$\frac{3}{8} \times \frac{2}{3} = \frac{6}{24} = \frac{1}{4} \quad \text{or} \quad \frac{\cancel{3}^{1}}{\cancel{8}_{4}} \times \frac{\cancel{2}^{1}}{\cancel{3}_{1}} = \frac{1}{4}$$

Dividing Fractions

Example: $\dfrac{3}{4} \div \dfrac{5}{6} =$

1. Write the first fraction.

2. Use the reciprocal of the second fraction to write a multiplication problem.

$\dfrac{6}{5}$ is the reciprocal of $\dfrac{5}{6}$

$\dfrac{3}{4} \times \dfrac{6}{5}$

3. Multiply the numerators.

4. Multiply the denominators.

5. Simplify if possible (either before or after multiplying).

$$\frac{3}{4} \times \frac{6}{5} = \frac{18}{20} = \frac{9}{10} \quad \text{or} \quad \frac{3}{\cancel{4}_{2}} \times \frac{\cancel{6}^{3}}{5} = \frac{9}{10}$$

Did you know? If you multiply two proper fractions, the product is a fraction that is less than 1.

See List 3.21, Steps for Finding the Least Common Multiple; List 3.23, Renaming Mixed Numbers and Improper Fractions; List 3.24, Steps for Simplifying Fractions.

Copyright © 2010 by Gary Robert Muschla, Judith A. Muschla, and Erin Muschla

Copyright © 2010 by Gary Robert Muschla, Judith A. Muschla, and Erin Muschla

List 3.26 Steps for Adding, Subtracting, Multiplying, and Dividing Mixed Numbers

The basic operations with mixed numbers are similar to the basic operations with fractions. Once students have mastered fractions, working with mixed numbers becomes easier.

Adding Mixed Numbers with Like Denominators

Example: $7\dfrac{2}{5} + 6\dfrac{1}{5} =$

1. Add the numerators. (Do not add denominators.)
2. Place the sum over the denominator.
3. Add the whole numbers.
4. Rename any improper fractions as mixed numbers or whole numbers.
5. Simplify if possible.

$$\begin{array}{r} 7\dfrac{2}{5} \\ +\,6\dfrac{1}{5} \\ \hline 13\dfrac{3}{5} \end{array}$$

Adding Mixed Numbers with Unlike Denominators

Example: $2\dfrac{1}{3} + 6\dfrac{3}{4} =$

1. Find the least common denominator (LCD) by finding the least common multiple (LCM) of the denominators.
2. Write equivalent fractions with the common denominator.
3. Add the numerators. (Do not add denominators.)
4. Place the sum over the denominator.
5. Add the whole numbers.
6. Rename any improper fractions as mixed numbers or whole numbers.
7. Simplify if possible.

$$\begin{array}{r} 2\dfrac{1}{3} = 2\dfrac{4}{12} \\ +\,6\dfrac{3}{4} = 6\dfrac{9}{12} \\ \hline 8\dfrac{13}{12} = 8 + 1\dfrac{1}{12} = 9\dfrac{1}{12} \end{array}$$

Mathematics

Subtracting Mixed Numbers with Like Denominators Without Renaming

Example: $3\dfrac{4}{5} - 1\dfrac{1}{5} =$

1. Subtract the numerator of the second fraction from the first. (Do not subtract the denominators.)
2. Write the difference over the denominator.
3. Subtract the whole numbers.
4. Simplify if possible.

$$\begin{array}{r} 3\dfrac{4}{5} \\ -\,1\dfrac{1}{5} \\ \hline 2\dfrac{3}{5} \end{array}$$

Subtracting Mixed Numbers with Like Denominators with Renaming

Example: $6\dfrac{2}{7} - 3\dfrac{4}{7} =$

1. Renaming is necessary when the numerator of the second fraction is larger than the numerator of the first fraction.
2. Rename the first mixed number.
3. Subtract the numerators. (Do not subtract the denominators.)
4. Place the difference over the denominator.
5. Subtract the whole numbers.
6. Simplify if possible.

$$\begin{array}{rl} 6\dfrac{2}{7} = 5\dfrac{7}{7} + \dfrac{2}{7} = 5\dfrac{9}{7} \\ -\,3\dfrac{4}{7} = \qquad\qquad 3\dfrac{4}{7} \\ \hline \qquad\qquad\qquad 2\dfrac{5}{7} \end{array}$$

Subtracting Mixed Numbers with Unlike Denominators Without Renaming

Example: $5\dfrac{2}{3} - 1\dfrac{1}{2} =$

1. Find the least common denominator (LCD) by finding the least common multiple (LCM) of the denominators.
2. Write equivalent fractions with the common denominator.
3. Subtract the numerator of the second fraction from the first. (Do not subtract the denominators.)
4. Place the difference over the denominator.
5. Subtract the whole numbers.

Copyright © 2010 by Gary Robert Muschla, Judith A. Muschla, and Erin Muschla

6. Simplify if possible.

$$5\frac{2}{3} = 5\frac{4}{6}$$
$$-1\frac{1}{2} = 1\frac{3}{6}$$
$$\overline{\phantom{-1\frac{1}{2}=}\ 4\frac{1}{6}}$$

Subtracting Mixed Numbers with Unlike Denominators with Renaming

Example: $7\frac{1}{3} - 4\frac{3}{5} =$

1. Find the least common denominator (LCD) by finding the least common multiple (LCM) of the denominators.

2. Write equivalent fractions with the common denominator.

$$7\frac{1}{3} = 7\frac{5}{15}$$
$$-4\frac{3}{5} = 4\frac{9}{15}$$
$$\overline{\phantom{-4\frac{3}{5}=4\frac{9}{15}}}$$

3. Renaming is necessary when the numerator of the second fraction is larger than the numerator of the first fraction.

4. Rename the first mixed number.

5. Subtract the second numerator from the first. (Do not subtract the denominators.)

6. Place the difference over the denominator.

7. Subtract the whole numbers.

8. Simplify if possible.

$$7\frac{5}{15} = 6\frac{15}{15} + \frac{5}{15} = 6\frac{20}{15}$$
$$-4\frac{9}{15} = \qquad\qquad\qquad 4\frac{9}{15}$$
$$\overline{\phantom{-4\frac{9}{15}=}} \qquad\qquad \overline{2\frac{11}{15}}$$

Multiplying Mixed Numbers

Example: $2\frac{1}{5} \times 1\frac{1}{4} =$

1. Rename the mixed numbers as improper fractions.

$$\frac{11}{5} \times \frac{5}{4} =$$

2. Multiply the numerators.

3. Multiply the denominators.

4. Rename improper fractions as mixed numbers or whole numbers.

Copyright © 2010 by Gary Robert Muschla, Judith A. Muschla, and Erin Muschla

5. Simplify if possible. (If possible simplify before multiplying. Then follow the previous steps.)

$$\frac{11}{5} \times \frac{5}{4} = \frac{55}{20} = 2\frac{15}{20} = 2\frac{3}{4} \quad \text{or} \quad \frac{11}{\cancel{5}_1} \times \frac{\cancel{5}^1}{4} = \frac{11}{4} = 2\frac{3}{4}$$

Dividing Mixed Numbers

Example: $3\frac{1}{2} \div 1\frac{2}{3} =$

1. Rename the mixed numbers as improper fractions.

$$\frac{7}{2} \div \frac{5}{3} =$$

2. Use the reciprocal of the second fraction to write a multiplication problem.
3. Multiply the numerators.
4. Multiply the denominators.
5. Rename improper fractions as mixed numbers or whole numbers.
6. Simplify if possible (either before or after multiplying).

$$\frac{7}{2} \times \frac{3}{5} = \frac{21}{10} = 2\frac{1}{10}$$

Did you know? If you add or multiply mixed numbers, the answer is greater than 1. If you subtract or divide mixed numbers, the answer could be less than 1, equal to 1, or greater than 1, depending on the mixed numbers.

See List 3.21, Steps for Finding the Least Common Multiple; List 3.23, Renaming Mixed Numbers and Improper Fractions; List 3.24, Steps for Simplifying Fractions; List 3.25, Steps for Adding, Subtracting, Multiplying, and Dividing Fractions.

Copyright © 2010 by Gary Robert Muschla, Judith A. Muschla, and Erin Muschla

List 3.27   Steps for Changing Decimals to Fractions

Decimals can easily be converted to fractions, provided students understand place value. The following steps simplify the process.

1. Identify the place value of the last digit of the decimal.
2. Use the place value of this digit as the denominator of the fraction.
3. Any digits to the left of the decimal point are written as whole numbers. Any digits to the right of the decimal point are written as the numerator of the fraction.
4. Simplify if possible.

   Examples:

0.4	The 4 is in the tenths place.	$0.4 = \dfrac{4}{10} = \dfrac{2}{5}$
0.13	The 3 is in the hundredths place.	$0.13 = \dfrac{13}{100}$
0.125	The 5 is in the thousandths place.	$0.125 = \dfrac{125}{1000} = \dfrac{1}{8}$
3.06	The 3 is a whole number.	
	The 6 is in the hundredths place.	$3.06 = 3\dfrac{6}{100} = 3\dfrac{3}{50}$

 Did you know? Any decimal that terminates can be changed to a fraction.

See List 3.16, Place Value Chart for Decimal Numbers; List 3.24, Steps for Simplifying Fractions; List 3.28, Steps for Changing Fractions to Decimals.

Copyright © 2010 by Gary Robert Muschla, Judith A. Muschla, and Erin Muschla

Mathematics

List 3.28   Steps for Changing Fractions to Decimals

There are two methods for changing fractions to decimals. The first is to rewrite the fraction as an equivalent fraction whose denominator is 10, 100, 1,000, and so on. Then the fraction can be changed directly to a decimal. This method works only with fractions whose denominator is a factor of a power of 10. The second method is to divide the numerator of the fraction by the denominator. This method can be used for all fractions.

Rewriting the Fraction

Example: Change $\frac{1}{2}$ to a decimal.

1. Multiply the numerator and the denominator of the fraction by the same number so that the denominator is a power of 10.

2. Change the fraction to an equivalent decimal.

$$\frac{1}{2} \times \frac{5}{5} = \frac{5}{10} = 0.5$$

Dividing the Numerator by the Denominator

Example: Change $\frac{1}{2}$ to a decimal.

1. Set up a division problem by dividing the numerator by the denominator.

$$2\overline{)1}$$

2. Add a decimal point after the dividend and add 1 zero.

3. Divide. (Add more zeros if necessary.)

$$\begin{array}{r} 0.5 \\ 2\overline{)1.0} \\ \underline{1\,0} \end{array} \qquad \frac{1}{2} = 0.5$$

4. For repeating decimals, be sure to indicate the repeating digits by placing a bar over the digit or digits that repeat.

$$\frac{2}{3} \qquad \begin{array}{r} 0.66 \\ 3\overline{)2.00} \\ \underline{1\,8} \\ 20 \\ \underline{18} \\ 2 \end{array} \qquad \frac{2}{3} = 0.\overline{6}$$

 Did you know? A thorough understanding of multiplication facts and divisibility rules is essential for rewriting fractions as equivalent decimals.

See List 3.19, Steps for Adding, Subtracting, Multiplying, and Dividing Decimals; List 3.25, Steps for Adding, Subtracting, Multiplying, and Dividing Fractions; List 3.27, Steps for Changing Decimals to Fractions.

Copyright © 2010 by Gary Robert Muschla, Judith A. Muschla, and Erin Muschla

List 3.29   Steps for Changing Decimals to Percents

Percent means hundredths and is denoted by the % symbol. Writing a decimal as a percent requires that the decimal is expressed as hundredths. You may do this in one of two ways: Change the decimal to an equivalent fraction, or change the decimal to an equivalent percent directly. Both methods are shown below.

Changing the Decimal to an Equivalent Fraction, Then to a Percent

Example: Change 0.8 to a percent.

1. Write the decimal as a fraction.

$$0.8 = \frac{8}{10}$$

2. If necessary, change the fraction to an equivalent fraction with a denominator of 100.

$$\frac{8}{10} \times \frac{10}{10} = \frac{8}{100}$$

3. Change the fraction to a percent.

$$\frac{80}{100} = 80\%$$

Changing the Decimal Directly to a Percent

Example: Change 0.5 to a percent.

1. Move the decimal point two places to the right and include any placeholders. (This is the same as multiplying by 100.)

2. Change the decimal directly to the percent.

$$0.5\,0 = 50\%$$

Did you know? You can remember that percent means hundredths by thinking that there are 100 cents in a dollar.

See List 3.27, Steps for Changing Decimals to Fractions; List 3.30, Steps for Changing Percents to Decimals; List 3.31, Steps for Changing Fractions to Percents.

Copyright © 2010 by Gary Robert Muschla, Judith A. Muschla, and Erin Muschla

List 3.30   Steps for Changing Percents to Decimals

Since percent means hundredths, percents can easily be converted to decimals. This can be done by writing an equivalent fraction or by moving the decimal point. Both methods follow.

Changing the Percent to a Decimal by Writing an Equivalent Fraction

1. Write the percent as an equivalent fraction with a denominator of 100.
2. Do not simplify.
3. Express the fraction as a decimal.

   Examples:

   $$58\% = \frac{58}{100} = 0.58 \qquad 34\% = \frac{34}{100} = 0.34$$

   $$2\% = \frac{2}{100} = 0.02 \qquad 125\% = \frac{125}{100} = 1.25$$

Changing the Percent Directly to a Decimal

Move the decimal point two places to the left. (This is the same as dividing by 100.)

Examples:

$$58\% = 0.58 \qquad 34\% = 0.34 \qquad 2\% = 0.02 \qquad 125\% = 1.25$$

Did you know? Giving a job 110% of you attention, although mathematically incorrect, is a common expression for trying very hard.

See List 3.28, Steps for Changing Fractions to Decimals; List 3.29, Steps for Changing Decimals to Percents.

Copyright © 2010 by Gary Robert Muschla, Judith A. Muschla, and Erin Muschla

List 3.31   Steps for Changing Fractions to Percents

Every fraction can be changed to a percent. One method is to change the fraction to a percent by writing an equivalent fraction. This can be done only if 100 is divisible by the denominator of the fraction. The other method is to change a fraction to a decimal, and then change the decimal to a percent.

Changing the Fraction to a Percent by Using an Equivalent Fraction

Example: Change $\frac{3}{4}$ to a percent.

1. If 100 is divisible by the denominator of the fraction, write an equivalent fraction with a denominator of 100.

2. Change the equivalent fraction to a percent.

$$\frac{3}{4} \times \frac{25}{25} = \frac{75}{100} = 75\%$$

Changing the Fraction to a Percent by Using the Decimal Method

Example: Change $\frac{3}{4}$ to a percent.

1. Divide the numerator of the fraction by the denominator.

2. Add a decimal point and two zeros. (The two zeros are necessary to change the fraction to a percent because percent means hundredths.)

$$\begin{array}{r} .75 = 75\% \\ 4\overline{)3.00} \\ \underline{2\ 8} \\ 20 \\ \underline{20} \end{array}$$

3. Divide and express the quotient as a percent.

4. If there is a remainder, write the remainder as a fraction. Simplify if necessary.

$$\frac{7}{8} \qquad \begin{array}{r} 0.87\frac{4}{8} = 87\frac{1}{2}\% \\ 8\overline{)7.00} \\ \underline{6\ 4} \\ 60 \\ \underline{56} \\ 4 \end{array}$$

 Did you know? Every proper fraction can be changed to a percent that is less than 100%. Improper fractions and whole numbers can be changed to percents that are greater than or equal to 100%.

See List 3.19, Steps for Adding, Subtracting, Multiplying, and Dividing Decimals; List 3.28, Steps for Changing Fractions to Decimals; List 3.29, Steps for Changing Decimals to Percents; List 3.32, Steps for Changing Percents to Fractions.

Copyright © 2010 by Gary Robert Muschla, Judith A. Muschla, and Erin Muschla

List 3.32   Steps for Changing Percents to Fractions

When changing percents to fractions, remember that the % symbol means hundredths. Percents can easily be changed directly to fractions by writing equivalent fractions.

1. Change the percent to an equivalent fraction with a denominator of 100.
2. Rename any improper fractions as mixed numbers.
3. Simplify if possible.

Examples:

$$30\% = \frac{30}{100} = \frac{3}{10} \qquad 8\% = \frac{8}{100} = \frac{2}{25} \qquad 135\% = \frac{135}{100} = 1\frac{35}{100} = 1\frac{7}{20}$$

 Did you know? *Percent* comes from two Latin words, *per* meaning "by" and *centum* meaning "hundred."

See List 3.24, Steps for Simplifying Fractions; List 3.31, Steps for Changing Fractions to Percents.

Copyright © 2010 by Gary Robert Muschla, Judith A. Muschla, and Erin Muschla

List 3.33   The Customary System of Measures

The United States uses the customary system of measures to measure length, weight, and capacity. When you think of inches, pounds, and pints, you are using the customary system. For example, a paper clip is about 1 inch long, a piece of notebook paper is about a foot long, and a baseball bat is about a yard long. A slice of bread weighs about 1 ounce and a loaf of bread (16 slices) weighs about a pound. A glass of water contains 8 fluid ounces and 4 glasses of water are the same as one quart. Following are basic units of measurement, how they are related, and their abbreviations.

Units of Measure	Abbreviations
Length	*Length*
12 inches = 1 foot	inch: in or ″
3 feet = 1 yard	foot: ft or ′
36 inches = 1 yard	yard: yd
1,760 yards = 1 mile	mile: mi
5,280 feet = 1 mile	
Weight	*Weight*
16 ounces = 1 pound	ounce: oz
2,000 pounds = 1 ton	pound: lb
	ton: T
Capacity (Liquid Measure)	*Capacity (Liquid Measure)*
3 teaspoons = 1 tablespoon	teaspoon: t or tsp
2 tablespoons = 1 fluid ounce	tablespoon: T or tbsp
8 fluid ounces = 1 cup	fluid ounce: fl oz
2 cups = 1 pint	cup: c
16 fluid ounces = 1 pint	pint: pt
2 pints = 1 quart	quart: qt
4 cups = 1 quart	gallon: gal
32 fluid ounces = 1 quart	
4 quarts = 1 gallon	
128 fluid ounces = 1 gallon	

 Did you know? The customary system of measures is also referred to as the English system of measurement.

See List 3.34, Steps for Converting Units in the Customary System of Measures; List 3.35, Steps for Computing with the Customary System of Measures.

Copyright © 2010 by Gary Robert Muschla, Judith A. Muschla, and Erin Muschla

List 3.34   Steps for Converting Units in the Customary System of Measures

In order to change from one unit of measurement to another in the customary system, it is necessary to know the equivalencies. The guidelines for conversions follow.

To Convert from a Larger Unit to a Smaller Unit

Example: Convert 5 ft 2 in to inches.

1. Find an equivalent measure by referring to a table or by learning the equivalent values.

   $1\,\text{ft} = 12\,\text{in}$

2. Multiply.

   $5\,\text{ft} = 5 \times 12 = 60\,\text{in}$

3. Add if necessary.

   $5\,\text{ft}\ 2\,\text{in} = 60\,\text{in} + 2\,\text{in} = 62\,\text{in}$

To Convert from a Smaller Unit to a Larger Unit

Example: Convert 20 oz to pounds and ounces.

1. Find an equivalent measure by referring to a table or by learning the equivalent values.

   $16\,\text{oz} = 1\,\text{lb}$

2. Divide.

$$
\begin{array}{r}
1\,\text{R}4 \\
16\overline{)20} \\
\underline{16} \\
4
\end{array}
$$

3. Express the remainder as the smaller unit of the equivalency.
   $20\,\text{oz} = 1\,\text{lb}\ 4\,\text{oz}$

 Did you know? The abbreviation for pound, lb, is not a shortened form of the word pound. Instead it is a shortened form of an old Roman weight, *libra*, which is about 12 ounces.

See List 3.33, The Customary System of Measures.

Copyright © 2010 by Gary Robert Muschla, Judith A. Muschla, and Erin Muschla

The Elementary Teacher's Book of Lists

Copyright © 2010 by Gary Robert Muschla, Judith A. Muschla, and Erin Muschla

List 3.35   Steps for Computing with the Customary System of Measures

Special rules must be followed to add, subtract, multiply, and divide in the customary system of measures. The lists below summarize the procedures.

Adding Units of Measurements

Example: Find the sum of 4 yd 2 ft and 3 yd 2 ft.

1. Line up the units in each column.
2. Add each column separately.

$$
\begin{array}{r}
4 \text{ yd } 2 \text{ ft} \\
+\ 3 \text{ yd } 2 \text{ ft} \\
\hline
7 \text{ yd } 4 \text{ ft}
\end{array}
$$

3. Express the sum in terms of the larger quantity if necessary.
   Since 1 yd = 3 ft, divide 4 ft by 3.

$$
\begin{array}{r}
1 \text{ yd } 1 \text{ ft} \\
3\overline{)4 \text{ ft}} \\
\underline{3} \\
1
\end{array}
$$

   4 ft = 1 yd + 1 ft
   7 yd 4 ft = 7 yd + 1 yd + 1 ft = 8 yd 1 ft

Subtracting Units of Measurements

Example: Find the difference between 6 lb 2 oz and 2 lb 7 oz.

1. Line up the units in each column. Remember to write the larger quantity on the top.

$$
\begin{array}{r}
6 \text{ lb } 2 \text{ oz} \\
-\ 2 \text{ lb } 7 \text{ oz}
\end{array}
$$

2. If necessary, rename the values of the larger quantity using equivalent values.
   Since 16 oz = 1 lb, 6 lb 2 oz = 5 lb + 16 oz + 2 oz = 5 lb 18 oz
3. Subtract.
4. Express the difference in terms of the larger quantity if necessary.

$$
\begin{array}{r}
5 \text{ lb } 18 \text{ oz} \\
-\ 2 \text{ lb }\ \ 7 \text{ oz} \\
\hline
3 \text{ lb } 11 \text{ oz}
\end{array}
$$

Mathematics   183

Multiplying Units of Measurements

Example: Multiply 1 ft 8 in by 2.

1. Set up a multiplication problem.

2. Multiply from right to left, multiplying each column separately.

$$
\begin{array}{r}
1\text{ ft }\quad 8\text{ in} \\
\times\ 2 \\
\hline
2\text{ ft }16\text{ in}
\end{array}
$$

3. Express the product in terms of the larger quantity if necessary. Since 12 in = 1 ft, divide 16 in by 12.

$$
\begin{array}{r}
1\text{ ft }4\text{ in} \\
12\overline{)\,16\text{ in}} \\
\underline{12\phantom{\text{ in}}} \\
4
\end{array}
$$

2 ft 16 in = 2 ft + 1 ft + 4 in = 3 ft 4 in or 1 yd 4 in

Dividing Units of Measurements

Example: Divide 9 lb 12 oz by 4.

1. Express the quantity in terms of the smaller unit.
Since 16 oz = 1 lb, 9 lb 12 oz = 9 × 16 oz + 12 oz = 156 oz

2. Set up the division problem.

3. Divide.

$$
\begin{array}{r}
39\text{ oz} \\
4\overline{)\,156\text{ oz}} \\
\underline{12} \\
36 \\
\underline{36} \\
\end{array}
$$

4. Express the quotient in terms of the larger quantity if necessary.

$$
\begin{array}{r}
2\text{ lb }7\text{ oz} \\
16\overline{)\,39\text{ oz}} \\
\underline{32\phantom{\text{ oz}}} \\
7
\end{array}
$$

39 oz = 2 lb 7 oz

Did you know? A knowledge of equivalent measures is helpful when computing in the customary system.

See List 3.33, The Customary System of Measures.

Copyright © 2010 by Gary Robert Muschla, Judith A. Muschla, and Erin Muschla

List 3.36   Visualizing the Metric System

The metric system of measurement is used throughout the world. Because American students are more familiar with customary units of measure such as feet, quarts, and pounds, they may have trouble visualizing metric measurements. The following examples can help.

- The *meter* (m) is used for measuring length. A meter is equal to about 1.1 yards, a little over 3 feet. The length of a baseball bat and the width of your classroom door are each about a meter.

- The *liter* (L) is used for measuring liquid capacity. A liter is equal to 1.06 quarts. A large bottle of water contains 1 liter of water.

- The *gram* (g) is used for measuring mass. A paper clip, a dime, a raisin, and a jelly bean each weigh about a gram. Because a gram is so small, kilograms (kg) are commonly used to measure mass. A kilogram is equal to 1000 grams or about 2.2 pounds, roughly equal to the weight of an adult's pair of sneakers.

 Did you know? The metric system was adopted in France in the 1790s.

See List 3.37, Metric System Units and Prefixes; List 3.38, Steps for Converting Units in the Metric System.

Copyright © 2010 by Gary Robert Muschla, Judith A. Muschla, and Erin Muschla

List 3.37   Metric System Units and Prefixes

The metric system is a system of measurement that is used throughout the world. Prefixes representing powers of ten are used to indicate larger or smaller units. Three of the most important units of the metric system are the meter, liter, and kilogram.

Length is measured in meters (m).

Capacity is measured in liters (L).

Mass is measured in kilograms (kg).

Common Metric Prefixes and Values

kilo = one thousand or 1,000

hecto = one hundred or 100

deca or deka = ten or 10

deci = one-tenth or 0.1

centi = one-hundredth or 0.01

milli = one-thousandth or 0.001

Common Units of Measure in the Metric System

Length

10 millimeters (mm) = 1 centimeter (cm)

10 centimeters = 1 decimeter (dm)

10 decimeters = 1 meter (m)

1 meter = 100 centimeters = 1,000 millimeters

1000 meters = 1 kilometer (km)

Capacity

1000 milliliters (mL) = 1 liter (L)

1,000 liters = 1 kiloliter (kL)

Mass

1000 grams (g) = 1 kilogram (kg)

 Did you know? Capacity and mass are related in the metric system. One milliliter of pure water has a mass of one gram. Stated another way: 1 liter of pure water has a mass of 1,000 grams or 1 kilogram.

See List 3.36, Visualizing the Metric System.

Copyright © 2010 by Gary Robert Muschla, Judith A. Muschla, and Erin Muschla

List 3.38   Steps for Converting Units in the Metric System

The values of the metric system are based on powers of ten. Once the basic values are understood, conversions become quite easy. The following steps show how to convert the metric units of length, liquid capacity, and mass.

To Convert a Larger Unit to a Smaller Unit

Example: Convert 3 kg to g.

1. Start with the number of the larger unit (3 kilograms).
2. Find the number of smaller units in the larger unit. (There are 1,000 grams in each kilogram.)
3. Multiply.
   $3 \times 1,000 = 3,000$ grams
   $3\,kg = 3,000\,g$

To Convert a Smaller Unit to a Larger Unit

Example: Convert 357 mL to L.

1. Start with the number of the smaller unit (357 milliliters).
2. Find the number of smaller units in the larger unit. (There are 1,000 milliliters in a liter.)
3. Divide the smaller unit by the larger.
4. Insert placeholders if necessary.
   $357 \div 1000 = 0.357\,L$
   $357\,mL = 0.357\,L$

Did you know? The metric system is a decimal system. This is why larger and smaller units can be defined by multiplying or dividing basic units by powers of 10.

See List 3.37, Metric System Units and Prefixes.

Copyright © 2010 by Gary Robert Muschla, Judith A. Muschla, and Erin Muschla

List 3.39   Steps for Computing in the Metric System

It is easy to add, subtract, multiply, and divide units of measure in the metric system. Just follow the rules below.

Addition

Example: Find the sum of 3.4 cm and 5 mm.

1. Convert to the larger unit. Since cm is the larger unit, convert 5 mm to 0.5 cm.

2. Add.
$$
\begin{array}{r}
3.4 \text{ cm} \\
+\ \underline{0.5} \text{ cm} \\
3.9 \text{ cm}
\end{array}
$$

Subtraction

Example: Find the difference between 0.9 km and 35 m.

1. Convert to the larger unit. Since km is the larger unit, convert 35 m to 0.035 km.

2. Subtract. (If necessary, add zeros and regroup.)
$$
\begin{array}{r}
0.900 \text{ km} \\
-\ \underline{0.035} \text{ km} \\
0.865 \text{ km}
\end{array}
$$

Multiplication

Example: Multiply 4.3 mL by 5.

1. Set up the multiplication problem.

2. Multiply as you would multiply decimals.
$$
\begin{array}{r}
4.3 \text{ mL} \\
\times\ \underline{5} \\
21.5 \text{ mL}
\end{array}
$$

Division

Example: Divide 7.4 m by 8.

1. Write the division problem.

2. Divide. (If necessary, add zeros as placeholders.)
$$
\begin{array}{r}
.925 \text{ m} \\
8\,\overline{)7.400} \text{ m} \\
\underline{7\,2} \\
20 \\
\underline{16} \\
40 \\
\underline{40}
\end{array}
$$

 Did you know? Many people think that computing with metric units is easier than using the customary system of measures because there are no equivalencies to remember or look up.

See List 3.19, Steps for Adding, Subtracting, Multiplying, and Dividing Decimals; List 3.37, Metric System Units and Prefixes; List 3.38, Steps for Converting Units in the Metric System.

Copyright © 2010 by Gary Robert Muschla, Judith A. Muschla, and Erin Muschla

A ruler is used to measure length. There are two basic types of rulers: a customary ruler and metric ruler. The customary ruler is numbered in inches, and tick marks represent a half, a fourth, an eighth, or a sixteenth of an inch. Metric rulers are numbered in centimeters, and tick marks represent millimeters. Many rulers have customary units along one edge of the ruler and metric units along the other. The procedures for measuring are the same.

- Decide if you will need a customary ruler or metric ruler for the object you wish to measure.
- If you are using a customary ruler, decide if the tick marks are marked for every half, fourth, eighth, or sixteenth of an inch.
- If you are using a metric ruler, the tick marks are most likely marked for each millimeter.
- Place the beginning of the scale of your ruler on one end of the object you will measure. (Note: The scale may not begin at the edge of the ruler.)
- Start at the beginning of the scale and measure to the end of the object.
- If the length of the object does not end at a whole number on the ruler, find the largest whole number before the end of the object. Then count the tick marks. Include both the number and the proper unit: for example, $4\frac{3}{8}$ inches or 10.3 centimeters.
- If you are measuring a large object use a yardstick, meter stick, or tape measure.

 Did you know? Before measurements were standardized, an inch was often defined as the length of three barley grains placed end to end, and a foot was the length of a king's foot.

See List 3.33, The Customary System of Measures; List 3.37, Metric System Units and Prefixes.

Copyright © 2010 by Gary Robert Muschla, Judith A. Muschla, and Erin Muschla

We measure time in several ways. Unfortunately, no matter how we measure it, there never seems to be enough. This is certainly true of teachers, for whom there are never enough hours in the day. Following are time equivalencies.

$$60 \text{ seconds (sec)} = 1 \text{ minute (min)}$$
$$60 \text{ minutes} = 1 \text{ hour (hr)}$$
$$24 \text{ hours} = 1 \text{ day (d)}$$
$$7 \text{ days} = 1 \text{ week (wk)}$$
$$4 \text{ weeks} \approx 1 \text{ month (mn)}$$
$$52 \text{ weeks} = 1 \text{ year (yr)}$$
$$12 \text{ months} = 1 \text{ year}$$
$$365\frac{1}{4} \text{ days} = 1 \text{ year}$$
$$366 \text{ days} = 1 \text{ leap year}$$
$$10 \text{ years} = 1 \text{ decade}$$
$$100 \text{ years} = 1 \text{ century}$$
$$1{,}000 \text{ years} = 1 \text{ millennium}$$

Some Timely Facts

- **Gregorian calendar:** The calendar in use throughout much of the world, instituted by Pope Gregory XIII in 1582.

- **A.M. or a.m.:** *ante meridiem*, meaning "before noon."

- **P.M. or p.m.:** *post meridiem*, meaning "after noon."

- **Solar time:** A measurement of time in which noon occurs when the sun is at the highest point over a given location.

- **Standard Time:** The mean solar time at the central meridian in any of the 24 time zones.

- **Daylight Saving Time:** In most states of the United States, Standard Time plus one hour, which seems to make daylight last an hour longer.

- **The days in the months:** April, June, September, and November are the only months that have 30 days. February has 28 days, except for a leap year when it has 29. All of the other months have 31 days.

Did you know? The measurement of a year is based on one revolution of the Earth around the sun. A year is 365 days, 5 hours, 48 minutes, and 45.5 seconds, which is typically rounded to $365\frac{1}{4}$. That extra quarter of a day requires a leap year once every four years to ensure that the calendar remains accurate.

Copyright © 2010 by Gary Robert Muschla, Judith A. Muschla, and Erin Muschla

List 3.42 Measuring Temperature

Two of the most common scales used to measure temperature are the Celsius and Fahrenheit Scales. To change from one scale to the other, follow these procedures.

- To change degrees Fahrenheit to degrees Celsius, use the formula
  $C = (F - 32) \div 1.8$.
- To change degrees Celsius to degrees Fahrenheit, use the formula
  $F = (C \times 1.8) + 32$.

The following list shows some common temperatures and their measures in both scales.

Degrees Fahrenheit	Degrees Celsius	Common Examples
374° F	190° C	a hot oven
212° F	100° C	water boils
151° F	66° C	hot faucet water
104° F	40° C	a high fever
98.6° F	37° C	normal body temperature
95° F	35° C	a hot day
45° F	7° C	cold water
32° F	0° C	water freezes
12° F	−11° C	frozen yogurt

 Did you know? There is a third scale for measuring temperature, the Kelvin Scale, which is used to measure temperature in scientific experiments.

Copyright © 2010 by Gary Robert Muschla, Judith A. Muschla, and Erin Muschla

List 3.43   Angles

An *angle* is formed by two rays that have the same endpoint. Following are angle facts and examples of common angles.

Angle Facts

- The common endpoint of the rays that form an angle is called the *vertex* of the angle.
- An angle can be named by its vertex or by three points: a point on one of the rays, the vertex, and a point on the other ray.
- The symbol $\angle$ indicates angle. In $\angle ABC$ point B is the vertex. The symbol and letters are read "angle ABC." $\angle ABC$ may also be named $\angle CBA$ or $\angle B$.
- All angles are measured in degrees. The symbol $^\circ$ indicates degrees.

Common Angles

Acute angle: An angle whose measure is less than 90°.

Right angle: An angle whose measure is 90°. A box in the vertex of an angle is sometimes used to show a right angle.

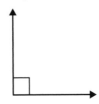

Obtuse angle: An angle whose measure is greater than 90°.

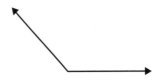

Straight angle: An angle whose measure is 180°. It is the same as a straight line.

 Did you know? The corner of a text book or the corner of a piece of paper is an example of a right angle. Acute angles are small enough to fit inside the corner. Obtuse angles are too large to fit in the corner.

See List 3.44, Steps for Measuring and Drawing Angles.

Copyright © 2010 by Gary Robert Muschla, Judith A. Muschla, and Erin Muschla

List 3.44   Steps for Measuring and Drawing Angles

A *protractor* is a tool used to measure and draw angles. All angles are measured in degrees.

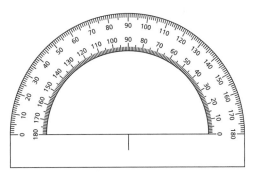

To measure an angle, do the following:

1. Place the center point of the protractor on the vertex of the angle. The vertex is the point where the two rays of the angle meet.
2. Line up the center point and the 0° mark on the protractor with one of the rays of the angle.
3. Find the point where the other ray passes through the scale. You may have to extend the side of the angle so that it crosses the scale.
4. Use the scale that starts with 0°.
5. Find the measure of the angle where ray passes through the scale.
6. Label the measure with the degree symbol °.

To draw an angle, do the following:

1. Draw and label one ray.
2. Place the center point of the protractor on the endpoint of the ray.
3. Line up the ray with the 0° mark on the protractor.
4. Use the scale that starts with 0°.
5. Mark a point on the paper of the measure of the angle you want to draw. For example, to draw a 50° angle, mark your point at 50°. For a 120° angle, mark your point at 120°.
6. Draw a ray from the endpoint through the point you marked.
7. Label a point on the ray.

 Did you know? Forms of the protractor that is used today were used in ancient times.

See List 3.43, Angles.

Copyright © 2010 by Gary Robert Muschla, Judith A. Muschla, and Erin Muschla

List 3.45   Polygons

A *polygon* is a special type of closed figure whose sides are straight line segments. (A closed figure begins and ends at the same point.) Polygons are named according to the number of their sides. The diagonal of a polygon is a line segment drawn from one vertex to another non-adjacent vertex. The following list contains some useful information about polygons.

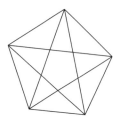

Polygon	Number of Sides	Number of Angles	Number of Diagonals
Triangle	3	3	0
Quadrilateral	4	4	2
Pentagon	5	5	5
Hexagon	6	6	9
Heptagon	7	7	14
Octagon	8	8	20
Nonagon	9	9	27
Decagon	10	10	35

 Did you know? You can find the number of diagonals of any polygon by using the formula $(n^2 - 3n) \div 2$, where n represents the number of sides.

See List 3.46, Classifying Triangles; List 3.47, Classifying Quadrilaterals.

Copyright © 2010 by Gary Robert Muschla, Judith A. Muschla, and Erin Muschla

List 3.46   Classifying Triangles

A *triangle* is a polygon that has three sides and three angles. All triangles can be classified by the length of their sides or the types of their angles.

Classification by the Length of the Sides

- If a triangle has 3 congruent sides, it is an *equilateral triangle*.
- If a triangle has 2 congruent sides, it is an *isosceles triangle*.
- If a triangle has no congruent sides, it is a *scalene triangle*.

Equilateral Triangle   Isosceles Triangles   Scalene Triangles

Classification by the Types of Angles

- If a triangle has 3 acute angles, it is an *acute triangle*.
- If a triangle has 1 right angle, it is a *right triangle*.
- If a triangle has 1 obtuse angle, it is an *obtuse triangle*.

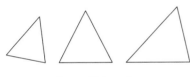      

Acute Triangles   Right Triangles   Obtuse Triangles

 Did you know? All right triangles have one right angle and two acute angles.

See List 3.43, Angles.

Copyright © 2010 by Gary Robert Muschla, Judith A. Muschla, and Erin Muschla

Mathematics   **195**

List 3.47   Classifying Quadrilaterals

A *quadrilateral* is a polygon that has four sides and four angles. All quadrilaterals can be classified by the length of their sides, number of right angles, and parallel sides. Following are some quadrilaterals and their properties.

Trapezoid

- One pair of sides is parallel.

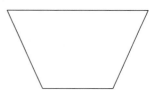

Parallelogram

- Opposite sides are parallel.
- Opposite sides are congruent.

Rectangle

- Opposite sides are parallel.
- Opposite sides are congruent.
- All angles are right angles.

Square

- Opposite sides are parallel.
- All sides are congruent.
- All angles are right angles.

Rhombus

- Opposite sides are parallel.
- All sides are congruent.

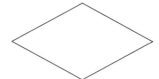

 Did you know? The plural of *rhombus* is "rhombuses" or "rhombi."

Copyright © 2010 by Gary Robert Muschla, Judith A. Muschla, and Erin Muschla

Copyright © 2010 by Gary Robert Muschla, Judith A. Muschla, and Erin Muschla

List 3.48   Tangrams

A *tangram* is a geometric puzzle consisting of seven figures: five triangles, a square, and a parallelogram. It is thought to have been invented in China at least several hundred years ago and has been amusing and amazing people ever since. Thousands of shapes can be formed with the figures of a tangram, stimulating both visualization skills and creativity. That students are working with geometric shapes is another benefit. The tangram that follows can be used as a template for making tangrams for your students.

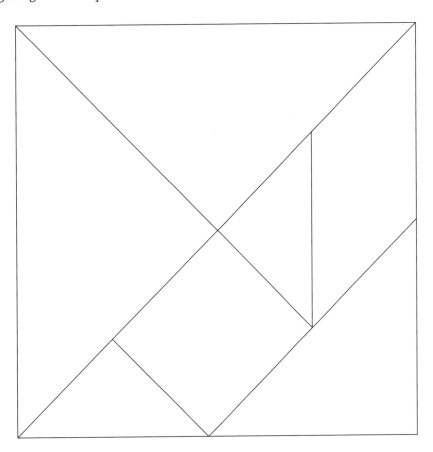

Tangram Facts (and Speculations)

- No one knows exactly when the tangram was invented. One story tells how a servant of a Chinese emperor dropped an expensive square tile. Worried of his fate should the emperor discover what happened, the servant desperately tried to put the pieces back together. Although he was unable to make a square, he made several other shapes, which became the idea for tangrams. (No one knows what happened to the servant.) In time, tangrams spread around the world, arriving in America in the early 1800s.

- Some people believe that the word *tangram* comes from the word *trangram*, which means "puzzle" or "trinket."

- Each piece of the puzzle is called a *tan*.

- There are many interesting geometric aspects about tangrams, including:
    - The two largest triangles of a tangram are congruent.
    - The two smallest triangles are congruent.
    - All of the triangles are similar.
    - All of the triangles are right isosceles triangles.
    - The area of each large triangle is $\frac{1}{4}$ of the area of the puzzle.
    - The area of the medium triangle is $\frac{1}{8}$ of the area of the puzzle.
    - The area of each of the small triangles is $\frac{1}{16}$ of the area of the puzzle.
    - The area of the square is $\frac{1}{8}$ of the area of the puzzle.
    - The area of the parallelogram is $\frac{1}{8}$ of the area of the puzzle.

Following are three shapes—a dog, a tree, and a candle—that can be formed from the tans with just a little imagination.

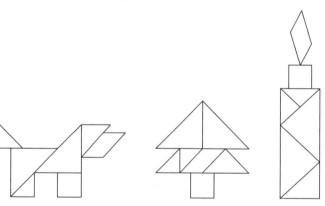

 Did you know? Taking a tangram apart and reassembling the pieces into a square is a good warm-up for creating other shapes and figures.

See List 3.46, Classifying Triangles; List 3.47, Classifying Quadrilaterals.

Copyright © 2010 by Gary Robert Muschla, Judith A. Muschla, and Erin Muschla

List 3.49   Tessellations

A *tessellation* is a design that covers a plane (a flat surface) without any gaps or any overlaps. Think of tiles on a floor. When a plane is covered by a tessellation, it is called "tessellating the plane" or "tiling the plane." Working with tessellations gives students a chance to use their creativity, visualization skills, and develop an understanding of geometric figures. Following are facts about tessellations.

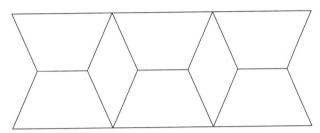

- A tessellation that uses only one shape to tile the plane is a pure tessellation. *Example*: rectangular tiles on a floor.

- A regular tessellation uses only one regular polygon to tile the plane. (In a regular polygon, all sides are congruent and all angles are congruent.) Only a square, an equilateral triangle, or a regular hexagon can be used to form a regular tessellation.

- A semi-regular tessellation uses two or more types of regular polygons to tile the plane. Examples of polygons that form a semi-regular tessellation include: an equilateral triangle and a regular hexagon; square and a regular octagon; a regular hexagon, a square, and an equilateral triangle.

 Did you know? M. C. Escher (1898–1972) was a Dutch artist noted for his use of tessellations.

See List 3.45, Polygons.

Copyright © 2010 by Gary Robert Muschla, Judith A. Muschla, and Erin Muschla

List 3.50   Circle Words and Facts

A *circle* is a closed plane figure with all points being the same distance from the center point. To understand circles, your students will need to understand the following words and facts.

Circle Words

- *Center*: A fixed point from which all points on a circle are equidistant
- *Central angle*: An angle whose vertex is at the center of a circle
- *Chord*: A line segment that connects any two points on a circle
- *Circumference*: The distance around a circle
- *Compass*: A tool for constructing circles
- *Diameter*: A chord through the center that connects any two points on a circle
- *Radius*: A line segment from the center of a circle to a point on the circle
- *Semicircle*: One-half of a circle
- *Tangent*: A line that intersects a circle at one point and only one point

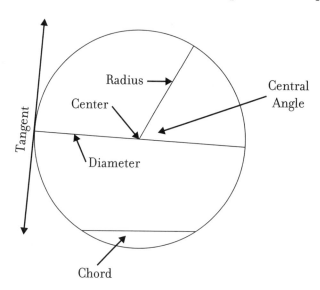

Copyright © 2010 by Gary Robert Muschla, Judith A. Muschla, and Erin Muschla

Circle Facts

- A circle is named by its center point.
- The radius is $\frac{1}{2}$ of the diameter. The diameter is 2 times the radius.
- The diameter is the longest chord of a circle.
- There are $360°$ in a circle.
- The measure of a central angle is less than or equal to $180°$.
- The ratio of the circumference to the diameter of a circle is called *pi*. The symbol for *pi* is π. The decimal value for *pi* is about 3.14. The fraction value for *pi* is about $\frac{22}{7}$.
- The formula for finding the circumference of a circle is $C = \pi \times d$.
- The formula for finding the area of a circle is $A = \pi \times r^2$ or $A = \pi \times r \times r$.

 Did you know? A circle is often used as a metaphor for something that has no beginning and no end.

Copyright © 2010 by Gary Robert Muschla, Judith A. Muschla, and Erin Muschla

List 3.51 Solid Figures

Solid figures, also called *space figures*, are three-dimensional shapes. They have length, width, and height. Following are facts about solid figures.

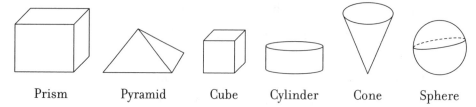

| Prism | Pyramid | Cube | Cylinder | Cone | Sphere |

- A *face* is the flat surface of a solid.
- An *edge* is the line segment at which two faces intersect.
- The *vertex* is a point at which the edges of the solid meet.
- A *polyhedron* is a solid figure whose flat surfaces are polygons. Some types of polyhedra include prisms, pyramids, and regular polyhedra.
- A *prism* is a polyhedron with two faces (called *bases*) that are polygons and which are both parallel and congruent. The other faces (called *lateral faces*) are parallelograms. Some common types of prism include:
  - A triangular prism has two triangular bases and three lateral faces.
  - A rectangular prism has two rectangular bases and four lateral faces.
- A *pyramid* is a polyhedron that has one base. The lateral faces are triangles that have a common vertex.
- A *regular polyhedron* has congruent faces. There are only five regular polyhedra:
  1. A *tetrahedron* has four faces, each of which is an equilateral triangle.
  2. A *cube* has six faces, each of which is a square.
  3. An *octahedron* has eight faces, each of which is an equilateral triangle.
  4. A *dodecahedron* has twelve faces, each of which is a regular pentagon.
  5. An *icosahedron* has twenty faces, each of which is an equilateral triangle.
- Solid figures can have curved surfaces. They are not polyhedra. Some of these include:
  - A *cylinder* has two congruent circular bases. The bases are parallel.
  - A *cone* has one circular base and one vertex.
  - A *sphere* is a set of points in space that are equidistant from the center.

 Did you know? There are two plural forms of polyhedron: polyhedra and polyhedrons.

See List 3.45, Polygons.

Copyright © 2010 by Gary Robert Muschla, Judith A. Muschla, and Erin Muschla

List 3.52   Cubes

Visualizing a three-dimensional figure from a two-dimensional drawing requires a special skill. You can use pentominoes and hexominoes with your students to promote this skill.

A *pentomino* is a figure formed by joining five congruent squares in a way that each square shares at least one side with another square. If cut out and folded along the shared line segments, the eight pentominoes below will form an open box.

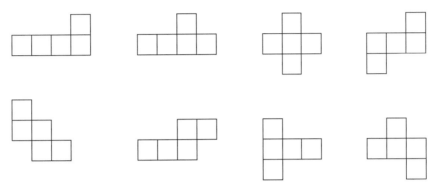

A *hexomino* is a figure formed by joining six congruent squares in the manner described previously. If cut out and folded along the shared line segments, the eleven hexominoes below will form a cube.

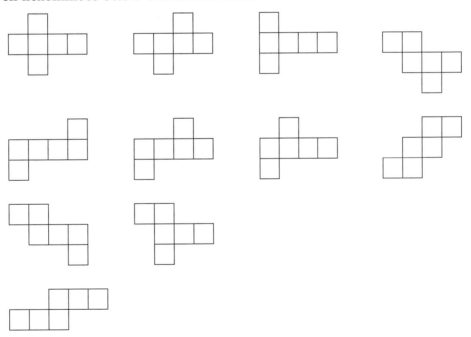

 Did you know? A domino is a figure formed by two squares in a way that both squares share a common side.

Copyright © 2010 by Gary Robert Muschla, Judith A. Muschla, and Erin Muschla

A figure is *symmetric* if there is balance or regularity to it. Two types of symmetry are line symmetry and rotational symmetry.

A figure has *line symmetry* if a line can be drawn through it, dividing it into two parts that are the same but facing in opposite directions. Following are facts about line symmetry.

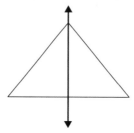

- Line symmetry is also called *reflectional symmetry*.
- A line of symmetry is the line that divides the figure into two identical parts that face in opposite directions.
- If a figure is folded along a line of symmetry, each part of the figure will coincide with the other part.
- An equilateral triangle has three lines of symmetry. Each line of symmetry is drawn from a vertex of the triangle to the midpoint of the opposite side.
- A square has four lines of symmetry. Two are the diagonals. The other two are each drawn from the midpoint of a side to the midpoint of the opposite side.
- A rectangle that is not a square has two lines of symmetry. Each is drawn from the midpoint of a side to the midpoint of the opposite side. (The diagonals of a rectangle are not lines of symmetry.)
- All regular polygons have the same number of lines of symmetry as the number of sides.
- Some figures have no lines of symmetry. A scalene triangle is one example.

A rotation is a movement of a figure in a circular motion around a point. A figure has *rotational symmetry* if it can be rotated around a point so that resulting figures match the original figure. Following are facts about rotational symmetry.

- The order of rotational symmetry is the number of different ways that a figure can be rotated to match itself. (A rotation cannot be more than 360°.)

Copyright © 2010 by Gary Robert Muschla, Judith A. Muschla, and Erin Muschla

- The order of rotational symmetry of an equilateral triangle is three.

- The order of rotational symmetry of a square is four.

- The order of rotational symmetry of a rectangle that is not a square is two.

- The order of rotational symmetry of a regular polygon equals the number of its sides.

- All figures have at least one order of rotational symmetry. (Rotating a figure 360° will always match the original figure.)

- A special type of rotational symmetry is *point symmetry*. A figure has point symmetry if it can be rotated 180° around a point to match the original figure. It looks the same upside down as right side up.

Did you know? Symmetry is found throughout nature. A leaf, for example, has line symmetry. A daisy has line symmetry, rotational symmetry, and point symmetry.

See List 3.45, Polygons; List 3.46, Classifying Triangles; List 3.47, Classifying Quadrilaterals.

Copyright © 2010 by Gary Robert Muschla, Judith A. Muschla, and Erin Muschla

A *formula* is a set of numbers and symbols that expresses a mathematical rule. Being able to apply formulas to solve problems is a critical skill in a student's overall mathematical competence. The following formulas are useful for elementary math students.

- Perimeter of a polygon:
  P = the sum of the lengths of its sides
- Perimeter of a rectangle:
  $P = (2 \times l) + (2 \times w)$
- Perimeter of a square:
  $P = 4 \times s$
- Circumference of a circle:
  $C = \pi \times d$
- Area of a rectangle:
  $A = l \times w$
- Area of a parallelogram:
  $A = b \times h$
- Area of a triangle:
  $A = \dfrac{1}{2} \times b \times h$
- Area of a circle:
  $A = \pi \times r^2$ or $A = \pi \times r \times r$
- Volume of a rectangular prism:
  $V = l \times w \times h$
- Surface area of a rectangular prism:
  $SA = 2 \times (l \times w) + 2 \times (l \times h) + 2 \times (w \times h)$

Did you know? Being able to apply mathematical formulas is more important than memorizing them. Formulas can always be found in math texts and reference books. Application, however, is dependent upon understanding.

Copyright © 2010 by Gary Robert Muschla, Judith A. Muschla, and Erin Muschla

List 3.55   The Number Line

The *number line* is a line on which points correspond to numbers. It is a useful tool for showing relationships between numbers. Following are facts about number lines and ways to use them in your classroom.

Number Line Facts

- The number line extends infinitely in both directions.
- Arrows are used to show continuation.
- Successive numbers are 1 unit apart, for example, 2 is one unit from 3, 3 is one unit from 4, and so on.
- Every whole number, fraction, mixed number, decimal, and integer can be located on the number line.
- Every number to the right is larger than any number to the left. Conversely, every number to the left is smaller than any number to the right.
- Positive numbers are located to the right of zero.
- Negative numbers are located to the left of zero.

Practical Uses of Number Lines in the Classroom

- Locating numbers
- Estimating
- Comparing numbers
- Ordering numbers
- Finding sums, differences, products, and quotients
- Skip counting
- Exploring patterns
- Rounding numbers
- Determining distance (in terms of units)
- Finding absolute value

 Did you know? You can think of a ruler as a part of a number line.

See List 3.40, Steps for Measuring Length.

Copyright © 2010 by Gary Robert Muschla, Judith A. Muschla, and Erin Muschla

List 3.56   Transformations

A *transformation* is a movement of a figure. Some ways you can transform a figure are by translation, reflection, and rotation. Each of these is a rigid movement in which the figure does not change its shape or size.

- *Translation*: An image of a figure is formed by moving every point on the figure the same distance in the same direction. Another name for a translation is a *slide*.

- *Reflection*: An image of a figure is flipped over a line. All of the points of the new image of the figure are the same distance from the line as the original figure. Another name for a reflection is a *flip*.

- *Rotation*: An image of a figure is formed by turning a figure around a fixed point. Another name for a rotation is a *turn*.

 Did you know? Your image in a mirror is a reflection of yourself.

Copyright © 2010 by Gary Robert Muschla, Judith A. Muschla, and Erin Muschla

See List 3.53, Symmetry.

List 3.57   Common Graphs

Graphs provide the means for organizing, displaying, and relating data. There are several types of graphs students should be able to construct and interpret. Many of the most common are included in the list that follows.

- *Bar graph*: Uses vertical or horizontal bars to compare data
- *Double bar graph*: Compares two sets of data in the same graph
- *Circle graph*: Shows how parts of the data are related to the whole and to each other. The entire circle equals 100% of the data. Circle graphs are sometimes called *pie graphs*.
- *Histogram*: A special bar graph that shows the number of times data occur within specific intervals
- *Line graph*: Displays data as points that are connected by line segments. Line graphs show changes in the relationship between items of data.
- *Line plot*: Shows the frequency of data along a number line
- *Pictograph*: Displays data with pictures or symbols. A key is used to show how many each picture represents.
- *Scattergram*: Displays relationships among data in the form of unconnected points

Tips for Constructing a Graph

1. Decide what information you want to show.
2. Decide what data you will use.
3. Decide which graph will best display your data.
4. Construct your graph accurately. Be sure to include a title, scale, labels for data, accurate data, and a key, if necessary.
5. Construct your graph neatly.

 Did you know? Bar graphs, line graphs, circle graphs, and pictographs are the most commonly used graphs.

Copyright © 2010 by Gary Robert Muschla, Judith A. Muschla, and Erin Muschla

List 3.58   Mean, Median, and Mode

Measures of central tendency—the mean, median, and mode—are useful for analyzing numerical data. When you present a lesson to your students on measures of central tendency, be sure to include clear explanations of the terminology and offer plenty of examples.

- *Data*: The facts and numbers collected.
- *Outlier*: One or more numbers that appear unusually large or small and out of place when compared with the other data. Some data sets do not have any outliers.
- *Frequency*: The number of times a number or group of numbers occurs.
- *Mean*: The average of all the numbers in the data. The mean, also called the *average*, is found by adding all the numbers and dividing by the amount of numbers in the data.
- *Median*: The number in the middle when the numbers are ordered from least to greatest or greatest to least. (If there is no middle number, the median is found by finding the average of the two middle numbers.)
- *Mode*: The number that appears most often in the group. There may be no mode, one mode, or several modes, depending on the data.
- *Range*: The difference between the largest and smallest numbers in a set of data.

Examples of the Mean, Median, and Mode

Consider the scores on a recent math test:
    80, 75, 95, 80, 88, 92, 52, 78, 98, 88, 95, 80, 90, 95, 98, and 92

- In this example, the data set is the test scores.
- The outlier is 52, since it is significantly less than any of the other scores.
- The frequency of 80 is 3; 95 is 3; 88 is 2; 92 is 2; and 98 is 2. The frequency of each of the other scores is 1.
- The mean is 86.
- The median is 89. This is found by arranging the scores in ascending or descending order. Since there is no middle number, the scores closest to the middle are 88 and 90. Their average is 89.
- The modes are 95 and 80, since each occurs three times. This is more than any other score.
- The range is 46. This is found by subtracting the smallest number, 52, from the largest, 98.

Did you know? The method of collecting, organizing, and analyzing data is called *descriptive statistics*.

Copyright © 2010 by Gary Robert Muschla, Judith A. Muschla, and Erin Muschla

List 3.59   Math Manipulatives for Your Classroom

In addition to basic materials for math instruction such as rulers, meter sticks, protractors, and compasses, manipulatives can greatly enhance your instruction by allowing you to demonstrate properties or involve your students with hands-on activities for exploring concepts and relationships. The manipulatives that follow prove useful in math programs.

- *Attribute blocks*: Plastic blocks that include circles, squares, rectangles, triangles, and hexagons. The blocks can be used to classify shapes.
- *Base 10 blocks*: Cubes that represent 1, 10, 100, and 1,000. The cubes can help students develop an understanding of the decimal system.
- *Centimeter cubes*: 1-centimeter cubes, each of which has a volume of 1 cubic centimeter and weighs 1 gram. The cubes can be used to explore surface area, volume, and equivalent measures.
- *Bills and coins*: Paper bills and plastic coins in various monetary denominations can demonstrate computation with money, including making change.
- *Color tiles*: 1-inch square tiles. Available in different colors, these tiles can be used for generating and completing patterns and finding the probability of an event.
- *Cuisenaire® Rods*: A set of ten rectangular rods in various lengths, ranging from 0.1 unit, 0.2 unit, 0.3 unit, and so on to 1 unit. The rods can be used for modeling the basic operations, computing with decimals and fractions, and enhancing spatial problem-solving skills.
- *Decimal Squares®*: Small squares that represent a whole unit, 0.1, 0.01, and 0.001. They can be used in exploring operations with decimals and percents.
- *Dice*: Ordinary dice, with the numbers 1 to 6 expressed in dot notation. They can be used in probability.
- *Fraction circles*: A set of several circles. One circle represents a whole. The other circles are divided into parts, for example, halves, thirds, fourths, sixths, and eighths. They can be used to model fractions, equivalencies, and operations with fractions.
- *Fraction squares*: Several squares, one of which represents a whole with the others being divided into parts, for example, halves, thirds, fourths, sixths, and eighths. They can be used to model fractions, equivalencies, and operations with fractions.
- *Geoboards and rubber bands*: Circular and square boards with pegs on which rubber bands can be placed. Circular geoboards can be used to discover properties of circles and congruence. Square geoboards can be used in graphing, creating shapes, and finding area.
- *Geometric solids*: Wooden or plastic models of geometric figures including prisms, pyramids, cylinders, and spheres. They can be used to help students visualize vertices, faces, and edges of polyhedra and also to explore surface area and volume.

Copyright © 2010 by Gary Robert Muschla, Judith A. Muschla, and Erin Muschla

- *Liter cube*: A 1,000-milliliter cube, graduated in 100-milliliter increments. It can be used to measure capacity and demonstrate equivalent units.
- *MIRA*™: A transparent geometric tool with reflective properties. It can be used with symmetry, congruence, and transformations.
- *Mirror*: Any type of nonbreakable mirror can be used to explore reflections.
- *Multilink*® *cubes*: Cubes of various colors that snap together. The cubes can be used for exploring squares and cubes of numbers, visualizing three-dimensional figures, and finding surface area and volume.
- *Operations dice*: Six-sided dice that include +, -, ×, ÷, =, and > . They can be used to practice math facts.
- *Pattern blocks*: A set of figures, including hexagons, squares, trapezoids, triangles, parallelograms, and rhombi. They can be used to investigate patterns, congruence, and symmetry.
- *Patty paper*: Translucent paper that can be used to trace figures and investigate congruence, symmetry, and transformations.
- *Pentominoes*: Twelve shapes scored in 1-inch square sections. They can be used to explore area, perimeter, symmetry, congruence, and transformations.
- *Playing cards*: A deck of 52 cards. The cards can be used to demonstrate the probability of an event.
- *Polyhedra dice*: Four-, six-, eight-, ten-, twelve-, and twenty-sided dice that are labeled with numbers ranging from 1 to the number of sides. They can be used to explore probability.
- *Spinners*: Available in different sizes and shapes, each spinner has an arrow that can be spun and lands on a specific section of the base. Spinners can be used to find the probability of an event.
- *Tangrams*: A set of seven geometric figures: two large isosceles triangles, two small isosceles triangles, one parallelogram, one square, and one isosceles triangle that is not congruent to either of the other isosceles triangles. Tangrams can be used to develop visualization skills, spatial sense, and understanding of the geometric figures that compose the tangram.
- *Thermometer*: A Celsius/Fahrenheit thermometer can be used to show similarities between the two temperature scales.
- *Timer*: A digital timer can be used to measure elapsed time or record time in experiments.
- *Two-color counters*: Circular disks, one side of which is red and the other side yellow. They can be used with probability, estimation, and modeling operations with integers.
- *Unifix*® *cubes*: Interlocking cubes that link in only one way. They can be used to create and extend patterns, and model decimals and fractions.

Did you know? Because they support conceptual understanding, manipulatives are beneficial for most students, but they are especially beneficial to students who are kinesthetic learners.

Copyright © 2010 by Gary Robert Muschla, Judith A. Muschla, and Erin Muschla

List 3.60   Tips for Reading and Solving Math Word Problems

Many students have trouble solving math word problems. For many of these students, much of the trouble is rooted in reading, in weak vocabulary or poor comprehension skills. Yet, the first step to solving a math word problem is reading it accurately. Understanding the words that follow can help your students determine what the problem is asking, which will enable them to proceed with finding its answer.

Addition	Subtraction	Multiplication	Division
add	decreased by	double (times two)	divided by
all together	deduct	multiply	(a) half (divide by two)
both	difference	product	(a) fourth (divide by four)
combine	fewer	of	
gain	left	quadruple (times four)	quotient
greater than	less than	times	ratio of
in all	lose	twice (times two)	(a) third (divide by three)
increased by	loss	triple (times three)	
larger than	lower	square (times itself)	
longer than	minus		
more than	reduced by		
plus	remain		
rise	remove		
sum	shorten		
total	smaller than		
	subtract		

Tips for Solving Math Word Problems

1. Always read the problem carefully.
2. Reread the problem if necessary.
3. Be sure you understand the information and what you are asked to find.
4. Look for key words that can help you decide to add, subtract, multiply, or divide.
5. If you are given a worksheet, underline key words.
6. If you are using a book, list the key words of a problem on a separate sheet of paper.
7. Show your work.
8. Check that your answer makes sense in the context of the problem.

 Did you know? Solving math word problems requires a variety of reading and math skills.

See List 3.61, Math Problem-Solving Strategies.

Copyright © 2010 by Gary Robert Muschla, Judith A. Muschla, and Erin Muschla

List 3.61   Math Problem-Solving Strategies

Students who approach problem-solving in a deliberate, methodical manner are more successful at finding solutions than students who work on problems without a plan. Teaching the following problem-solving strategies to your students can provide them with the means and confidence to solve the most challenging problems.

1. Read and study the problem carefully.
2. Identify the important information.
3. Decide what you must find.
4. Circle or write down the facts needed to solve the problem.
5. To help you understand the problem, look for patterns, draw a picture, or make a table or chart for data.
6. Think of similar problems you have solved in the past. How might what you did then help you solve this problem?
7. Plan what operation or operations you will need to use to solve the problem.
8. Work out the problem.
9. Double check your work.
10. Make sure that your answer has the proper units.
11. Be sure that your answer is logical and makes sense.
12. Check that you answered the question completely.

 Did you know? When you teach your students problem-solving skills, you are providing them with skills that they can adapt to other areas of their lives.

See List 3.60, Tips for Reading and Solving Math Word Problems.

Copyright © 2010 by Gary Robert Muschla, Judith A. Muschla, and Erin Muschla

List 3.62   Math and Literature

Literature has the potential to spark students' interest in mathematics. Whether students are engaged in a compelling story or are introduced to a new concept, incorporating books into your math program can only enhance your program. Following are books you might consider.

Alexander, Who Used to Be Rich Last Sunday by Judith Viorst

Amanda Bean's Amazing Dream by Cindy Neuschwander

Anno's Math Games by Mitsumasa Anno

Anno's Mysterious Multiplying Jar by Masaichiro Anno and Mitsumasa Anno

Beanstalk: The Measure of a Giant by Ann McCallum

The Best of Times by Greg Tang

Betcha! by Stuart J. Murphy

Can You Count to a Googol? by Robert E. Wells

A Cloak for the Dreamer by Aileen Friedman

Counting on Frank by Rod Clement

Divide and Ride by Stuart J. Murphy

Equal Shmequal by Virginia L. Kroll

Follow the Money! by Loreen Leedy

Fraction Action by Loreen Leedy

A Grain of Rice by Helena Clare Pittman

Grandfather Tang's Story by Ann Tompert

The Grapes of Math: Mind-Stretching Math Riddles by Greg Tang

The Great Divide: A Mathematical Marathon by Dayle Ann Dodds

The Great Graph Contest by Loreen Leedy

The Greedy Triangle by Marilyn Burns

How Big Is a Foot? by Rolf Myller

How Big Is It? by Ben Hillman

How Much Is a Million? by David M. Schwartz

How Tall, How Short, How Far Away? by David A. Adler

The I Hate Mathematics Book by Marilyn Burns

If You Made a Million by David M. Schwartz

Inchworm and a Half by Elinor J. Pinczes

It's Probably Penny by Loreen Leedy

Jim and the Beanstalk by Raymond Briggs

The King's Commissioners by Aileen Friedman

The Librarian Who Measured the Earth by Kathryn Lasky

Mapping Penny's World by Loreen Leedy

Math Appeal by Greg Tang

Math Curse by Jon Scieszka

Copyright © 2010 by Gary Robert Muschla, Judith A. Muschla, and Erin Muschla

Math Fables by Greg Tang

Math Fables Too by Greg Tang

Math for All Seasons by Greg Tang

Math Potatoes: Mind Stretching Brain Food by Greg Tang

Math-terpieces: The Art of Problem-Solving by Greg Tang

Measuring Penny by Loreen Leedy

Mission: Addition by Loreen Leedy

The Monster Money Book by Loreen Leedy

Multiplying Menace: The Revenge of Rumpelstiltskin by Pam Calvert

Mummy Math: An Adventure in Geometry by Cindy Neuschwander

The Number Devil: A Mathematical Adventure by Hans Magnus Enzensberger

One Hundred Hungry Ants by Elinor J. Pinczes

Pastry School in Paris: An Adventure in Capacity by Cindy Neuschwander

Patterns in Peru: An Adventure in Patterning by Cindy Neuschwander

A Place for Zero: A Math Adventure by Angeline Sparagna LoPresti

Rabbits Rabbits Everywhere: A Fibonacci Tale by Ann McCallum

A Remainder of One by Elinor J. Pinczes

Sir Cumference and All the King's Tens: A Math Adventure by Cindy Neuschwander

Sir Cumference and the Dragon of Pi: A Math Adventure by Cindy Neuschwander

Sir Cumference and the First Round Table: A Math Adventure by Cindy Neuschwander

Sir Cumference and the Great Knight of Angleland: A Math Adventure by Cindy Neuschwander

Sir Cumference and the Isle of Immeter: A Math Adventure by Cindy Neuschwander

Sir Cumference and the Sword in the Cone: A Math Adventure by Cindy Neuschwander

Spaghetti and Meatballs for All! A Mathematical Story by Marilyn Burns

Subtraction Action by Loreen Leedy

Sweet Clara and the Freedom Quilt by Deborah Hopkinson

Tiger Math: Learning to Graph from a Baby Tiger by Ann Whitehead Nagda and Cindy Bickel

2 x 2 = Boo: A Set of Spooky Multiplication Stories by Loreen Leedy

A Very Improbable Story by Edward Einhorn

What's Your Angle, Pythagoras? by Julie Ellis

Zachary Zormer: Shape Transformer by Joanne Anderson Reisberg

 Did you know? Charles Lutwidge Dodgson, who, under the pen name of Lewis Carroll, wrote *Alice in Wonderland* and *Through the Looking Glass*, also wrote a book called *Symbolic Logic*, which introduced children to logic.

Copyright © 2010 by Gary Robert Muschla, Judith A. Muschla, and Erin Muschla

List 3.63   Checklist for a Successful Math Program

A successful math program is one in which students are actively engaged in learning the concepts and skills that lead to competence in mathematics. Evaluating your math program according to the following criteria will help you to build a math program that is satisfying and rewarding to both you and your students.

- ☑ The classroom is inviting, bright, and cheerful.
- ☑ Classroom activities are built around practical and effective routines.
- ☑ Math is taught as a relevant subject; activities are meaningful; critical thinking is fostered.
- ☑ Explanations and directions are clear.
- ☑ Homework reinforces the skills and concepts students learned in class.
- ☑ Various methods of instruction address the diverse learning styles of students.
- ☑ Lessons are interesting and their delivery is clear and concise.
- ☑ There are opportunities for students to work individually, in pairs, or in groups.
- ☑ Students are encouraged to solve problems in a variety of ways.
- ☑ Cooperative learning is fostered as a way to share ideas.
- ☑ Students are given the opportunity to use manipulatives to explore math concepts.
- ☑ Students have access to technology to find information, organize and analyze data, and solve problems.
- ☑ Good study skills are taught and fostered.
- ☑ Discussion about mathematics is encouraged.
- ☑ Students have the opportunity to share and reflect upon the solutions to problems.
- ☑ Conferencing with students is a regular part of your math program.
- ☑ Students are encouraged to come for extra help when necessary.
- ☑ The class is orderly, disruptions are minimal, and disruptions that occur are handled efficiently.
- ☑ Writing and literature are important parts of your class.
- ☑ Various methods of assessment are used.
- ☑ Students are encouraged to apply math to other subjects, as well as to aspects of their lives outside of school.
- ☑ It is assumed (and made apparent) that every student, regardless of gender or ethnicity, can succeed at math.

Did you know? Galileo, the Italian physicist and astronomer, summed up the importance of mathematics about 450 years ago when he described the universe as being "written in the language of mathematics."

Copyright © 2010 by Gary Robert Muschla, Judith A. Muschla, and Erin Muschla

Science

It is through the observations, investigations, and experimentations of science that we are able to determine how and why things work as they do. A strong foundation in science enables students to discover, understand, and appreciate the world in which they live.

List 4.1   Characteristics of Living Things

Although life on Earth is incredibly diverse and widespread, all living things share basic characteristics. The following criteria separate living things from nonliving things.

- Living things are made of cells. The simplest organisms are single-celled, while complex organisms such as human beings are composed of trillions of cells that make up specialized tissues and organs.
- Living things exchange gases with the environment through respiration. Animals inhale oxygen and release carbon dioxide as a waste product. Plants absorb carbon dioxide and release oxygen as a waste product.
- Living things need food for energy. Animals hunt or find food. Plants, through photosynthesis, make their own food. One-celled organisms absorb food.
- Living things grow and develop. Living things have a life cycle.
- Living things reproduce. Animals may bear live young or lay eggs from which young hatch. Plants produce seeds from which new plants will grow. Bacteria multiply by cell division.
- Living things react to their environment. Animals find shelter or build nests. Deciduous plants lose their leaves in fall. Bacteria infect hosts.

 Did you know? Biology is the science of living things.

See List 4.3, What Animals Need to Survive.

List 4.2   The Kingdoms of Life

All living things on Earth are grouped in kingdoms. Although some scientists use slightly different classification systems, the standard system recognizes five basic kingdoms of life.

Kingdom	Examples of Members
Animalia	Animals
Plantae	Flowering plants, mosses, ferns, cone-bearing plants
Fungi	Yeasts, molds, mushrooms
Protista	Algae, protozoa, water molds
Prokaryotae (Monera)	Bacteria

 Did you know? Scientists still have not discovered all of the different living things on Earth. Each year brings new discoveries.

Copyright © 2010 by Gary Robert Muschla, Judith A. Muschla, and Erin Muschla

List 4.3   What Animals Need to Survive

Although every animal is adapted to living in a particular environment, all animals share some important characteristics. These characteristics follow.

All animals:

- Require food
- Require water
- Require living space, usually in a specific environment or habitat
- Require shelter—from the weather, a place to bear young, and a place to rest
- Require oxygen for respiration

Special types of animals include:

- *Carnivores*—eat only meat
- *Herbivores*—eat only plants
- *Omnivores*—eat plants and animals
- *Predators*—hunt and eat other animals for food
- *Scavengers*—eat the remains of animals killed by predators

 Did you know? Loss of habitat is one of the greatest threats to the survival of many animals.

See List 4.1, Characteristics of Living Things.

Copyright © 2010 by Gary Robert Muschla, Judith A. Muschla, and Erin Muschla

List 4.4   Traits of Common Types of Animals

Animals belong to one of two groups: vertebrates and invertebrates. *Vertebrates* have a backbone with a spinal column; *invertebrates* have no backbone. While invertebrates account for most of the animals on Earth, vertebrates are usually larger and have more complex bodies and bigger brains. The major groups of vertebrates and invertebrates follow.

Vertebrates

Mammals

- Mammals have the most highly developed nervous system of all animals.
- All mammals are warm-blooded.
- Most are born live and are nursed by their mother's milk. (Exceptions: The platypus and echidna hatch from eggs.)
- Most mammals have body hair.

    Examples of mammals: dogs, cats, elephants, whales, kangaroos

Birds

- All birds are warm-blooded.
- Birds have feathers and wings.
- Birds have beaks.
- Most birds can fly. (Exceptions: ostriches and penguins)

    Examples of birds: sparrows, hawks, owls, vultures

Amphibians

- Amphibians are cold-blooded.
- Most live in water for part of their lives, breathing with gills. They live on land for the other part of their lives, breathing with lungs.

    Examples of amphibians: frogs, toads, salamanders

Fish

- Fish live in water and breathe through gills.
- They have scales.
- Most are cold-blooded.
- Most fish lay eggs. (Exception: Sharks bear live young.)

    Examples of fish: salmon, swordfish, trout, cod

Reptiles

- Reptiles are cold-blooded.
- They breathe with lungs.
- They are covered with scaly skin.
- Most reptiles lay eggs. (Exceptions: Some lizards give birth to live young.)

    Examples of reptiles: turtles, tortoises, alligators, snakes, lizards

Copyright © 2010 by Gary Robert Muschla, Judith A. Muschla, and Erin Muschla

List 4.4   continued

Invertebrates

Arthropods

- Arthropods are the biggest animal group on Earth.
- They have segmented bodies, protected by a hard exoskeleton (external skeleton).
  Examples of arthropods: insects, spiders, shrimp, lobsters

Mollusks

- Mollusks have soft bodies.
- Most mollusks have hard shells.
- Some mollusks live on land; others live in water.
  Examples of mollusks: snails, squid, octopuses, oysters, clams, scallops

Worms

- Worms have long, soft bodies.
- There are many different kinds of worms. Some worms may be only an inch or two long; others may be several feet in length.
- Worms live in many habitats, including in the soil, in water, and even inside the bodies of other animals.
  Examples of worms: earthworms, roundworms, flatworms

Echinoderms

- Echinoderms live in sea water.
- Their bodies consist of a central disk with arms radiating outward.
- They have external skeletons.
  Examples of echinoderms: starfish, sea urchins, sea cucumbers

Coelenterates

- Coelenterates are very primitive animals.
- They take in food and release wastes through their mouths.
- Their mouths are surrounded by tentacles that sting.
  Examples of coelenterates: jellyfish, corals, sea anemones

Sponges

- Sponges are the most primitive of animals. The first sponges appeared on Earth about 600 million years ago.
- Unlike most animals, they do not move.
- They obtain food by filtering very small organisms out of the water.
  Examples of sponges: red sponge, brown tube sponge, boring sponge

Did you know? Warm-blooded animals use energy from food to maintain a constant body temperature. Cold-blooded animals are dependent on their environment for their body temperature.

Copyright © 2010 by Gary Robert Muschla, Judith A. Muschla, and Erin Muschla

List 4.5   Animal Names

Some animals have special names for males, females, and young. They also have special words for groups of the same animals. The following list offers the names for the members of families of common animals.

Animal	Male	Female	Young	Group
Antelope	buck	doe	calf	herd
Bear	boar	sow	cub	sleuth, sloth
Buffalo	bull	cow	calf	herd, gang
Camel	bull	cow	calf	flock
Cat	tom	queen	kitten	clutter, clowder
Chicken	rooster	hen	chick	flock
Cow	bull	cow	calf	herd, drove, flock
Deer	buck	doe	fawn	herd
Dog	dog	bitch	pup	pack
Duck	drake	duck	duckling	brace, team, flock
Elephant	bull	cow	calf	herd, gang
Elk	bull	cow	calf	gang
Falcon	tercel, terzel	falcon	chick	cast
Fox	Reynard, dog	vixen	cub, pup	leash, skulk
Goat	billy	nanny	kid	herd, trip
Goose	gander	goose	gosling	gaggle, flock, skein
Horse	stallion	mare	colt, foal	herd
Kangaroo	buck	doe	joey	troop, mob
Leopard	leopard	leopardess	cub	leap, prowl
Lion	lion	lioness	cub	pride
Moose	bull	cow	calf	herd
Pig	boar	sow	piglet	litter, sounder
Rabbit	buck	doe	bunny	nest
Seal	bull	cow	pup, calf	pod
Sheep	ram, buck	ewe	lamb	flock, drove, herd
Swan	cob	pen	cygnet	bevy, wedge
Tiger	tiger	tigress	cub	streak, ambush
Whale	bull	cow	calf	gam, pod
Zebra	stallion	mare	colt	herd, crossing

Did you know? There is a special name for a group of kittens. They are called a *kindle* or a *litter*.

Copyright © 2010 by Gary Robert Muschla, Judith A. Muschla, and Erin Muschla

Many species of animals migrate periodically or seasonally seeking food, mates, a place to lay eggs or bear and raise young. They may migrate from colder to warmer climates, sometimes traveling hundreds or thousands of miles. The Arctic tern is a spectacular migrator, breeding near the North Pole and spending the northern winter in Antarctica. Following are examples of migratory animals.

American Eel (fish)
American Goldfinch (bird)
Arctic Tern (bird)
Blue Whale (mammal)
Canada Goose (bird)
Caribou (mammal)
Dolphin (mammal)
Duck (bird)
Eastern Meadowlark (bird)
Flycatcher (bird)
Gray Whale (mammal)
Green Sea Turtle (reptile)
Hummingbird (bird)
Humpback Whale (mammal)
Loon (bird)

Monarch Butterfly (insect)
Mule Deer (mammal)
Porpoise (mammal)
Red Bat (mammal)
Reindeer (mammal)
Robin (bird)
Salmon (fish)
Sandpiper (bird)
Seal (mammal)
Swallow (bird)
Tuna (fish)
Walrus (mammal)
Warbler (bird)
Wildebeest (mammal)
Zebra (mammal)

Did you know? Birds are the champion migrators, as many species in the Northern Hemisphere fly south from the Arctic and temperate zones to avoid harsh winters.

Copyright © 2010 by Gary Robert Muschla, Judith A. Muschla, and Erin Muschla

List 4.7 Hibernating Animals

To survive long cold winters, many animals become inactive and reduce their body processes. This period of reduced metabolism is *hibernation*. Following are facts about hibernation and examples of animals that spend their winters hibernating.

Facts About Hibernation

- During hibernation, animals enter a state called *torpor*. In torpor an animal may appear to be in a deep sleep or dead.
- The heart rate of a hibernating animal is decreased to a few beats per minute.
- The breathing rate is greatly reduced.
- The animal's body temperature falls to near freezing.
- The animal does not need food during hibernation.
- Many animals come out of hibernation several times during the winter for brief periods. They may eat some stored food, but then they return to hibernation.
- Some frogs and fish in hot climates enter a sleeplike state to protect themselves from extreme heat. This state is called *estivation*. They may burrow into mud or become inactive until the heat of the summer passes.

True Hibernators

Members of the following animal groups are considered to be true hibernators.

badgers	hedgehogs	shrews
bats	some lizards	skunks
chipmunks	marmots	some snakes
some frogs	mice	some toads
ground squirrels	possums	some turtles
hamsters	prairie dogs	woodchucks

 Did you know? Most biologists do not consider bears to be true hibernators. Bears sleep through much of the winter, but their body temperature decreases only a few degrees. They may awaken several times during the winter.

Copyright © 2010 by Gary Robert Muschla, Judith A. Muschla, and Erin Muschla

List 4.8   Nocturnal Animals

Nocturnal animals sleep or rest during the day and become active at night. Many nocturnal animals have special adaptations for night activities. Owls, for instance, are known for their excellent eyesight, which enables them to see in the dark. The following animals are most active at night.

aardvark	firefly	mouse	scorpion
anteater	gerbil	opossum	skunk
armadillo	hamster	owl	slug
badger	hedgehog	porcupine	tarantula
bat	mink	raccoon	toad
cricket	moth	rat	weasel

 Did you know? Diurnal animals are most active during the day.

Copyright © 2010 by Gary Robert Muschla, Judith A. Muschla, and Erin Muschla

List 4.9   Animal Superstars

It is estimated that more than four million species of animals live on Earth. All have developed special traits that enable them to survive in their habitats. Some animals, however, have developed especially noteworthy traits. These are the superstars of animals.

- Biggest and heaviest animal: blue whale; about 110 ft, 210 tons (33 m, 189 metric tons)
- Biggest land animal: African elephant; about 10 ft, 6 in; 6.25 tons (3.1 m, 5.6 metric tons)
- Biggest land carnivore: polar bear; 7–8 ft, 900–1,600 lbs (2.2–2.5 m, 410–720 kg)
- Tallest animal: giraffe; 14–20 ft tall (4.5–6 m)
- Smallest mammal: bumblebee bat; 0.07 oz (1.96 g)
- Biggest ears: male African elephant; 3 ft wide (0.9 m)
- Biggest eyes: blue whale; diameter of 5 in (12.7 cm)
- Fastest animal on land (short distance): cheetah; 70 mph (112 kmph)
- Fastest animal on land (long distance): pronghorn antelope; 35 mph (56 kmph)
- Slowest moving animal: snail, 0.03 mph; (0.05 kmph)
- Biggest bird: North African ostrich; 9 ft tall, 345 lb (2.7 m, 155 kg)
- Fastest bird: peregrine falcon; diving speed up to 200 mph (320 kmph)
- Fastest bird (while flying): spine-tailed swift; 106 mph (170 kmph)
- Longest fish: whale shark; 41 ft (12.5 m)
- Smallest fish: tiny goby; a half-inch (1.27 cm)
- Fastest fish: sailfish; 68 mph (109 kmph)
- Biggest turtle: leatherback; 5 ft long, 1,300 lb (1.5 m, 585 kg)
- Biggest lizard: Komodo dragon; 10 feet long, 300 lbs (3 m, 135 kg)
- Longest snake: reticulated python; 32 ft long (9.6 m)
- Fastest insect: dragonfly; 36 mph (58 kmph)
- Longest insect: stick insect; 15 in long (38 cm)
- Sleepiest animal: koala, about 22 hours each day

 Did you know? Measuring the length of a live reticulated python can be very dangerous.

See List 4.10, Some Incredible Animal Facts.

Copyright © 2010 by Gary Robert Muschla, Judith A. Muschla, and Erin Muschla

List 4.10   Some Incredible Animal Facts

Animals are diverse in their traits and behaviors. The following facts are certainly interesting if not incredible.

- Despite its name, the whale shark is not a whale. Instead of hunting prey, it scoops up plankton in its large mouth.
- Box turtles are long-lived, capable of surviving up to a century.
- Female marsupials such as kangaroos carry their young in pouches.
- Hummingbirds are the only bird that can fly straight up, straight down, and backward. They can even hover.
- Some eels can swim backward.
- The typical slug has four noses.
- The bola spider fires a sticky wad of saliva at its prey. The saliva is attached to a length of silk, which the spider then reels back like a fisherman pulling in his catch.
- Sharks are constantly growing new teeth to replace those that are lost in attacking prey. In its lifetime, a shark may grow several thousand teeth.
- A chameleon can move its two eyes individually, in different directions at the same time.
- An albatross can sleep while flying.
- The head of a woodpecker is filled with pockets of air that serve as cushions to protect the bird's brain when it is pecking at wood for insects.
- A cockroach can live for several days without a head.
- A lion's roar can be heard five miles away.
- A dog's sense of smell can detect one molecule of a scent in a million.
- Butterflies can travel up to 600 miles (960 km) without stopping.
- The duck-billed platypus is considered to be a mammal, though it has the traits of several creatures. It is warm-blooded and covered with fur as a mammal. It has webbed feet and the beak of a duck. And it lays eggs.
- A bee sucks nectar from flowers through its long, hollow tongue.
- Bats use echolocation to fly at night. They send out high-frequency sound waves. When the sound waves echo back to them, they adjust their flight.

 Did you know? Zoologists are scientists who study animals.

See List 4.4, Traits of Common Types of Animals; List 4.9, Animal Superstars.

Copyright © 2010 by Gary Robert Muschla, Judith A. Muschla, and Erin Muschla

List 4.11   Metamorphosis

Some animals undergo *metamorphosis*, major changes in form as they develop. Although metamorphosis varies among different species, the general pattern for all animals is similar.

Stages of Complete (or True) Metamorphosis

1. An adult female lays eggs.
2. An egg develops into a larva. A larva has little or no resemblance to the adult it will become.
3. The larva changes in body and structure as it matures into an adult.
4. The adult begins the cycle again by mating.

Example of the Metamorphosis of a Butterfly

1. The adult female lays eggs.
2. An egg develops into a larva, which is a caterpillar.
3. The larva changes into a pupa (also known as a chrysalis). The insect is enclosed in a cocoon.
4. The caterpillar tissues are broken down, and the body of the adult butterfly is formed.
5. The butterfly emerges from the cocoon.
6. The adult continues the cycle.

Example of the Metamorphosis of a Frog

1. The adult female lays eggs.
2. A tadpole (larva) hatches from an egg. The tadpole is fishlike, breathing with gills. It also has a tail.
3. The tadpole grows. It develops legs and webbed feet.
4. The tadpole develops lungs for breathing air.
5. When the tadpole loses its tail and breathes with lungs, its metamorphosis is complete. It is now a frog.
6. The adult continues the cycle.

Did you know? Some insects undergo incomplete metamorphosis, which has fewer stages. An example is the chinch bug. The chinch bug hatches from an egg as a nymph, which is a smaller, undeveloped form of an adult. In stages the nymph matures and develops wings. It is then capable of mating.

Copyright © 2010 by Gary Robert Muschla, Judith A. Muschla, and Erin Muschla

List 4.12   What Plants Need to Live

Plants are organisms that have special requirements for growth. Most plants depend on the following for their survival and reproduction.

- Light
- Water
- Carbon dioxide
- Oxygen

- Minerals
- Suitable range of temperatures
- Suitable medium (usually soil) in which to grow

 Did you know? Plants are the beginning of the food chain. Without plants, the food chain would collapse, and life on Earth would die off.

See List 4.13, Photosynthesis.

List 4.13   Photosynthesis

Photosynthesis is the process through which green plants use the energy of sunlight to turn carbon dioxide and water into food. Following are the facts about photosynthesis.

- Chlorophyll, a substance found in a plant's leaves, enables a plant to use the sun's energy.
- Chlorophyll gives leaves their green color.
- Chlorophyll gains energy by absorbing sunlight.
- The plant uses the energy absorbed by chlorophyll to break down water molecules that it has absorbed from the soil.
  - Breaking down water molecules leaves hydrogen and oxygen atoms.
  - Hydrogen atoms combine with atoms of carbon dioxide that have been absorbed through the plant's leaves. The combination of hydrogen and carbon dioxide forms glucose, a type of sugar.
  - The glucose molecules combine to form starch.
  - The glucose also combines with minerals the plant has absorbed from the soil to form complex proteins.
  - The plant uses the starch to form new cells and to grow.
- Leftover oxygen atoms are released through the leaves into the air.

 Did you know? The oxygen plants release to the air as a waste product is essential for animal life.

See List 4.12, What Plants Need to Live; List 4.42, The Carbon Oxygen Cycle.

Copyright © 2010 by Gary Robert Muschla, Judith A. Muschla, and Erin Muschla

List 4.14   The Food Chain

A *food chain* is a series of living things, each using the organism on the chain before it as a source of food. Energy from food is transferred from organisms lower in the chain to organisms higher in the chain. The following words are the vocabulary of food chains.

- *Community*: All the different species that live and interact with each other in a particular habitat
- *Decomposers*: Bacteria and fungi that feed on dead plants and animals, breaking the remains down into nutrients that can be reused by primary producers
- *Food web*: The interconnections between several food chains
- *Green plants*: Primary producers on land
- *Organism*: A living thing
- *Photosynthesis*: The process through which green plants obtain energy from the sun to turn carbon dioxide and water into food
- *Plankton*: Primary producers in water
- *Predators*: Animals that hunt and kill other animals for food; carnivores
- *Primary consumers*: Herbivores, which are plant-eating animals
- *Primary producers*: Plants, which make their own food through photosynthesis and are at the beginning of a food chain
- *Secondary consumers*: Carnivores, which are meat-eating animals that feed mostly on primary consumers

Example of a Food Chain

An insect eats the leaf of a plant.

A spider eats the insect.

A bird eats the spider.

A hawk eats the bird.

The hawk dies.

Decomposers feed on the remains of the hawk.

The remains are broken down into nutrients that are reused by plants.

 Did you know? Without primary producers, there would be no food chains.

Copyright © 2010 by Gary Robert Muschla, Judith A. Muschla, and Erin Muschla

List 4.15   Biomes of the World

A *biome* is a community of plants and animals that live in a large area of the Earth's surface. Biomes are the result of climate in a region. Following are descriptions of the world's major biomes.

Coniferous Forest

- Found in northern temperate zones, south of the Arctic, from Alaska across North America, through northern Europe and northern Asia

  Examples of plant life: mostly cone-bearing trees such as spruce, fir, and hemlock

  Examples of animal life: moose, elk, bears, snowshoe rabbits, various birds

Deciduous Forest

- Found in mild temperate zones, especially eastern North America, Europe, and eastern Asia

  Examples of plant life: trees and shrubs that lose their leaves in the fall, including oak, maple, and ash; variety of flowers

  Examples of animal life: squirrels, rabbits, raccoons, deer, many species of birds

Rain Forests

- Found near the equator, especially in Asia, Africa, South America, Central America, and many islands in the Pacific Ocean
- Most receive at least 70 in (1,780 mm) of rainfall per year
- Have more species of plants and animals than any other biome

  Examples of plant life: thick vegetation, including tall trees, vines, herbs, mosses

  Examples of animal life: anteaters, jaguars, sloths, monkeys, parrots

Grasslands

- Found throughout the world
- Most receive between 10 in (254 mm) and 40 in (1,016 mm) of rainfall per year

  Examples of plant life: grasses, cereal crops; few trees

  Examples of animal life: grazing animals, prairie dogs (North America), giraffes, zebras, and lions (Africa)

Mountains

- Found on all continents

  Examples of plant life: trees, shrubs, wild flowers in lower elevations; little plant life in higher elevations

  Examples of animal life: mountain goats, sheep, pumas

Copyright © 2010 by Gary Robert Muschla, Judith A. Muschla, and Erin Muschla

Deserts

- Found on every continent but Europe
- Receive less than 10 in (254 mm) of rainfall per year
- May be hot, such as the Sahara in Africa, or cold, as in Antarctica

  Examples of plant life: varieties of cactuses

  Examples of animal life: snakes, lizards, camels

Tundra

- Found in the Arctic
- Is the coldest biome on Earth

  Examples of plant life: small shrubs and lichen; flowers that bloom in short summer when the top layer of the permafrost melts; too cold for trees

  Examples of animal life: polar bears, caribou, grey wolves

Did you know? Deserts cover about one-fifth of the Earth's surface.

See List 4.16, Rain Forests.

Copyright © 2010 by Gary Robert Muschla, Judith A. Muschla, and Erin Muschla

List 4.16   Rain Forests

Rain forests are large areas of land thick with trees and underlying vegetation. There are two types of rain forests: *tropical rain forests* and *temperate rain forests*. Following are facts about them, as well as areas of the world where major rain forests are found.

Rain Forest Facts

- About 6% of the world's surface is covered with rain forests.
- It is estimated that rain forests supply 30%–40% of the world's oxygen. (The oxygen is released as a by-product of photosynthesis.)
- Although rain forests are found in more than 70 countries, close to half of the land covered with rain forests is located in Brazil, Zaire, and Indonesia.
- About half of all species of plants and animals on Earth live in rain forests.
- Rain forests have three levels:
    1. *Canopy*: The tallest level, with the tops of trees reaching between 100 and 200 ft (30 and 60 m)
    2. *Understory*: A mix of small trees, vines, shrubs, and ferns
    3. *Forest floor*: Populated mostly with herbs, mosses, and fungi
- The biggest rain forests are found in tropical regions, between the Tropic of Cancer and the Tropic of Capricorn.
- Many rain forests receive more than 80 in (1,500 mm) of rainfall each year. The Amazon Rain Forest receives around 100 in (2,540 mm).
- The average annual temperature of tropical rain forests is 77° F (25° C).
- Tropical rain forests may be described as tall, dense jungles.
- The growing season in tropical rain forests is year-round. This supports the great growth of vegetation.
- Temperate rain forests are farther from the equator and lie in the Temperate Zone. They are located in coastal areas.
- Temperate rain forests receive significant amounts of rainfall, but less than tropical rain forests.
- Temperate rain forests are dense, but they do not have the appearance of a jungle.

Copyright © 2010 by Gary Robert Muschla, Judith A. Muschla, and Erin Muschla

The Elementary Teacher's Book of Lists

Locations of Major Tropical Rain Forests	Locations of Major Temperate Rain Forests
Brazil (Amazon Basin)	Pacific Northwest (USA)
Central America	Southeast Australia
Southeast Asia	New Zealand
Equatorial Africa	Southern Chile
Northeast Australia	Europe (coasts of Ireland, Scotland, Norway)
Many Pacific Islands	

 Did you know? Despite the vegetation it supports, the soil of rain forests is nutrient poor.

See List 4.17, Why Rain Forests Are Important; List 4.18, How to Save the Rain Forests.

Copyright © 2010 by Gary Robert Muschla, Judith A. Muschla, and Erin Muschla

List 4.17   Why Rain Forests Are Important

Many scientists consider rain forests to be among the most important areas on Earth. They are vital to the plants and animals that live within them, to people, and to the Earth as a whole.

- Because rain forests are home to half of the world's plants and animals, the destruction of rain forests would result in mass extinctions.
- The plants in rain forests absorb carbon dioxide, a greenhouse gas. By removing carbon dioxide from the air, rain forests help to control the Earth's temperature.
- As a by-product of photosynthesis, rain forests release oxygen. Scientists estimate that rain forests may account for 30%–40% of the Earth's atmospheric oxygen.
- Rain forests provide many agricultural products, including:
  - Coffee
  - Sugarcane
  - Cacao for chocolate
  - Coconuts
  - Bananas
  - Pineapples
  - Cinnamon
- Rain forests supply many vital products, including:
  - Timber for construction and furniture
  - Rubber for tires
  - Dyes for coloring
  - Ingredients for many medicines

 Did you know? If rain forests disappeared, the Earth's climate would change. The rate of global warming would likely increase.

See List 4.16, Rain Forests; List 4.18, How to Save the Rain Forests.

Copyright © 2010 by Gary Robert Muschla, Judith A. Muschla, and Erin Muschla

List 4.18   How to Save the Rain Forests

It has been estimated that the size of the Earth's rain forests are decreasing by about 80,000 acres per day. If deforestation continues, the rain forests will eventually vanish and so will the benefits they give to the Earth. Following are the primary causes of rain forest destruction and ways to save the forests.

Causes of Rain Forest Destruction

- Logging
- Clearing of land for agriculture
- Clearing of land for animal grazing
- Road building
- Expansion of human population
- Illegal trade in animals and resources

Ways to Save the Rain Forests

- Learn about the importance of the rain forests.
- Teach others about the importance of the rain forests.
- Support the planting of trees to replace trees cut down during logging.
- Support the establishment of parks to protect rain forests and the wildlife within them.
- Only purchase rain forest products from companies that work in ways that do not damage rain forests.
- Support laws that protect the rain forests, while taking into account the needs of the people that live there.

 Did you know? Every year, an area of rain forest equal to the area of New Jersey is cut down.

See List 4.16, Rain Forests; List 4.17, Why Rain Forests Are Important.

Copyright © 2010 by Gary Robert Muschla, Judith A. Muschla, and Erin Muschla

List 4.19   Facts About Endangered Species

Endangered species are animals and plants that are in danger of becoming extinct. Species that are likely to become endangered are described as being threatened. Many threatened species eventually become endangered. Following are facts about endangered species.

- More than 1,000 animals are considered to be endangered.
- About 20,000 plants are endangered.
- In the past 400 years, some 500 species of plants and animals that lived in North America have become extinct.
- Factors that can lead to plants and animals becoming endangered and extinct include:
  - Destruction of habitats
  - Pollution
  - Illegal hunting and poaching
  - Introduction of new species that upsets the balance in the environment
  - Climate change
- Many governments and organizations are working to save endangered species.
  - Laws have been established to protect endangered species.
  - Many zoos and animal reserves have programs that try to breed endangered animals in captivity, then reintroduce them to the wild.

 Did you know? You can find a current list of endangered species at the Web site of the U.S. Fish and Wildlife Service, www.fws.gov/endangered.

See List 4.20, Examples of Endangered Animals; List 4.21, Some Extinct Animals; List 4.22, Examples of Endangered Plants.

Copyright © 2010 by Gary Robert Muschla, Judith A. Muschla, and Erin Muschla

List 4.20   Examples of Endangered Animals

The animals on the following list are only a small portion of the roughly 1,000 that are endangered. Still, the list will provide your students with many examples.

Albatross, Short-Tailed (bird)
Bat, Gray (mammal)
Beetle, American Burying (insect)
Bobwhite, Masked (bird)
Butterfly, Lotis Blue (insect)
Caribou, Woodland (mammal)
Condor, California (bird)
Deer, Columbian White-Tailed (mammal)
Dragonfly, Hine's Emerald (insect)
Ferret, Black-Footed (mammal)
Gecko, Monito (reptile)
Goby, Tidewater (fish)
Goose, Hawaiian (bird)
Jaguar (mammal)
Moth, Blackburn's Sphinx (insect)
Mouse, Pacific Pocket (mammal)
Ocelot (mammal)
Otter, Northern Sea (mammal)
Otter, Southern Sea (mammal)

Owl, Northern Spotted (bird)
Panther, Florida (mammal)
Plover (bird)
Prairie Dog, Utah (mammal)
Pronghorn, Sonora (mammal)
Puma (mammal)
Salamander, Reticulated Flatwoods (amphibian)
Salmon, Atlantic (fish)
Salmon, Sockeye (fish)
Sea Turtle, Green (reptile)
Sea-Lion, Steller (mammal)
Snake, San Francisco Garter (reptile)
Sturgeon, Alabama (fish)
Toad, Arroyo (amphibian)
Whale, Blue (mammal)
Wolf, Gray (mammal)
Woodpecker, Ivory-Billed (bird)

Did you know? Some animals, benefitting from the protection afforded by being on the endangered species list, have increased in numbers enough so that they are no longer endangered. Two examples are the American alligator and the American bison.

See List 4.19, Facts About Endangered Species; List 4.21, Some Extinct Animals; List 4.22, Examples of Endangered Plants.

Copyright © 2010 by Gary Robert Muschla, Judith A. Muschla, and Erin Muschla

List 4.21   Some Extinct Animals

When the last living member of a species dies, the species is extinct. Over Earth's history, millions of animals have become extinct. While natural causes—global disasters such as asteroid strikes, massive volcanic eruptions, great floods, and major climate change—have been responsible for countless extinctions, humans are the cause of many others.

American Mastodon, 8000 B.C.

Arizona Jaguar, 1905

Bali Tiger, 1937

Bear-Eared Hopping Mouse, 1843

Caspian Tiger, 1957

Cave Lion, 8000 B.C.

Dodo Bird, 1681

Florida Black Wolf, 1917

Giant Short-Faced Bear, 10,500 B.C.

Great Auk, 1844

Kamchutka Bear, 1920

Martinique Lizard, 1830s

Mexican Silver Grizzly Bear, 1967

Passenger Pigeon, 1914

Pig-Footed Bandicoot, 1950s

Round Island Boa, 1980

Saber-Toothed Tiger, 8000 B.C.

Steller's Sea Cow, 1768

Tasmanian Tiger, 1936

Tasmanian Wolf, 1933

Texas Red Wolf, 1970

Wooly Mammoth, 2000 B.C.

The Mystery of Mass Extinctions

The Earth has suffered at least five mass extinctions in which high percentages of life at the time perished. The most recent occurred 65 million years ago. Some scientists believe that an asteroid a few miles wide slammed into the Earth near the Yucatan Peninsula, resulting in a dust cloud that blocked sunlight and caused global temperatures to plunge. This destroyed much plant life, which in turn caused many animals to starve, including all of the dinosaurs. No one knows with certainty if that is true, or what caused the other mass extinctions, which include:

- *End Triassic Extinction* about 205 million years ago
- *Permian-Triassic Extinction* about 251 million years ago
- *Late Devonian Extinction* about 365 million years ago
- *Ordovician-Silurian Extinction* about 445 million years ago

 Did you know? Occasionally a member of a species thought to be extinct is discovered. In 1938, scientists found a coelacanth (fish) off the southeastern coast of South Africa. The coelacanth had been thought to be extinct for about 70 million years. Such discoveries, however, are rare.

See List 4.19, Facts About Endangered Species; List 4.20, Examples of Endangered Animals; List 4.22, Examples of Endangered Plants.

Copyright © 2010 by Gary Robert Muschla, Judith A. Muschla, and Erin Muschla

The Elementary Teacher's Book of Lists

List 4.22   Examples of Endangered Plants

It is estimated that some 20,000 plants around the world are endangered. Many of these plants occupy important parts of their habitats, and their loss can affect the balance of nature. The following list contains examples of plants that are endangered in the United States.

Ambrosia, San Diego
Aster, Florida Golden
Barberry, Nevin's
Bellflower, Brooksville
Blazingstar, Scrub
Bluegrass, Napa
Buttercup, Autumn
Cactus, Bakersfield
Cactus, Star
Clover, Monterrey
Coneflower, Smooth
Cypress, Gowen
Daisy, Willamette
Dogwood, Ashy
Fern, Aleutian Shield
Goldenrod, Short's
Irisette, White

Larkspur, Baker's
Lichen, Rock Gnome
Lily, Western
Mint, Longspurred
Morning-Glory, Stebbins'
Onion, Munz's
Phlox, Yreka
Plum, Scrub
Prairie-Clover, Leafy
Rhododendron, Chapman
Rosemary, Etonia
Snowbells, Texas
Spineflower, Sonoma
Sumac, Michaux's
Wallflower, Ben Lomond
Watercress, Gambell's
Wild-Rice, Texas

 Did you know? Global warming is a serious threat to plant species that are finely attuned to climate.

See List 4.19, Facts About Endangered Species; List 4.20, Examples of Endangered Animals.

Copyright © 2010 by Gary Robert Muschla, Judith A. Muschla, and Erin Muschla

List 4.23   Dinosaur Facts

For well over a hundred million years, dinosaurs were the dominant form of life on Earth. They became extinct about 65 million years ago, making way for the rise of mammals, and, of course, us. Your students will no doubt be fascinated by the following facts about dinosaurs.

- Dinosaurs appeared on the Earth about 230 million years ago.
- Dinosaurs lived on all continents of the Earth. (The shapes and positions of the continents at that time were quite different than they are today. Also, the Earth was generally warmer then.)
- In 1822, Mary Mantell, an Englishwoman, found some very big teeth and bones that turned out to be the first fossils of a dinosaur. Because the teeth resembled those of a modern iguana, the creature was named *Iguanodon*.
- The earliest dinosaur fossils, dating to about 230 million years ago, were found in Argentina and Brazil.
- Scientists who study fossils are known as *paleontologists*. Many paleontologists search for the fossils of dinosaurs.
- In the past, scientists believed that dinosaurs were cold-blooded, like modern lizards. Some scientists have begun to think that at least some dinosaurs were warm-blooded.
- Dinosaurs may be divided into two large groups: *Saurischian* and *Ornithischian*.
    1. Saurischian dinosaurs had lizardlike hips. This group includes both herbivores (plant-eating) and carnivores (meat-eating). The famous *Tyrannosaurus* was a meat-eating Saurischian. The *Apatosaurus* was an example of a plant-eater.
    2. Ornithiscian dinosaurs had birdlike hips. Ornithiscians were herbivores. An example is *Iguanodon*.
- Many paleontologists believe that modern birds descended from dinosaurs. In 2001, a fossil of a small *dromaeosaur* was found in China. Imprints of what were probably feathers were found around the body.
- Many theories are offered for the extinction of the dinosaurs, including:
    - Climate change that destroyed habitats, including plants that were the beginning of the dinosaur food chain
    - An asteroid that struck the Earth, causing a massive cloud of dust and smoke that blocked the light of the sun and caused the Earth's temperature to drop, killing most plant life
    - An exploding star (supernova) in nearby space that washed the Earth with lethal radiation

 Did you know? The word *dinosaur* was first used by Richard Owen, an English scientist, in 1841. It comes from the Greek *deinos*, meaning "terrible," and *sauros*, meaning "lizard." Thus, *dinosaur* means "terrible lizard."

See List 4.24, Dinosaur Superstars.

Copyright © 2010 by Gary Robert Muschla, Judith A. Muschla, and Erin Muschla

List 4.24   Dinosaur Superstars

All dinosaurs were impressive creatures. But some were exceptionally impressive, even by dinosaur standards.

- Biggest: *Seismosaurus*, about 120 ft long head to tail (36 m), 18 ft high (5.5 m)
- Smallest: *Microraptor*, about 16 in (40 cm)
- Fastest: *Ornithomimus*, about 40 mph (64 kmph) for short distances
- Most intelligent (probably, based on brain to body ratio which was equivalent to a modern bird): *Troodon*
- Least intelligent (probably, with a brain the size of a walnut in a body of three tons): *Stegosaurus*
- Greatest predator (probably, based on size, teeth, and claws): *Tyrannosaurus*
- Most heavily armored (with thick plates covering skin, rows of defensive spikes, large horns on head, and clublike tail): *Ankylosaurus*
- Longest neck: *Mamenchisaurus*, about 45 ft (14 m)
- Longest-lived: *Sauropods*, about 100 years
- Heaviest: *Arentinosaurus*, about 100 tons
- Longest tail: *Diplodocus*, about 43 ft (13 m)
- Tallest: *Sauroposeidon*, about 60 ft (18 m)
- Most teeth: *Hadrosaurus*, about 960

Did you know? Mammals that lived during the time of the dinosaurs were small, rodent-like creatures that no doubt spent much of their time hiding from dinosaurs.

See List 4.23, Dinosaur Facts.

Copyright © 2010 by Gary Robert Muschla, Judith A. Muschla, and Erin Muschla

The human body is made up of trillions of cells. Cells that have the same function form tissues, such as muscles. Tissues that work together form organs, such as the lungs. Organs that work together form systems, such as the circulatory system. All of the body's systems working together make human beings truly remarkable creatures. Following are descriptions of the major systems of the human body.

Circulatory System

- This system includes the heart, arteries, veins, and blood.
- The heart pumps blood, which is transported through arteries (away from the heart) and veins (back to the heart).
- Blood carries oxygen and nutrients to the cells and waste products from the cells.
- Capillaries are the smallest blood vessels. It is through the walls of capillaries that oxygen, nutrients, and wastes pass to and from cells.

Respiratory System

- This system includes the nose, trachea, and lungs.
- Air enters the body through the nose and passes through the trachea.
- The trachea branches into two bronchial tubes that go into the lungs.
- In the lungs, oxygen is absorbed and enters the blood stream. Carbon dioxide, a waste product of the cells carried to the lungs in the bloodstream, is exhaled.

Digestive System

- This system includes the mouth, esophagus, stomach, small intestine, and large intestine.
- The process of digestion breaks down food and converts it into substances the body can uses for energy, growth, and repair.
- Food is chewed in the mouth and travels through the esophagus to the stomach, where it is broken down by digestive acids. From the stomach it travels to the small intestine, where it is broken down further into proteins, minerals, carbohydrates, fats, and vitamins.
- Nutrients are absorbed through the walls of the small intestine and enter the bloodstream.
- Food that is not needed goes to the large intestine from which it is eliminated as waste.

Nervous System

- This system includes the brain, spinal cord, and nerves.
- The system sends and receives nerve impulses. These impulses enable a person to use his senses and control his body.

Copyright © 2010 by Gary Robert Muschla, Judith A. Muschla, and Erin Muschla

Copyright © 2010 by Gary Robert Muschla, Judith A. Muschla, and Erin Muschla

List 4.25 **continued**

- The brain has three major parts:
    1. The *cerebrum*, which controls thinking and the senses
    2. The *cerebellum*, which controls physical coordination
    3. The *brain stem*, which controls the body's involuntary actions such as heartbeat

Skeletal System

- This system includes bones, ligaments, and tendons.
- It provides strength and support for the body. It also protects organs.
- Working with muscles, the skeletal system helps the body move.

Muscular System

- This system has tissues that work with the bones to move the body.
- Some muscles are voluntary—for example, the muscles of your arm—which you can control.
- Some muscles are involuntary—the muscles that keep your heart beating—which you cannot control.

Endocrine System

- This system includes numerous glands such as the thyroid gland, pituitary gland, and adrenal glands.
- The glands produce hormones, which are chemicals that keep the body working normally.

Urinary System

- This system, which includes the kidneys, cleans waste from the body.
- It expels liquid waste as urine.
- It also helps regulate the amount of water in the body.

Did you know? Proper nutrition and regular exercise help to keep all of the body's systems in top condition.

See List 4.26, Some Amazing Facts About the Human Body; List 4.27, The Five Senses and Beyond.

List 4.26   Some Amazing Facts About the Human Body

Most students, and many adults, take their bodies for granted. They do not consider how truly wondrous the human body is. The following facts will likely amaze your students.

- The average human body is 70% water.
- The most common elements that make up the body are carbon dioxide, hydrogen, nitrogen, and oxygen.
- The human heart weighs less than a pound, but pumps about 2,000 gallons of blood every day.
- A person's heart beats about 100,000 times per day.
- The adult human body contains about 8 pints of blood.
- A drop of blood can circulate through the body in about 30 seconds.
- Red blood cells live about 120 days before being replaced. Bone cells live about 25 to 30 years before being replaced. Brain cells are never replaced. They last a lifetime.
- Most people breathe about 20 times per minute, which works out to be about 10 million times per year.
- The average person blinks about 20,000 times each day.
- An eyelash falls out after about 150 days.
- The adult body has about 6 pounds of skin.
- Skin is an incredible organ. It grows, repairs itself, and is waterproof. During their lifetime, people shed their skin about 40 times.
- Most people have (or had at one time) about 100,000 hairs on their head.
- A baby is born with more than 300 bones. Because some bones fuse together as the child grows, the typical adult has 206.
- Babies have 20 teeth but adults have 32.
- An adult's large intestine is about 5 feet long, while the small intestine is about 25 feet long.
- When a person sneezes, air is forced through the nose at a rate of about 100 mph.
- Billions of bacteria are on our bodies, and billions more are inside us. Many of the bacteria inside us reside in our stomach and intestines where they help us digest food.

 Did you know? It is easier to smile than to frown. About 17 muscles are needed to smile, and 43 are needed to frown. We should all be smiling more.

See List 4.25, Major Systems of the Human Body; List 4.27, The Five Senses and Beyond.

Copyright © 2010 by Gary Robert Muschla, Judith A. Muschla, and Erin Muschla

List 4.27   The Five Senses and Beyond

We experience the world through our senses. Although we typically think of the five senses, scientists recognize several more.

The Five Senses
- Sight
- Hearing
- Touch
- Smell
- Taste

More Senses
- Sense of time or time passing
- Sense of equilibrium, position of the body, and weight
- Sense of acceleration and motion
- Sense of temperature outside and within the body
- Senses of needs of the body, for example, hunger, thirst, and fatigue
- Sense of pain

Did you know? Aristotle, the Greek philosopher and scientist, identified the five senses back in the third century B.C.

See List 4.25, Major Systems of the Human Body.

List 4.28   Healthy Habits

It is never too early for children to develop positive habits. Following are some habits that will lead to good health.

- Get enough sleep each night. For children ages 3–5, 12–14 hours; children ages 5–12, 9–11 hours; adolescents, 8.5–9.5 hours; adults, 7–9 hours.
- Eat a solid breakfast each morning.
- Eat a balanced diet.
- Eat healthy snacks; fruits are a good choice.
- Brush teeth at least twice a day; if possible, brush after every meal. Clean regularly between teeth with dental floss.
- Wash your hands often and your body regularly.
- Get some exercise each day.
- Be active. Take part in sports, dance, or play a musical instrument.
- Drink plenty of water. Water is necessary for many of your body's functions.
- Treat others with respect and kindness. You will feel good about yourself and have many friends.

Did you know? Habits begun in childhood often become the habits of a lifetime.

Copyright © 2010 by Gary Robert Muschla, Judith A. Muschla, and Erin Muschla

Eating a balanced diet is essential to maintaining good health. Following are the major food groups.

Grains

Examples: Whole grain bread, cereal, crackers, rice, and pasta

Vegetables

Examples: Green and orange vegetables, dry beans and peas

Fruits

Examples: Various fruits

Oils

Examples: Oils and solid fats such as butter, margarine, shortening, and lard

Milk

Examples: Low-fat or fat-free milk; if necessary, lactose-free products may be substituted

Meat and Beans

Examples: Low-fat or lean meat and poultry, fish, beans, peas, nuts, and seeds

Did you know? To help people select the right foods to eat, the U.S. government has developed MyPyramid, which highlights the foods that a person should eat each day. The wider parts of the pyramid indicate foods that should be eaten in larger amounts, while the smaller parts indicate foods that should be eaten in smaller amounts. You can find much more information as well as activities about MyPyramid at the U.S. Department of Agriculture's Web site http://mypyramid.gov.

Copyright © 2010 by Gary Robert Muschla, Judith A. Muschla, and Erin Muschla

Copyright © 2010 by Gary Robert Muschla, Judith A. Muschla, and Erin Muschla

Matter is anything that has mass and occupies space. It is found throughout the universe. Use the following facts to introduce your students to matter.

- All matter is made up of atoms.
  Matter is commonly found in one of three forms, or states:
    1. *Solid*, which resists changes in shape or size. The atoms in solids are densely packed and do not move easily. They vibrate in place.
    2. *Liquid*, which takes the shape of the container that holds it. The atoms in liquids are less densely packed than atoms in solids. They easily slide over each other and change places.
    3. *Gas*, which expands to fill a container or space. The atoms in gases have no definite shape or volume. They spread out as far as possible.
- All forms of matter are affected by temperature. A good example is water. At or below 32° F (0° C), water freezes and is a solid (ice). Between 32° F (0°C) and 212° F (100° C), water is a liquid. At or above 212° F (100° C), water boils and becomes a gas (water vapor or steam).
- All matter expands when heated and contracts when cooled. Exception: water, which expands when frozen.
- The *melting point* is the temperature at which a solid turns to a liquid.
- The *freezing point* is the temperature at which a liquid turns to a solid.
- The *boiling point* is the temperature at which a liquid turns to a gas.
- *Condensation* occurs when a gas cools and turns into a liquid.
- *Volume* is the amount of space any form of matter takes up.
- *Mass* is the amount of matter in an object. It is not the same as ''weight.''
- *Weight* is the force of gravity on an object.

 Did you know? A change from one state of matter to another is called a *physical change*.

See List 4.31, Elements and Atoms.

List 4.31   Elements and Atoms

An *element* is the smallest piece of any form of matter that cannot be broken down into anything smaller and still be the same substance. Every element is made of atoms. The atoms of a specific element are identical and are different from the atoms that make up other elements. The following facts will help your students understand elements and atoms.

- Every element is a pure substance. Examples of elements include carbon, oxygen, nitrogen, aluminum, iron, and sulfur.
- Atoms, which make up elements, are made of subatomic particles, including:
  - *Protons*, which have positive electrical charges
  - *Electrons*, which have negative electrical charges
  - *Neutrons*, which have neither a positive nor negative charge and are electrically neutral
- Scientists classify elements according to the number of protons an element has, which is called the element's *atomic number*.
- Because each element is different from any other element, each has a different atomic number. A hydrogen atom has 1 proton. The atomic number of hydrogen is 1. A carbon atom has 6 protons. The atomic number of carbon is 6. An iron atom has 26 protons. The atomic number of iron is 26.
- Most atoms have an equal number of protons and electrons. The numbers of neutrons in some atoms do not equal the number of protons and electrons.
- The *atomic mass* of an atom is the amount of matter in the atom.
- In 1869, Dmitri I. Mendeleev, a Russian chemist, published a periodic table of the elements. He organized elements according to their atomic weights and chemical properties.
- As of 2010, there were 112 elements. The first 92 (from hydrogen with an atomic number of 1 to uranium with an atomic number of 92) are found naturally on the Earth. The others are produced in laboratories and are highly unstable.
- Scientists use chemical symbols when writing the names of elements. *Examples*: hydrogen, H; oxygen, O; nitrogen, N; neon, Ne; carbon, C; cobalt, Co. Most symbols are derived from the English name for the element. Some come from the Latin name for the element. For example, the Latin name for gold is *aurum*, and the symbol for gold is Au.

Did you know? The periodic table of elements contains all of the elements, according to their atomic number. You can find an example of the periodic table which you can use with your students at a Website maintained by the Los Alamos National Laboratory's Chemical Division at http://periodic.lanl.gov/default.htm.

See List 4.30, Facts About Matter.

Copyright © 2010 by Gary Robert Muschla, Judith A. Muschla, and Erin Muschla

List 4.32   Magnetism and Magnets

Magnetism is an invisible force. It enables magnetized objects to attract or repel other magnetized objects and also attract some nonmagnetic metallic objects. A magnet is an object that attracts specific metals. The following facts provide the basics about magnetism.

- Since ancient times, lodestone (an oxide of iron) has been known to have magnetic properties.
- Magnets are made of metal, usually a combination of iron, steel, nickel, or cobalt.
- The only naturally occurring metals that can be magnetic are iron, nickel, and cobalt.
- Most metals do not have magnetic properties. Some examples: aluminum, silver, lead, gold, copper, tin, and zinc
- Magnets come in many shapes, including bar, U, horseshoe, and square.
- The strongest magnetic effects of any magnet are at its poles. In a bar magnet, the poles are on opposite ends.
- The poles are identified as north and south. Around each pole is a magnetic field.
- Unlike poles attract and like poles repel. This phenomenon is known as the Law of Magnetism.
- In the early 1800s, scientists learned that sending an electric current through a wire produced an electromagnet. Because electromagnets can be turned on and off, they are used in countless devices and machines, including motors, telephones, and computers.
- The Earth is a giant magnet. It has two magnetic poles, much like a bar magnet. The Earth's north magnetic pole is close to the geographical north pole, and the south magnetic pole is close to the geographic south pole. The needle of a compass reacts to the Earth's magnetic field.
- Some animals, particularly birds, can sense the Earth's magnetic field. They use it to guide them when migrating or traveling long distances.

 Did you know? Allowing your students to explore the properties of magnets is a wonderful activity for a lesson about magnetism.

See List 4.33, Electricity.

Copyright © 2010 by Gary Robert Muschla, Judith A. Muschla, and Erin Muschla

List 4.33   Electricity

Scientists believe that electricity is the flow of electrons along a common pathway, for example, copper wire. Sharing the following information with your students as they study electricity can broaden the scope of your lesson.

- There are two types of electricity: static and current.
  - *Static electricity* is best described as a buildup of electrons.

    Examples: lightning; the shock you receive from a metal doorknob after walking across a wool rug; the "cling" in clothes
  - *Current electricity* is a flow of electrons through a closed circuit.

    Examples: power for lights, TVs, computers, stereos, air conditioners

- A *conductor* is a material that allows electrons to flow easily.

  Examples: metals, especially copper, live trees, animals, water

  (*Note*: It is the impurities in water that make water an excellent conductor. Pure water is actually a poor conductor; however, most people never encounter pure water. Even "pure" spring water contains natural minerals that will make it a fine conductor of electricity.)

- Poor conductors are materials that block or impede the flow of electrons. These materials are called insulators.

  Examples: nonmetals, rubber, glass, plastic

- Thales, an ancient Greek scientist in the sixth century B.C., was one of the first people to observe electricity. He rubbed amber, which is fossilized tree resin, with a wool cloth, after which the amber attracted lint. This, of course, was static electricity.

- In the nineteenth century, the English scientist Michael Faraday discovered that he could generate an electrical charge by moving a magnet inside a coil of wire. His work eventually led to electrical generators.

 Did you know? The word *electricity* is derived from the Greek word for "amber" (Thales's experiment), which is *elektron*.

See List 4.32, Magnetism and Magnets.

Copyright © 2010 by Gary Robert Muschla, Judith A. Muschla, and Erin Muschla

List 4.34   Facts About Energy

Energy is the ability to do work. We use energy to do everything we do. Following are facts about energy.

- There are two kinds of energy: potential energy and kinetic energy.
  - *Potential energy* is stored energy. An example of potential energy is a ball positioned at the top of a hill.
  - *Kinetic energy* is energy that moves things. A ball rolling down a hill is an example of kinetic energy. The potential energy of the ball while motionless at the top of the hill has been changed to kinetic energy.
- Energy comes in different forms, including:
  - Heat energy
  - Light energy
  - Mechanical energy
  - Electrical energy
  - Chemical energy
  - Sound energy
  - Nuclear energy

 Did you know? Energy cannot be created or destroyed, but it can be converted into different forms.

See List 4.35, Renewable and Nonrenewable Sources of Energy.

Copyright © 2010 by Gary Robert Muschla, Judith A. Muschla, and Erin Muschla

List 4.35 Renewable and Nonrenewable Sources of Energy

We use the energy stored in natural resources to produce the energy we need every day. These sources of energy can be divided into two groups: renewable and nonrenewable energy. Following are facts and examples of each.

Facts About Energy

- An energy source that can be replenished in a relatively short amount of time is renewable.
- An energy source that cannot be replenished in a relatively short amount of time is nonrenewable.
- Both renewable and nonrenewable energy sources can be used to produce other sources of energy such as heat and electricity.

Examples of Renewable Energy Sources

- *Solar energy*: Solar panels collect sunlight and can convert the light energy into heat or electricity.
- *Wind*: Modern windmills can generate electricity.
- *Geothermal*: Heat that arises from the molten rock deep beneath the surface of the Earth can be used to heat buildings or generate electricity.
- *Biomass*: When burned or allowed to decay, organic wastes such as wood from trees, animal wastes, and garbage produce methane, the main component in natural gas. The gas can then be used to produce heat or electricity.
- *Hydropower*: Powerfully running water can be used to generate electricity.
- *Tidal* (or *wave*): The power of ocean waves can be used to generate electricity.

Examples of Nonrenewable Energy Sources

- *Fossil fuels*: Oil, natural gas, and coal provide most of our energy. Fossil fuels were formed from the remains of dead plants and animals that lived millions of years ago. When these organisms died, their remains were covered by sediments and dirt. Over time, the remains were buried deep underground where pressure and heat eventually turned them into the fossil fuels we use today.
- *Uranium*: Atoms of uranium are split through a process called *nuclear fission*. The atoms release heat which can be used to create electricity.

 Did you know? Recycling reduces the amount of energy that is needed to make new products.

See List 4.34, Facts About Energy.

Copyright © 2010 by Gary Robert Muschla, Judith A. Muschla, and Erin Muschla

List 4.36   Simple Machines

Scientists define *work* as a force that moves an object. Simple machines are devices that are used to make work easier. Following are examples of machines that people have been using for thousands of years.

Inclined Plane

- Description: a plane surface that is tilted or inclined
- Uses: makes it easier to raise or lower heavy objects by pushing or pulling them up or down the inclined plane

    Examples: ramp, ladder, sliding board

Wedge

- Description: two inclined planes used together
- Uses: holds things together or separates or splits things

    Examples: axe head, cutting edge of a knife, tip of a screw driver, point of a nail, doorstop

Lever

- Description: a rigid bar that turns on a pivot, called a fulcrum
- Uses: amplifies strength or the ability to lift

    Examples: wheelbarrow, pliers, crowbar, scissors, seesaws

Screw

- Description: an inclined plane spiraled around a post
- Uses: converts rotational force to linear force; lifts or drives in by twisting

    Examples: car jack, piano stool, drill bit, nut and bolt

Copyright © 2010 by Gary Robert Muschla, Judith A. Muschla, and Erin Muschla

List 4.36   continued

Pulley

- Description: a grooved wheel that holds a rope or chain, which, when pulled, moves the wheel
- Uses: raises, lowers, or moves heavy loads

  Examples: flagpole, clothesline, block and tackle (which consists of fixed and moveable pulleys that can be used to lift very heavy objects)

Wheel and Axle

- Description: a wheel that turns around an axle (or rod); a kind of lever that can move 360°
- Uses: helps move objects easily

  Examples: wheels on cars, helicopter blades, doorknob

Gears

- Description: two or more wheels with sprockets (teeth) around the outer rims
- Uses: changes direction, speed, and/or power
- Examples: cars, bicycles, clocks, can openers

 Did you know? Compound machines are machines that are built of many simple machines working together. A truck is an example.

Copyright © 2010 by Gary Robert Muschla, Judith A. Muschla, and Erin Muschla

List 4.37   Facts About Earth: Our Home in Space

The Earth is our home in space. The following information describes our planet.

- Scientists believe that Earth was formed about 4.6 billion years ago, along with the sun and other planets of our solar system.
- The Earth is the third planet from the sun.
- The Earth is about 93 million mi (150 million km) from the sun.
- The Earth travels around the sun in a roughly circular orbit once in 365.25 days (1 year) at about 66,000 mph (106,200 kmph).
- The Earth's journey around the sun is about 600 million mi (965.6 million km).
- The Earth has one moon, which is about 240,000 mi (386,242 km) away.
- The Earth spins on its axis, an imaginary line from the North Pole to the South Pole, once every 24 hours (1 day).
- The Earth is roughly spherical, but flattened slightly at its poles.
- The diameter of the Earth is 7,926 mi (12,756 km) at the equator, its widest part.
- The circumference of the Earth (distance around its surface) is 24,902 mi (40,076 km).
- The Earth is made up of four layers:
  1. The *crust* is the top layer. It consists of dirt and rock. The thickness of the crust varies from about 22 mi (35 km) on landmasses to about 3 mi (4.8 km) beneath the oceans.
  2. The *mantle* is the middle layer. It consists of thick rocks and accounts for about 80% of the Earth's volume. The mantle extends down about 1,800 mi (2,897 km).
  3. The *outer core* extends down for another 3,000 mi (4,828 km). It is composed of super heated molten iron and nickel.
  4. The *inner core* is the center of the Earth. It consists of compressed iron and nickel. Scientists believe that the Earth's magnetic field arises from its core.
- The Earth is surrounded by a layer of atmosphere made up of several gases: nitrogen, 78%; oxygen, 21%; small amounts of carbon dioxide, argon, helium, hydrogen, and others.
- The average temperature of the Earth is about 59° F (15° C) at sea level.

 Did you know? The unique physical features of the Earth combined with its distance from the sun make Earth hospitable to life.

Copyright © 2010 by Gary Robert Muschla, Judith A. Muschla, and Erin Muschla

List 4.38   Kinds of Rock

The rocks found throughout the world can be divided into three types. Their classifications are based on how they were formed.

Igneous Rocks

- Igneous rocks are formed when magma (molten rock) from within the Earth rises to or close to the surface, cools, and hardens.
- There are two types of igneous rocks: intrusive, that cool and harden beneath the surface, and extrusive, that cool and harden at the surface.

    Examples: granite, obsidian, basalt

Sedimentary Rocks

- Sedimentary rocks are usually formed in seas and riverbeds. Parts of rock, shells, and sand become mixed and packed tightly together.

    Examples: sandstone, limestone, shale

Metamorphic Rocks

- Metamorphic rocks are formed when igneous or sedimentary rocks are transformed by heat and pressure.
- These rocks are usually formed deep within the Earth.

    Examples: marble, slate, quartzite

 Did you know? Most rocks are combinations of various minerals.

Copyright © 2010 by Gary Robert Muschla, Judith A. Muschla, and Erin Muschla

An earthquake is a shaking of the Earth's surface due to a sudden movement in the Earth's crust. The movement releases energy in the form of vibrations that pass through the Earth in waves. The following vocabulary and information can make lessons about earthquakes thorough and interesting.

Earthquake Vocabulary

- *Crust*: Outer layer of the Earth's surface
- *Epicenter*: The area on the Earth's surface directly above the origin of an earthquake and which often experiences the greatest effects
- *Fault*: A break or crack in the Earth's crust
- *Focus*: The point at which an earthquake begins
- *Magnitude*: The amount of energy released by an earthquake
- *Plates*: Immense pieces of the Earth's crust
- *Richter Scale*: The scale used to measure the magnitude of an earthquake
- *Seismic wave*: The vibrations (shaking movement) produced by an earthquake
- *Seismograph*: Instrument that measures the strength of an earthquake
- *Seismologist*: A scientist who studies movements of the Earth
- *Tsunami*: A tidal wave caused by an undersea earthquake

Why Earthquakes Happen

The Earth's crust is divided into enormous tectonic plates. The plates are in slow but constant movement. Some move toward each other and collide, some slide past each other in opposite directions, and some move away from each other. When plates come into contact, great pressure builds. When the pressure is released, the massive rocks deep below the surface shift suddenly, causing powerful vibrations. These vibrations can result in an earthquake.

Did you know? Thousands of earthquakes occur every year, but most are so weak that they are not felt at the surface. Only about one out of every five earthquakes causes damage.

See List 4.40, Facts About Volcanoes.

Copyright © 2010 by Gary Robert Muschla, Judith A. Muschla, and Erin Muschla

A *volcano* is an opening in the Earth's crust through which molten rock, gases, and ash erupt. Most volcanoes are mountains. When teaching about volcanoes, be sure to include the following information.

Volcano Vocabulary

- *Active volcano*: A volcano that is erupting or is likely to erupt
- *Crater*: The opening at the top of a volcano
- *Dormant volcano*: A volcano that is not erupting but is capable of erupting in the future
- *Eruption*: The process of lava flowing out of a volcano
- *Extinct volcano*: A volcano that is no longer capable of erupting
- *Lava*: Magma that flows out of a volcano
- *Magma*: Molten rock
- *Vent*: An opening in the Earth's surface through which magma flows
- *Volcanologist*: A scientist who studies volcanoes

Why Volcanoes Happen

Volcanoes occur when magma from deep within the Earth rises through weak spots in the Earth's crust. The magma usually cools before reaching the surface. But sometimes heat and pressure continue to force it upward. When the magma finally reaches a vent in the Earth's crust, it erupts, carrying with it rocks, steam, and hot gases. Eruptions can be violent explosions or slow flowing streams of lava. In time, the lava cools and builds up layers around the vent, forming a cone.

 Did you know? Many active volcanoes are located along the rim of the Pacific Ocean. The volcanoes there mark the boundaries between the tectonic plates under the Pacific Ocean and North America, South America, and Asia. These volcanoes are known as the Ring of Fire.

See List 4.39, Facts About Earthquakes.

Copyright © 2010 by Gary Robert Muschla, Judith A. Muschla, and Erin Muschla

List 4.41   The Water Cycle

Water is constantly moving through the environment. This process is called the *water cycle*. The basic stages of the water cycle follow.

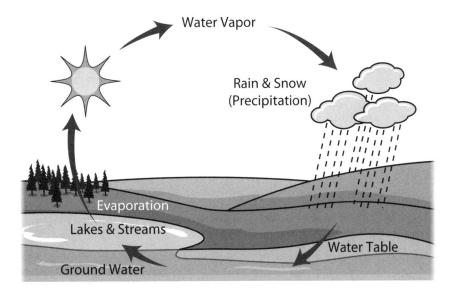

- Water on the surface of the Earth is heated by sunlight.
- Some of the heated water evaporates. It is now water vapor.
- The water vapor rises into the atmosphere.
- As the water vapor rises, it begins to cool.
- The water vapor condenses to form water droplets, which form clouds.
- When clouds cannot hold the water droplets any longer, the droplets fall. Depending on the temperature, the droplets fall as rain, snow, sleet, or hail.
- Some of the precipitation falls into bodies of water; the rest falls onto the ground and soaks into the soil.
- Some of the water that soaks into the ground is absorbed through the roots of plants.
- The plants use the water during photosynthesis. Excess water is released through the leaves of plants back to the atmosphere.
- Some of the water that soaked into the ground enters underground aquifers. From there it eventually flows to lakes, rivers, and oceans.
- The cycle continues.

 Did you know? The water cycle is also called the hydrologic cycle.

See List 4.42, The Carbon Oxygen Cycle.

Copyright © 2010 by Gary Robert Muschla, Judith A. Muschla, and Erin Muschla

List 4.42   The Carbon Oxygen Cycle

Carbon dioxide and oxygen are constantly moving through the environment. Plants require carbon dioxide for photosynthesis, and animals breathe oxygen. A basic summary of the carbon oxygen cycle follows.

- Plants absorb carbon dioxide through their leaves.
- Plants use the carbon dioxide in the process of photosynthesis to make their own food.
- During photosynthesis, oxygen is produced as a waste product. The plants release oxygen to the atmosphere.
- Animals and plants take in oxygen. During the process of respiration, the oxygen chemically combines with carbon compounds in foods. Energy and carbon dioxide are released.
- Animals take in carbon compounds when they consume plants.
- Decomposers break down the remains of dead plants and animals, releasing carbon dioxide to the air.
- The cycle then continues with plants using the carbon dioxide for photosynthesis.

 Did you know? The primeval Earth had little atmospheric oxygen. As plants evolved, the oxygen they released during photosynthesis accumulated in the air. In time, animals evolved with the capability to use oxygen during respiration.

See List 4.13, Photosynthesis; List 4.41, The Water Cycle.

Copyright © 2010 by Gary Robert Muschla, Judith A. Muschla, and Erin Muschla

Weather is the condition of the atmosphere around us. Few things vary as much as the weather or are as unpredictable. Predictably, then, we have a rather large vocabulary when speaking about the weather. When your students study the weather, they should become familiar with the words in the list that follows.

air	drizzle	humidity	snow
air mass	evaporation	hurricane	storm
air pressure	Fahrenheit scale	ice	storm warning
altitude	fair	intermittent	temperature
anemometer	fog	jet stream	thunder
atmosphere	freezing point	lightning	thunderstorm
barometer	freezing rain	low pressure	tornado
blizzard	frigid	meteorologist	twister
Celsius scale	front	meteorology	variably cloudy
chance	frost	overcast	visibility
climate	funnel cloud	partly cloudy	warm
clouds	global warming	precipitation	warning
cloudy	greenhouse	rain	water vapor
cold	effect	rainbow	weather
condensation	gust	relative	weather forecast
convection	hail	humidity	wind
dew	haze	seasons	wind chill
dew point	heat	shower	wind direction
Doppler radar	high pressure	sleet	wind vane
downpour	hot	smog	

 Did you know? The common belief that lightning never strikes the same place twice is *not* true.

See List 4.44, Types of Storms; List 4.45, Types of Clouds; List 4.46, The Highs and the Lows of Weather.

Copyright © 2010 by Gary Robert Muschla, Judith A. Muschla, and Erin Muschla

List 4.44   Types of Storms

Storms can be classified according to precipitation, wind speed, and location. Some storms can be weak; others, unfortunately, can be powerful and cause much destruction.

- *Blizzard*: Very heavy snow with visibility of less than a quarter mile and winds of 35 mph (56 kmph) or more
- *Extratropical low pressure*: A nontropical low pressure system
- *Gale*: A weather system with wind speeds of 39 to 54 mph (63 to 87 kmph)
- *Hurricane*: An intense storm with winds of at least 74 mph (118 kmph) and very heavy rain; can result in severe flooding of coastal areas
- *Nor'easter*: A major storm moving along the northeast coast of the United States with strong winds and heavy rain and/or snow
- *Thunderstorm*: A strong storm with heavy rains, thunder and lightning; often contains powerful wind gusts
- *Tornado*: A violent storm that rotates in the shape of a funnel and extends from the clouds to the ground
- *Tropical storm*: A storm that begins in the tropics and contains heavy rain and wind speeds of 39 to 73 mph (63 to 117 kmph)
- *Typhoon*: A hurricane located in the western Pacific Ocean

Did you know? About 1,000 tornadoes occur in the United States each year, mostly in the Midwest.

See List 4.43, Weather Words; List 4.45, Types of Clouds; List 4.46, The Highs and the Lows of Weather.

Copyright © 2010 by Gary Robert Muschla, Judith A. Muschla, and Erin Muschla

The Elementary Teacher's Book of Lists

The clouds in the sky are good indicators of the weather that can be expected. There are several different kinds of clouds. Following are the most common.

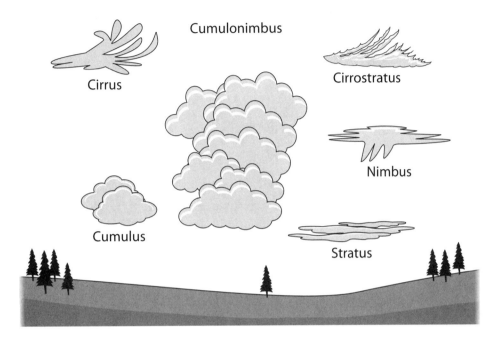

Cirrus

- Referred to as mare's tails because of their thin, wispy appearance
- High-altitude clouds, 4 mi (6.4 km) or higher
- Consist of ice crystals
- Generally occur with fair weather

Stratus

- Gray, much like a blanket
- Low-altitude clouds from near the surface to 1 mi (1.6 km) high
- Generally result in cloudy days

Cirrostratus

- Spread out like thin, white sheets
- Can cause a halo around the sun or moon as light tries to shine through
- About 4 mi (6.4 km) high
- Often indicates a coming storm

Copyright © 2010 by Gary Robert Muschla, Judith A. Muschla, and Erin Muschla

Cumulus

- White, flat on bottom, heaped and puffy on top
- Between 1,500 ft (450 m) to 4 mi (6.4 km) high
- Fair-weather clouds

Nimbus

- Heavy, dark clouds
- Often bring precipitation
- May be relatively near surface but may be 4 mi (6.4 km) or higher

Cumulonimbus

- Big storm clouds associated with thunderstorms
- May be relatively near to the surface but may extend several miles high
- Often bring heavy rain, strong winds, lightning, and thunder

 Did you know? A *ceilometer* is an instrument that measures the height of clouds.

See List 4.43, Weather Words; List 4.44, Types of Storms; List 4.46, The Highs and the Lows of Weather.

Copyright © 2010 by Gary Robert Muschla, Judith A. Muschla, and Erin Muschla

List 4.46   The Highs and the Lows of Weather

The weather of different places around the world can vary considerably. But sometimes the weather can be so extreme that the events are truly noteworthy.

- Highest recorded temperature in the world: 136° F (58° C) at El Azizia, Libya, Africa, September 13, 1922

- Highest recorded temperature in the United States: 134° F (57° C) at Death Valley, California, July 10, 1913

- Lowest recorded temperature in the world: –129° F (–89° C) at Vostok, Antarctica, July 21, 1983

- Lowest recorded temperature in the United States: –80° F (–62° C) at Prospect Creek, Alaska, January 23, 1971

- Highest recorded rainfall for one year in world: 1,042 in (2,647 cm) at Cherrapunji, India, August 1860–August 1861

- Highest recorded rainfall for one year in the United States: 739 in (1,878 cm) at Kukui, Maui, Hawaii, December 1981–December 1982

- Highest recorded rainfall for one day in the world: 72 in (183 cm) at Foc-Foc, La Réunion Island (near Africa), January 7–8, 1966

- Highest recorded rainfall for one day in the United States: 43 in (109 cm) at Alvin, Texas, July 25–26, 1979

- Greatest recorded amount of snowfall for one season in U.S.: 1,140 in (2,896 cm) at Rainier Paradise Ranger Station, Washington, 1971–1972

- Greatest recorded amount of snowfall for one day in the United States: 76 in (193 cm) at Silver Lake, Colorado, April 14–15, 1921

- Fastest recorded non-storm sustained winds: 231 mph (372 kmph) at Mt. Washington, New Hampshire, April 12, 1934

- Biggest recorded hail in the United States: 7 in diameter (18 cm) at Aurora, Nebraska, June 22, 2003

 Did you know? The climate of the Earth was quite different in the past and is likely to be quite different in the future.

See List 4.43, Weather Words; List 4.44, Types of Storms; List 4.45, Types of Clouds.

Copyright © 2010 by Gary Robert Muschla, Judith A. Muschla, and Erin Muschla

List 4.47   Our Solar System

Our solar system consists of the sun, the eight planets that orbit it, moons, asteroids, meteors, and comets. For a long time, ours was the only known solar system. But in recent years astronomers have found many planets orbiting many other stars. Astronomers now think that solar systems are common throughout our galaxy and probably the universe. We may not know much about these other solar systems, but we know quite a lot about ours.

The Sun

- *Location*: center of solar system
- *Diameter*: 870,000 mi (1,392,000 km); can hold 1 million earth-sized planets
- *Temperature*: estimated to be more than 27,000,000° F (15,000,000° C) at its core

Mercury

- Named after the Roman winged messenger of the gods
- *Mean distance from sun*: 36 million mi (57.9 million km)
- *Time to revolve around sun*: 88 days
- *Time to rotate on its axis*: 58 days, 15 hours, 30 minutes
- *Diameter*: 3,032 mi (4,880 km)
- *Surface*: rock and dust; plains, cliffs, craters
- *Atmosphere*: thin, mostly helium with some hydrogen
- *Mean temperature*: side facing the sun, 950° F (510° C); dark side, –346° F (–210° C)
- *Moons*: none
- *Interesting fact*: Mercury speeds around the sun at 30 mi per second (48 km per second).

Venus

- Named after the Roman goddess of love
- *Mean distance from sun*: 67.2 million mi (108.2 million km)
- *Time to revolve around sun*: 224.7 days
- *Time to rotate on its axis*: 243 days
- *Diameter*: 7,519 mi (12,100 km)
- *Surface*: rock and dust; mountains, canyons, plains
- *Atmosphere*: mostly carbon dioxide
- *Mean temperature*: 860° F (460° C)
- *Moons*: none
- *Interesting fact*: Because Venus is visible in the early morning and evening, it is known as the "morning star" and "evening star."

Copyright © 2010 by Gary Robert Muschla, Judith A. Muschla, and Erin Muschla

The Elementary Teacher's Book of Lists

Earth

- From the old English word *eorthe*, meaning "ground or soil"
- *Mean distance from sun*: 92.9 million mi (149.6 million km)
- *Time to revolve around sun*: 365.25 days
- *Time to rotate on its axis*: 23 hours, 56 minutes, 4.1 seconds
- *Diameter*: 7,926.2 mi (12,756 km)
- *Surface*: rock, soil, mountains, plains, valleys, water
- *Atmosphere*: nitrogen (78%), oxygen (21%), mix of other gases, including carbon dioxide
- *Mean temperature*: 59° F (15° C) at sea level
- *Moons*: 1
- *Interesting fact*: Earth is the only planet we know of that has life.

Mars

- Named after the Roman god of war because of reddish color of surface dust
- *Mean distance from sun*: 141.7 million mi (227.9 million km)
- *Time to revolve around sun*: 687 days
- *Time to rotate on its axis*: 24 hours, 37 minutes, 26 seconds
- *Diameter*: 4,194 mi (6,794 km)
- *Surface*: rocks, mountains, volcanoes, dust; ice at poles
- *Atmosphere*: carbon dioxide
- *Mean temperature*: –82° F (–63° C)
- *Moons*: two
- *Interesting fact*: In the past Mars had flowing water that may have supported life. Some scientists believe that bacteria may still live beneath the surface of the planet.

Jupiter

- Named after the king of the Roman gods
- *Mean distance from sun*: 483.9 million mi (778.3 million km)
- *Time to revolve around sun*: 11.9 years
- *Time to rotate on its axis*: 9 hours, 55 minutes, 30 seconds
- *Diameter*: 88,736 mi (142,800 km)
- *Surface*: liquid hydrogen and gases

Copyright © 2010 by Gary Robert Muschla, Judith A. Muschla, and Erin Muschla

- *Atmosphere*: hydrogen, helium, methane, ammonia, water
- *Mean temperature*: –234° F (–148° C)
- *Moons*: more than 60 (many quite small)
- *Interesting fact*: The Great Red Spot, a storm on Jupiter, is bigger than the Earth. It has been observed for more than 350 years.

Saturn

- Named for the Roman god of farming
- *Mean distance from sun*: 887.14 million mi (1,427 million km)
- *Time to revolve around sun*: 29.5 years
- *Time to rotate on its axis*: 10 hours, 39 minutes, 22 seconds
- *Diameter*: 74,978 mi (120,660 km)
- *Surface*: gas and gases in a liquid state
- *Atmosphere*: hydrogen and helium
- *Mean temperature*: –288° F (–178° C)
- *Moons*: 47 (many quite small)
- *Interesting fact*: Saturn is circled by rings of ice and rocks. The rings might be the remains of a moon that never formed, or one that was destroyed.

Uranus

- Named after the ancient Greek god of the heavens
- *Mean distance from sun*: 1,783.98 million mi (2,870 million km)
- *Time to revolve around sun*: 84 years
- *Time to rotate on its axis*: 17 hours, 14 minutes
- *Diameter*: 32,193 mi (51,810 km)
- *Surface*: covered with methane gas
- *Atmosphere*: mixture of hydrogen, helium, and methane
- *Mean temperature*: –353° F (–214° C)
- *Moons*: 27
- *Interesting fact*: Unlike the other planets that were known in ancient times, Uranus was the first planet discovered with a telescope. William Herschel discovered it in 1781.

Neptune

- Named after the Roman god of the sea
- *Mean distance from sun*: 2,796.5 million mi (4,497 million km)
- *Time to revolve around sun*: 164.8 years
- *Time to rotate on its axis*: 16 hours, 6 minutes

Copyright © 2010 by Gary Robert Muschla, Judith A. Muschla, and Erin Muschla

Copyright © 2010 by Gary Robert Muschla, Judith A. Muschla, and Erin Muschla

List 4.47   **continued**

- *Diameter*: 30,775 mi (49,528 km)
- *Surface*: gases in a liquid state
- *Atmosphere*: hydrogen, helium, methane, ammonia
- *Mean temperature*: –353° F (–214° C)
- *Moons*: 8
- *Interesting fact*: Triton, Neptune's largest moon, is thought to be the coldest place in the solar system at –393° F (–236° C)

Did you know? In 2006, Pluto, once the ninth planet, was reclassified as a dwarf planet. In 2008, the term *plutoid* was first used to describe "Pluto-like" dwarf planets.

See List 4.48, Beyond Our Solar System.

List 4.48   Beyond Our Solar System

We are most familiar with our own star (the sun), planets, moons, and other objects that make up our solar system. But space extends far beyond our solar system and contains billions of galaxies, each containing billions of stars. The following are all beyond our solar system.

- *Binary stars*: A pair of stars that travel through space together around a common center of gravity; also known as double stars
- *Black hole*: A region of space around a once massive star that has collapsed and where gravity is so intense that not even light can escape
- *Constellation*: One of eighty-eight groups of stars that appear as a pattern when viewed from Earth
- *Exoplanets* (also *extrasolar planets*): Planets beyond our solar system that orbit a star other than our sun
- *Galaxy*: A group of billions of stars that move together through space
- *Milky Way*: Our galaxy
- *Nebula*: An interstellar cloud of gas and dust; the birthplace of stars
- *Neutron star*: A small dense star that results from a supernova
- *Pulsar*: A rapidly spinning neutron star that emits regular bursts of radiation
- *Quasars*: Distant objects that give off energy equal to that of thousands of galaxies
- *Stars*: Immense, bright hot balls of gas that give off light and heat generated by nuclear fusion
- *Supernova*: A violent explosion of a massive star
- *Universe*: Space and all existing things

 Did you know? Most scientists believe that the universe has been expanding ever since the Big Bang. Many think that it will keep expanding. Some, however, think that one day the expansion will stop and reverse, leading to a massive collapse appropriately described as the Big Crunch. (Fortunately, should that happen, it will not be for several billion years.)

See List 4.47, Our Solar System.

Copyright © 2010 by Gary Robert Muschla, Judith A. Muschla, and Erin Muschla

Inventions make our lives easier. They help us to work efficiently, enable us to communicate with each other, or simply entertain and amuse us. The following list contains some of these inventions and the inventors.

Invention	Date	Inventor
Paper	105	Ts'ai Lun
Magnifying glass	1250	Roger Bacon
Eyeglasses (wearable)	1284	Salvino D'Armate
Movable type	1447	Johann Gutenberg
Microscope	1590	Zacharias Janssen
Telescope	1608	Hans Lippershey
Adding machine	1642	Blaise Pascal
Piano	1709	Bartolomeo Cristofori
Mercury thermometer	1714	Gabriel Fahrenheit
Sunglasses	1752	James Ayscough
Steam engine	1769	James Watt
Bifocal lenses (for glasses)	1780	Benjamin Franklin
Parachute	1785	Jean Pierre Blanchard
Cotton gin	1794	Eli Whitney
Modern pencil	1795	Nicolas Jacques Conté
Electric battery	1800	Alessandro Volta
Kaleidoscope	1817	Sir David Brewster
Stethoscope	1819	René T.M.H. Laënnec
Elastic fastenings	1820	Thomas Hancock
Balloons (toy)	1824	Michael Faraday
Matches	1827	John Walker
Lawn mower	1831	Edwin Budding and John Ferrabee
Postage stamp	1837	Rowland Hill
Steel plow	1838	John Deere
Vulcanized rubber	1844	Charles Goodyear
Sewing machine	1846	Elias Howe
Safety pin	1849	Walter Hunt
Safety elevator	1852	Elisha G. Otis
Potato chips	1853	George Crum
Telephone	1876	Alexander G. Bell
Microphone	1877	Emile Berliner
Phonograph	1877	Thomas A. Edison
Electric light bulb	1879	Thomas A. Edison
Electric iron	1882	Henry Seely
Bicycle	1885	James Starley
Motorcycle	1885	Gottlieb Daimler
Coca-Cola	1886	Dr. John Pemberton
Dishwasher	1886	Josephine Cochran
Record player	1887	Emile Berliner
Portable camera	1888	George Eastman

Copyright © 2010 by Gary Robert Muschla, Judith A. Muschla, and Erin Muschla

List 4.49   continued

Invention	Date	Inventor
Ballpoint pen	1888	John Loud
Drinking straws	1888	Marvin Stone
Zipper	1891	Whitcomb L. Judson
Motion picture projector	1894	Charles F. Jenkins
Automobile (gasoline)	1892	Charles E. Duryea and J. Frank Duryea
Wireless telegraph	1895	Guglielmo Marconi
X-ray	1895	Wilhelm Roentgen
Pepsi-Cola	1898	Caleb Bradham
Propeller airplane	1903	Orville and Wilbur Wright
Windshield wipers	1903	Mary Anderson
Ice cream cones	1904	Ernest Hamwi
Popsicles	1905	Frank Epperson
Vacuum cleaner	1907	J. Murray Spangler
Air conditioning	1911	Willis H. Carrier
Toaster (automatic pop-up)	1919	Charles Strite
Band-Aid®	1920	Earle Dickson
Lie detector (polygraph)	1921	John Larson
Frozen packaged foods	1924	Clarence Birdseye
Television (iconoscope)	1924	Vladimir K. Zworykin
Kool-Aid	1927	Edwin Perkins
Television (electronic)	1927	Philo Taylor Farnsworth
Animated cartoons	1928	Walt Disney
Penicillin	1928	Alexander Fleming
Chocolate chip cookies	1930	Ruth Wakefield
Parking meter	1932	Carl Magee
Ice cube trays	1933	Guy Tinkham
Computer	1936	Konrad Zuse
Helicopter	1939	Igor Sikorsky
Microwave oven	1945	Percy L. Spencer
Velcro	1948	Georges D. Mestral
Play-Doh	1956	Noah McVicker and Joseph McVicker
AstroTurf	1965	James Faria and Robert Wright
Word processor	1965	IBM
Video game (Pong)	1972	Nolan Bushnell
Compact disk (CD)	1972	RCA
Electronic pocket calculator	1972	Van Tassel
CAT scanner	1973	Godfrey N. Hounsfield
Space shuttle	1977	NASA
World Wide Web	1990	Tim Berners-Lee
Segway Personal Transporter	2001	Dean Kamen
Hybrid car	2003	Toyota

Copyright © 2010 by Gary Robert Muschla, Judith A. Muschla, and Erin Muschla

 Did you know? With 1,093 patents to his credit, Thomas A. Edison is probably the greatest inventor of all time.

List 4.50 Checklist for a Successful Science Program

A successful science program is the result of a variety of important conditions. Evaluating your program according to the following can help you develop a science program that is interesting, stimulating, and enjoyable for your students.

- ☑ Science is a fundamental part of your overall curriculum.
- ☑ Content and material are organized around broad scientific concepts.
- ☑ Equipment, materials, and supplies for demonstrations and experiments are available.
- ☑ Instruction is geared to the students' capabilities and preferred learning styles.
- ☑ Science activities involve students in investigation and exploration.
- ☑ Activities foster problem-solving skills.
- ☑ Opportunities are provided for individual and group work.
- ☑ Mathematics is an essential component of your science program.
- ☑ Communication, both written and oral, is encouraged and supported.
- ☑ Students are provided opportunities to discuss and share ideas about procedures and results.
- ☑ Technology is integrated with lessons and activities whenever possible.
- ☑ Assessment includes problem-solving, application of concepts, process skills, and general knowledge of topics.
- ☑ The classroom environment promotes positive attitudes about science and curiosity about our world.

Did you know? Science offers us the chance to understand all that is.

Copyright © 2010 by Gary Robert Muschla, Judith A. Muschla, and Erin Muschla

Social Studies

Social studies examines the development of civilizations and all that affects them. It enables us to learn about and understand the past so that we can understand the present and plan for the future. It is through social studies that your students will come to know the world.

List 5.1   Continents of the Earth

A *continent* is a very large land mass. There are seven continents that together cover about 30% of the Earth's surface. The continents are listed here from largest to smallest, with useful facts about each.

Asia

- Contains about 30% of the world's land area and more than 60% of its population
- Area: 17,383,000 sq mi (45,024,300 sq km)
- Highest point above sea level: Mt. Everest, Nepal-China, 29,035 ft (8,850 m)
- Lowest point below sea level: Dead Sea, Israel-Jordan, 1,312 ft (400 m)

Africa

- Contains about 20% of the world's land area and about 12% of its population.
- Area: 11,667,000 sq mi (30,225,400 sq km)
- Highest point above sea level: Mt. Kilimanjaro, Tanzania, 19,340 ft (5,895 m)
- Lowest point below sea level: Lake Assal, Djibouti, 512 ft (156 m)

North America

- Contains about 16% of the world's land area and about 8% of its population
- Area: 9,417,000 sq mi (23,396,400 sq km)
- Highest point above sea level: Mt. McKinley, United States, 20,320 ft (6,194 m)
- Lowest point below sea level: Death Valley, United States, 282 ft (86 m)

South America

- Contains about 12% of the world's land area and about 6% of its population
- Area: 6,879,000 sq mi (17,821,200 sq km)
- Highest point above sea level: Mt. Aconcagua, Argentina, 22,834 ft (6,960 m)
- Lowest point below sea level: Peninsula Valdez, Argentina, 131 ft (40 m)

Antarctica

- Contains about 9% of the world's land area and 0% of its population (except for a small number of scientists)
- Area: 5,400,000 sq mi (13,989,600 sq km)
- Highest point above sea level: Vinson Massif, 16,864 ft (5,140 m)
- Lowest point below sea level: Unknown because of thick ice sheet

Copyright © 2010 by Gary Robert Muschla, Judith A. Muschla, and Erin Muschla

Europe

- Contains about 7% of the world's land area and 13% of its population
- Area: 3,807,000 sq mi (9,856,900 sq km)
- Highest point above sea level: Mt. Elbrus, Russia, 18,510 ft (5,642m)
- Lowest point below sea level: Caspian Sea, Russia, 94 ft (29 m)

Australia

- Contains about 5% of the world's land area and 0.5% of its population
- Area: 2,968,000 sq mi (7,686,900 sq km)
- Highest point above sea level: Mt. Kosciusko, 7,310 ft (2,228 m)
- Lowest point below sea level: Lake Eyre, 49 ft (15 m)

  Note: Some geographers consider Australia to be part of Oceania, which also includes New Zealand and many Pacific islands.

Did you know? Because of shifting tectonic plates, the Earth's continents are in slow but constant motion. Over geologic time, their shape, size, and locations have varied greatly. Some 200 million years ago, for example, the continents were massed together in a supercontinent called Pangaea. Since then, they have separated and moved apart to their present locations.

See List 5.2, Oceans of the Earth.

Copyright © 2010 by Gary Robert Muschla, Judith A. Muschla, and Erin Muschla

List 5.2   Oceans of the Earth

The oceans cover about 70% of the Earth's surface. When sharing the following facts about oceans with your students, you might want to mention that the Pacific is nearly four times as big as the continent of Asia.

Pacific Ocean

- Area: 63,800,000 sq mi (165,250,000 sq km)
- Average depth: 14,040 ft (4,280 m)
- Deepest point: in the Mariana Trench off Guam, 36,201 ft (11,034 m)

Atlantic Ocean

- Area: 31,830,000 sq mi (82,440,000 sq km)
- Average depth: 10,925 ft (3,330 m)
- Deepest point: in the Puerto Rican Trench, 27,493 ft (8,380 m)

Indian Ocean

- Area: 28,360,000 sq mi (73,440,000 sq km)
- Average depth: 12,790 ft (3,900 m)
- Deepest point: in the Java Trench, 24,442 ft (7,450 m)

Arctic Ocean

- Area: 5,440,000 sq mi (14,090,000 sq km)
- Average depth: 3,950 ft (1,205 m)
- Deepest point: in the Eurasian Basin, 18,050 ft (5,502 m)

 Did you know? The ocean's tides are caused by the gravitational pull of the moon, and to a lesser extent by the sun.

See List 5.1, Continents of the Earth; List 5.5, The Earth's Largest Seas.

Copyright © 2010 by Gary Robert Muschla, Judith A. Muschla, and Erin Muschla

List 5.3   The Highest Mountains on Earth

Every continent on Earth has mountains. The greatest, however, are located in Asia.

- Everest, Nepal/Tibet:
  29,035 ft (8,850 m)
- K2, India/China:
  28,250 ft (8,611 m)
- Kanchenjunga, India/Nepal:
  28,208 ft (8,598 m)
- Lhotse, Nepal/Tibet:
  27,890 ft (8,501 m)
- Makalu I, Nepal/Tibet:
  27,790 ft (8,470 m)
- Dhaulagiri I, Nepal:
  26,810 ft (8,172 m)
- Manaslu I, Nepal:
  26,760 ft (8,156 m)
- Cho Oyu, Nepal:
  26,750 ft (8,153 m)
- Nanga Parbat, India:
  26,660 ft (8,126 m)
- Annapurna I, Nepal:
  26,504 ft (8,078 m)

 Did you know? Outside of Asia, the world's highest mountain is Mt. Aconcagua in South America. It is 22,834 ft (6,960 m) high.

See List 5.4, The Highest Mountains in North America.

Copyright © 2010 by Gary Robert Muschla, Judith A. Muschla, and Erin Muschla

List 5.4 The Highest Mountains in North America

Although none of North America's mountains rank among the world's highest, many surpass 15,000 ft (457 m) in elevation. Following are the highest.

- McKinley, Alaska, United States: 20,320 ft (6,194 m)
- Logan, Canada: 19,580 ft (6,050 m)
- Orizaba, Mexico: 18,700 ft (5,700 m)
- St. Elias, United States/Canada: 18,008 ft (5,489 m)
- Popocatéptl, Mexico: 17,887 ft (5,452 m)
- Foraker, United States: 17,400 ft (5,304 m)
- Ixtaccihuatl, Mexico: 17,343 ft (5,286 m)
- Lucania, Canada: 17,147 ft (5,226 m)
- King, Canada: 16,971 ft (5,173 m)
- Steele, Canada: 16,644 ft (5,073 m)
- Bona, United States: 16,552 ft (5,045 m)
- Blackburn, United States: 16,391 ft (4,996 m)

 Did you know? The highest mountain in Central America, which geographers consider to be a part of North America, is Volcán Tajumulco in Guatemala at 13,845 ft (4,220 m) in elevation.

See List 5.3, The Highest Mountains on Earth.

Copyright © 2010 by Gary Robert Muschla, Judith A. Muschla, and Erin Muschla

List 5.5   The Earth's Largest Seas

The typical *sea* is a large area of salt water within an ocean. Many seas are partially or almost completely surrounded by land. Most geographers consider major gulfs and bays to be seas. Following are notable seas located around the world.

- South China Sea: 1,148,500 sq mi (2,974,600 sq km)
- Caribbean Sea: 1,063,000 sq mi (2,753,000 sq km)
- Mediterranean Sea: 970,000 sq mi (2,510,000 sq km)
- Bering Sea: 890,000 sq mi (2,304,000 sq km)
- Sea of Okhotsk: 611,000 sq mi (1,580,000 sq km)
- Gulf of Mexico: 600,000 sq mi (1,550,000 sq km)
- Sea of Japan: 377,600 sq mi (978,000 sq km)
- Hudson Bay: 316,000 sq mi (819,000 sq km)
- East China Sea: 290,000 sq mi (750,000 sq km)
- Andaman Sea: 308,000 sq mi (798,000 sq km)
- North Sea: 220,000 sq mi (570,000 sq km)
- Black Sea: 163,000 sq mi (422,000 sq km)
- Red Sea: 174,000 sq mi (450,000 sq km)
- Baltic Sea: 149,000 sq mi (386,000 sq km)

 Did you know? The Caspian Sea, located in Europe and Asia, is not a sea but a vast saltwater lake. It is 143,630 square miles (372,000 square kilometers).

See List 5.2, Oceans of the Earth.

Copyright © 2010 by Gary Robert Muschla, Judith A. Muschla, and Erin Muschla

A *lake* is a large body of inland water. Although most lakes contain fresh water, some, such as the Great Salt Lake in Utah, are saltier than ocean water. Following are the world's largest natural lakes, the continents on which they are found, and their size.

- Caspian Sea, Asia and Europe: 143,630 sq mi (372,000 sq km)
- Superior, North America: 31,700 sq mi (82,103 sq km)
- Victoria, Africa: 26,828 sq mi (69,484 sq km)
- Huron, North America: 23,050 sq mi (59,699 sq km)
- Michigan, North America: 22,300 sq mi (57,757 sq km)
- Tanganyika, Africa: 12,700 sq mi (32,893 sq km)
- Baikal, Asia: 12,162 sq mi (31,499 sq km)
- Great Bear, North America: 12,028 sq mi (31,153 sq km)
- Nyasa, Africa: 11,100 sq mi (28,749 sq km)
- Great Slave, North America: 11,031 sq mi (28,570 sq km)
- Erie, North America: 9,910 sq mi (25,667 sq km)
- Winnipeg, North America: 9,417 sq mi (24,390 sq km)

Did you know? The Great Lakes—Superior, Huron, Michigan, Erie, and Ontario—collectively are the largest body of freshwater in the world.

See List 5.7, The Earth's Longest Rivers.

Copyright © 2010 by Gary Robert Muschla, Judith A. Muschla, and Erin Muschla

List 5.7   The Earth's Longest Rivers

Rivers are large natural streams of water that empty into another body of water, such as an ocean, lake, or another river. While most rivers are only a few miles long, some flow for thousands of miles. The following list contains the world's longest rivers, the continents on which they are found, and their length.

- Nile, Africa: 4,132 mi (6,650 km)
- Amazon, South America: 4,000 mi (6,437 km)
- Yangtze, Asia: 3,915 mi (6,300 km)
- Mississippi-Missouri, North America: 3,741 mi (6,020 km)
- Yenisey, Asia: 3,443 mi (5,540 km)
- Huang, Asia: 3,395 mi (5,464 km)
- Ob, Asia: 3,361 mi (5,409 km)
- Parana, South America: 3,032 mi (4,880 km)
- Congo, Africa: 2,900 mi (4,700 km)
- Amur, Asia: 2,761 mi (4,444 km)
- Lena, Asia: 2,734 mi (4,400 km)
- Mekong, Asia: 2,700 mi (4,400 km)

 Did you know? At 201 feet (61 meters), the Roe River in Montana is the shortest river in the world.

See List 5.6, The Earth's Largest Lakes.

Copyright © 2010 by Gary Robert Muschla, Judith A. Muschla, and Erin Muschla

Because of its size, the United States is often divided into regions. Along with general locations, states in particular regions may share similar geography, history, foods, and traditions. Following are six of the most common regions into which the United States is divided.

New England

Maine	Massachusetts	New Hampshire
Vermont	Connecticut	Rhode Island

Middle Atlantic

New York	New Jersey	Pennsylvania	Delaware	Maryland

South

Virginia	West Virginia	Kentucky	Missouri	
Tennessee	North Carolina	South Carolina	Georgia	
Alabama	Mississippi	Louisiana	Florida	Arkansas

Midwest

Ohio	Michigan	Wisconsin	Minnesota	North Dakota	
South Dakota	Iowa	Illinois	Indiana	Nebraska	Kansas

Southwest

Oklahoma	Texas	New Mexico	Arizona

West

Colorado	Wyoming	Montana	Washington	Oregon	
Idaho	Utah	Nevada	California	Alaska	Hawaii

Did you know? The regional terms "New England" and "Northeast" are often used synonymously. But there is a difference. The Northeast usually refers to the six New England states plus the Mid-Atlantic states of New York, New Jersey, and Pennsylvania.

Copyright © 2010 by Gary Robert Muschla, Judith A. Muschla, and Erin Muschla

List 5.9   Your Place in the World

The Earth is very big. Our homes occupy a very small place in the world. The following list shows a breakdown.

Earth
↓
Your Continent
↓
Your Country
↓
Your Geographic Region
↓
Your State or Province
↓
Your County
↓
Your City, Town, or Township
↓
Your Home

 Did you know? The Earth is a member of the solar system, which is a part of the Milky Way Galaxy, which is a part of the universe, which many scientists believe has no end.

Copyright © 2010 by Gary Robert Muschla, Judith A. Muschla, and Erin Muschla

The Elementary Teacher's Book of Lists

List 5.10   Pilgrim Facts

The Pilgrims left England for the New World in search of religious freedom. They established the first permanent English colony in what was to become New England. Following are facts about these early colonists.

- At the time of settlement, the colonists were not called Pilgrims. The term would not be used to describe them for nearly two hundred years.
- The colonists left Plymouth, England, on September 16, 1620.
- There were 102 colonists, including men, women, and children.
- Only 35 of the 102 colonists were members of the English Separatist Church seeking religious freedom. The others included personal servants, indentured servants, and adventurers.
- The colonists sailed on the *Mayflower*. It has been estimated that the *Mayflower* was only about 90 feet (27 m) long. That is less than one-third of the length of a football field from goal line to goal line.
- The colonists' original destination was the mouth of the Hudson River, near present-day New York City. But the *Mayflower* wandered off course during its voyage.
- The *Mayflower* dropped anchor off what is present-day Provincetown, Massachusetts, on November 21, 1620.
- The adult men soon drafted and signed the *Mayflower Compact*. This was the first constitution written in the New World.
- Searching for a good location for their colony, the colonists landed on Plymouth on December 21, 1620. That date is celebrated in New England as Forefather's Day.
- The first winter of the new colony brought much suffering. Forty-five of the 102 colonists died from disease, famine, and the harsh conditions.
- The first Thanksgiving was held in autumn, late 1621. But this hardly resembled the Thanksgivings most Americans celebrate. The colonists held a simple ceremony in which they gave thanks to God for their survival.

 Did you know? The early settlers of Plymouth were referred to as the Old Comers, and later as the Forefathers.

See List 5.11, The Thirteen Colonies.

Copyright © 2010 by Gary Robert Muschla, Judith A. Muschla, and Erin Muschla

List 5.11   The Thirteen Colonies

More than twenty early colonies were established in what was to become the United States. Of these, thirteen eventually emerged.

Colony	Date Founded	Founder
Connecticut	1636	Thomas Hooker
Delaware	1638	Peter Minuit
Georgia	1733	James Oglethorpe
Maryland	1634	George Calvert
Massachusetts	1630	John Winthrop
New Hampshire	1630	John Mason
New Jersey	1660	Lord Berkeley
New York	1626	Peter Minuit
North Carolina	1653	Group of proprietors
Pennsylvania	1682	William Penn
Rhode Island	1636	Roger Williams
South Carolina	1670	Group of proprietors
Virginia	1607	John Smith

Did you know? In 1663, King Charles II granted the Carolina territory to eight proprietors (nobles). The proprietors then divided the territory into North and South Carolina.

See List 5.10, Pilgrim Facts.

Copyright © 2010 by Gary Robert Muschla, Judith A. Muschla, and Erin Muschla

The Elementary Teacher's Book of Lists

List 5.12   Colonial Firsts

The thirteen colonies were unique in the world's history. Following are significant events that helped shaped their development and eventually led to the creation of the United States.

1507: The name "America" appears in a geography book for the first time. The name is based on Amerigo Vespucci, who is given credit for discovering what is recognized as a new continent.

1565: The Spanish found the first permanent European colony in North America at St. Augustine, Florida. The colony led the way for future English colonies in Virginia and Massachusetts.

1587: Virginia Dare is the first English child born in the New World. She is born on Roanoke Island off the coast of North Carolina on August 18. The colony, however, fails.

1607: The first permanent English colony is founded at Jamestown, Virginia.

1608: By the end of this year, Jamestown's trade with England includes lumber and iron ore.

1609: Tobacco is grown by the Virginia colonists. It soon becomes an important export product.

1619: The Virginia House of Burgesses convenes in Jamestown. It is the first legislative assembly in America.

1620: Colonists from England, eventually to be called the Pilgrims, land at Cape Cod, Massachusetts. The Mayflower Compact is written and signed by forty-one men. The Compact is the first written constitution in the New World.

1620: In Virginia, the first public library in the colonies is established. The books are donated by English landowners.

1624: Dutch colonists land in New York.

1626: Peter Minuit purchases Manhattan Island from Native Americans for about $24. He names the island New Amsterdam.

1633: The colonies' first town government is organized in Dorchester, Massachusetts.

1636: Roger Williams founds Rhode Island. Williams is a supporter of religious tolerance and Rhode Island soon becomes a destination for colonists seeking religious freedom.

1638: The first printing press in the colonies is set up in Cambridge, Massachusetts.

1652: Slavery is declared illegal in Rhode Island.

1664: The English seize control of the Dutch New Amsterdam and rename the colony New York.

1682: William Penn founds Pennsylvania.

1693: The College of William and Mary is founded in Virginia.

1701: Yale College is founded in Connecticut.

Copyright © 2010 by Gary Robert Muschla, Judith A. Muschla, and Erin Muschla

1704:   *The Boston News-Letter*, the first successful newspaper in the colonies, is published.

1714:   Tea is imported to the American colonies for the first time.

1729:   *The Pennsylvania Gazette* is first published by Benjamin Franklin. The paper eventually becomes the most popular paper in the colonies.

1731:   Benjamin Franklin founds the first public library in Philadelphia.

1732:   Benjamin Franklin begins publishing *Poor Richard's Almanac*.

1752:   The first general hospital in America is founded in Philadelphia.

1753:   With the establishment of a postal service, Benjamin Franklin and William Hunter are appointed as postmasters general for the colonies.

1764:   Colonists start protesting Parliament's increasing actions designed to raise money from the colonies. Calls for no taxation without representation are voiced.

1770:   Rising tensions result in British troops firing on a crowd in Boston in what becomes known as the Boston Massacre. Three Americans are killed and two others are mortally wounded.

1773:   After Parliament passes the Tea Act, giving British merchants an advantage in selling tea in America, a group of colonists disguised at Indians boards English ships in Boston harbor and throws tea overboard.

1774:   The first Continental Congress is held at Philadelphia. The Congress drafts a petition calling on King George III to rectify colonial grievances and calls for continued resistance against British unfair trade practices.

1775:   The American Revolution begins with the Battle of Lexington and Concord.

1776:   On July 4, the Declaration of Independence is approved by delegates from the thirteen colonies.

Did you know? In 1215, the Magna Carta was signed by King John in England. By limiting the power of the king and guaranteeing liberties to the people, the document was an important step toward democracy.

See List 5.13, Famous Men and Women of Colonial America.

Copyright © 2010 by Gary Robert Muschla, Judith A. Muschla, and Erin Muschla

Copyright © 2010 by Gary Robert Muschla, Judith A. Muschla, and Erin Muschla

List 5.13   Famous Men and Women of Colonial America

The colonial period in America was a remarkable time, dominated by remarkable people. A few of the most noteworthy are recalled in the following list.

- *John Adams* (1735–1826): A delegate to the First and Second Continental Congress, John Adams led the movement for independence. He later became the second president of the United States.

- *Samuel Adams* (1722–1803): An American patriot, Samuel Adams was one of the leaders of resistance to British policy in Massachusetts. He promoted the formation of the Boston Chapter of the Sons of Liberty.

- *Ethan Allen* (1738–1789): A patriot of the American Revolution, Ethan Allen was the leader of the Green Mountain Boys and a champion of statehood for Vermont.

- *Benedict Arnold* (1741–1801): An American military leader who was noted for distinguished service in the Continental Army, Benedict Arnold subsequently committed treason, an act for which he is most remembered.

- *Crispus Attucks* (c. 1723–1770): Of African American and Native American ancestry, Crispus Attucks was one of five people killed in the Boston Massacre. He is considered to be a heroic figure in American history.

- *John Berkeley* (1602–1678): Along with Sir George Carteret, John Berkeley, First Baron Berkeley of Stratton, founded the colony of New Jersey, naming it after the island of Jersey in the English Channel.

- *George Calvert* (c. 1580–1632): George Calvert, first Baron Baltimore, founded the colony of Maryland in 1634.

- *Charles Cornwallis* (1738–1805): A British general and statesman, Cornwallis suffered defeat at Yorktown, Virginia in 1781, an event that led to the end of the Revolutionary War.

- *Benjamin Franklin* (1706–1790): A printer, author, diplomat, philosopher, and scientist, Benjamin Franklin's contributions to the cause of the American Revolution and the new federal government were considerable. He is one of America's greatest statesmen.

- *Thomas Gage* (1721–1787): A British general and colonial governor in America, Thomas Gage was commander of all British forces in North America. His rigorous enforcement of unpopular British measures aggravated tensions with the colonists.

- *Thomas Hooker* (c. 1586–1647): A Congregationalist clergyman, Thomas Hooker was a founder of the colony of Connecticut.

- *King George III* (1738–1820): The king of Great Britain and Ireland, George III reigned during the Revolutionary War.

- *Alexander Hamilton* (1755–1804): An American statesman, Alexander Hamilton was the principal writer of *The Federalist Papers.*

- *John Hancock* (1737–1793): An American patriot and statesman, John Hancock was a member of the Continental Congress (serving as its president for the first two years) and the first man to sign the Declaration of Independence.

- *Patrick Henry* (1736–1799): An American orator and statesman, Patrick Henry, in 1775, urged the adoption of a resolution to establish a state of defense in Virginia. He is known for his famous quote: "I know not what course others may take, but as for me, give me liberty or give me death!"

- *John Jay* (1745–1829): An American statesman, John Jay was a member of the bar who represented American merchants protesting British restrictions on the commerce of the colonies. He became a member of Continental Congress, wrote a series of articles known as "The Federalist," and served as the first chief justice of the United States.

- *Thomas Jefferson* (1743–1826): An American revolutionary leader and political philosopher, Thomas Jefferson was the author of the Declaration of Independence and the third president of the United States.

- *Marquis de Lafayette* (1757–1834): A French military leader who fought on the side of the colonists during the American Revolution, Lafayette later played a prominent part in the French Revolution.

- *James Madison* (1751–1836): Known as the father of the Constitution because of his strong role in the Constitutional Convention, James Madison was secretary of state under Thomas Jefferson and became the fourth president of the United States.

- *Francis Marion* (c. 1732–1795): An American general who proved to be an excellent guerrilla leader, Francis Marion was called the Swamp Fox. After attacking British forces, he would retreat to the swamps of South Carolina, which were unfamiliar to the British and frustrated their pursuit.

- *John Mason* (1586–1635): John Mason served as a governor of an English colony in Newfoundland, helped colonize Maine, and founded the colony of New Hampshire.

- *Peter Minuit* (1580–1683): As a representative of the Dutch West India Company, Peter Minuit purchased Manhattan Island from Native Americans for about $24.

- *James Oglethorpe* (1696–1785): James Oglethorpe was the founder of the colony of Savannah, which became the colony of Georgia.

- *Thomas Paine* (1737–1809): An Anglo-American political philosopher, Thomas Paine wrote *Common Sense*, influencing public opinion to support the American Revolution.

- *William Penn* (1644–1718): The founder of the colony of Pennsylvania, William Penn planned and named the city of Philadelphia.

Copyright © 2010 by Gary Robert Muschla, Judith A. Muschla, and Erin Muschla

List 5.13   continued

- *Molly Pitcher* (1754–1832): Molly Pitcher was born Mary Ludwig. She came to be called Molly Pitcher as she carried pitchers of water to her husband, John Hays, and other soldiers at the Battle of Monmouth.

- *Paul Revere* (1735–1818): An American silversmith, engraver, patriot, and folk hero, Paul Revere participated in the Boston Tea Party and served as a messenger for the colonists. The events of his famous ride described in Henry Wadsworth Longfellow's poem "Paul Revere's Ride," however, were inaccurate. British scouts detained Revere, preventing him from completing his mission of warning patriots of approaching British troops. Fortunately, another rider was able to warn the patriots in time.

- *Betsy Griscom Ross* (1752–1836): Although Betsy Ross is the reputed maker of the first flag of the United States, there is no conclusive evidence that she actually did.

- *John Smith* (c. 1579–1631): John Smith was one of the men who established the first permanent English settlement in America at Jamestown, Virginia, in 1607. His able leadership of the colony through its first two years helped ensure its survival.

- *George Washington* (1732–1799): A member of the Continental Congress and the commander in chief of the Continental Army, George Washington became the first president of the United States.

- *Roger Williams* (1603–1683): Founder of the colony of Rhode Island, Roger Williams was an early believer in democracy and religious freedom.

- *John Winthrop* (1588–1649): An early leader of the colony of Massachusetts, Winthrop helped found the New England Confederation in 1643.

 Did you know? There is no evidence that George Washington cut down a cherry tree and later confessed his act to his father.

See List 5.12, Colonial Firsts; List 5.14, Causes of the Revolutionary War; List 5.15, Events Leading Up to the American Revolution; List 5.17, Great Events of the American Revolution.

Copyright © 2010 by Gary Robert Muschla, Judith A. Muschla, and Erin Muschla

Several factors in the relationship between the colonies and Great Britain moved the colonies to declare their independence. Following are the underlying causes of the war.

- The British viewed the colonies simply as colonies to be used for the benefit of Great Britain. The colonists believed that they were entitled to the full rights of Englishmen.

- As a result of several years of war with other nations of Europe, by 1760 Britain had substantial war debt. Britain hoped to raise money from its North American colonies.

- To raise money from the colonies, Britain attempted to control trade and increase taxes. But the colonists resented British control and what they considered to be taxation without representation.

- Having contributed men and money to the British war efforts against the French during the French and Indian Wars, the colonies had militias. Although the militias lacked the training of British soldiers, they had weapons and knew how to fight.

- Many American churches were founded by dissidents who had left England in search of religious freedom. Their ties to England were not strong.

- Many American leaders were influenced by the liberal thinking of the Enlightenment. They believed in republican ideas that a government's authority was derived from the governed.

- Having settled a frontier, many colonists tended to be rugged individuals. Most who were born in the colonies had never been to England. They believed in liberty and self-governance.

 Did you know? It has been estimated that up to 20% of the colonists remained loyal to Great Britain. After the war, many of these colonists returned to Great Britain or moved to Canada, Florida, or the British islands in the Indies.

See List 5.15, Events Leading up to the American Revolution.

Copyright © 2010 by Gary Robert Muschla, Judith A. Muschla, and Erin Muschla

List 5.15   Events Leading up to the American Revolution

Although the American Revolution started at the Battle of Lexington and Concord with what Emerson described as the "shot heard round the world," the steps toward revolution began several years earlier. The following events made war difficult to avoid.

1760: The population of the thirteen colonies is about 1.6 million. It is already large enough to support militias and an army.

1764: In seeking to raise revenues, Parliament passes the Sugar Act, which increases duties on non-British goods shipped to the colonies. Passage of the Currency Act prohibits the colonies from issuing their own currency. Both acts anger the colonists.

1765: Passage of the Quartering Act requires the colonies to provide barracks and supplies to British troops. The Stamp Act is the first direct tax on the colonies. Items including newspapers, almanacs, pamphlets, legal documents, dice, and playing cards are now taxable. Special stamps are placed on items to show that the tax has been paid. Colonists respond with organized protests. Secret organizations such as the Sons of Liberty are formed.

1766: Although Parliament repeals the Stamp Act, it passes the Declaratory Act, which states that Parliament can pass laws on the colonies.

1767: Parliament passes the Townshend Acts, which tax items including tea, glass, lead, paint, and paper. In response, the colonies discourage the purchase of imported British goods.

1768: With colonial opposition to British policies increasing, British troops are sent to Boston.

1770: The colonies boycott of imported British goods causes Parliament to repeal much of the Townshend Acts. But the tax on tea continues. Conflict between British troops and citizens in Boston results in the Boston Massacre.

1772: Committees of Correspondence are created throughout the colonies for the purpose of communicating events.

1773: Parliament reduces the tax on imported British tea. This gives British merchants an advantage in selling tea in America and leads to the Boston Tea Party.

1774: Great Britain responds to the Tea Party by tightening its control over the colonies, particularly Massachusetts. An expansion of the Quartering Act of 1765 further angers the colonists, who organize more protests. The first Continental Congress meets in Philadelphia to discuss a united resistance. As the British begin to fortify Boston, many colonists in New England conclude that war is inevitable. Preparations for war begin.

Copyright © 2010 by Gary Robert Muschla, Judith A. Muschla, and Erin Muschla

1775: Parliament passes the New England Restraining Act, which prohibits New England from trading with any country other than Great Britain. Tensions continue to mount. When the British attempt to destroy American munitions at Concord, the Battle of Lexington and Concord results. It is the beginning of the war.

 Did you know? The actual battle at Lexington erupted with a shot from a stray British gun.

See List 5.14, Causes of the Revolutionary War.

Copyright © 2010 by Gary Robert Muschla, Judith A. Muschla, and Erin Muschla

The following words have special significance to the American colonial period and Revolutionary War. They are necessary to any discussion about the times and events.

Act: A formal written record, statement, or law

Colonist: A settler or founder of a colony

Colony: A town, city, or territory controlled by a distant state

Commerce: Trade between states or nations

Committee: A group of people chosen to act on a matter

Congress: An assembly in which delegates represent regions or states

Crown (the): A reference to the king, George III

Delegate: A person chosen to formally represent others

Export: Goods sent to another country for sale

Frontier: An unsettled region; the lands west of the colonies

Import: Goods brought into a country for sale

Independence: Not being subject to the authority of another; autonomous

King: King George III, sovereign male ruler of Great Britain

Liberty: Freedom

Loyalist: A person remaining faithful to Great Britain and King George III

Militia: A military organization manned by ordinary citizens who are called up only when needed

Minutemen: Special groups of colonial militia who were ready for fast action

Musket: A rifle common during the colonial period

Neutralists: Colonists who did not take the side of loyalists or patriots

Parliament: The supreme law-making body of Great Britain

Patriot: A colonist who supported independence from Great Britain

Petition: A formal request for action, usually submitted to authorities

Protest: An objection

Rebel: A person who resists the authority of the government

Rebellion: Organized resistance to a government

Redcoats: A term describing British soldiers, who wore red coats

Representation: The act of serving others in a legislative body

Republic: A government in which sovereignty resides in the people and leaders are elected by the people

Resolution: The act of deciding or determining to do something

Revolution: The overthrow of a government by those governed

Sons of Liberty: An American patriotic society that supported independence

Copyright © 2010 by Gary Robert Muschla, Judith A. Muschla, and Erin Muschla

Tax: Money demanded by a government from its citizens to support the government

Town meeting: A general meeting in which the concerns of citizens are discussed

Trade: Commerce

Traitor: A person who betrays another or commits treason

Treason: A crime of disloyalty to a ruler

Tyrant: A person who holds great power; a ruler who exercises great power cruelly

Unalienable right: A basic right that cannot be taken away by government

Did you know? The phrase "No taxation without representation" was one of the greatest rallying cries during the colonial period.

See List 5.14, *Causes of the Revolutionary War*; List 5.15, *Events Leading up to the American Revolution*; List 5.17, *Great Events of the American Revolution*.

Copyright © 2010 by Gary Robert Muschla, Judith A. Muschla, and Erin Muschla

List 5.17 Great Events of the American Revolution

The American Revolution began in 1775 and formally ended with the Treaty of Paris in 1783. In the terms of the treaty, Great Britain recognized the independence of its former thirteen colonies as the United States of America. The boundaries of the new country extended west to the Mississippi, north to Canada, and south to Florida. The revolution was highlighted by many significant events. Some of the most significant and memorable follow.

- The British General Thomas Gage sends men to seize munitions that the colonists are gathering at Concord, Massachusetts. When the Boston Committee of Safety learns of this, they send Paul Revere and two other men on the night of April 18, 1775, to warn the patriots and gather the Minutemen.

- The war begins on April 19, 1775, with the Battle of Lexington and Concord.

- On May 10, the Second Continental Congress meets at Philadelphia. The delegates recognize that the war has begun, and they establish Congress as the central government of "the United Colonies of America." The delegates also unanimously vote to appoint George Washington as the commander in chief of what will become the Continental Army.

- In June 1775, the Battle of Bunker Hill takes place. This was the only battle in the siege of Boston. Although the Americans were forced to retreat, they proved to be an effective fighting force against a professional army.

- On January 1, 1776, *Common Sense*, written by Thomas Paine, appears. The pamphlet advances the movement toward independence.

- In March 1776, after the Battle of Dorchester Heights, the British are forced to leave New England.

- On July 4, 1776, the Continental Congress adopts the Declaration of Independence.

- On December 26, 1776, George Washington leads his men across the Delaware River and defeats Hessian soldiers in Trenton.

- On January 3, 1777, Washington defeats a British force under the command of General Charles Cornwallis in the Battle of Princeton. The British are forced to retreat to New York.

- In September and October 1777, after British victories in the Battles of Brandywine Creek and Germantown, the British seize Philadelphia.

- On October 17, 1777, colonial forces defeat the British at Saratoga, New York. Many historians believe this to be a turning point, because it convinces the French that the Americans have a chance of winning the war.

- In 1778, France recognizes American independence and joins the war on the side of the colonies.

- In June 1778, colonial forces defeat the British at Monmouth, New Jersey. During the battle, Molly Pitcher carries water to the colonial soldiers.

Copyright © 2010 by Gary Robert Muschla, Judith A. Muschla, and Erin Muschla

- In December 1778, the British seize Savannah, Georgia, in a campaign to seize the southern colonies.

- In 1779, Spain joins France in the war against Great Britain. The British now face major wars in America and Europe.

- In May 1780, the British capture Charleston and gain control of the South.

- In autumn of 1781, American and French forces defeat the British at Yorktown, Virginia. On October 19, Washington accepts the surrender of General Cornwallis at Yorktown. Except for minor hostilities, the war is over.

- On September 3, 1783, the Treaty of Paris is signed, officially ending the war.

Did you know? British concessions in the Treaty of Paris nearly doubled the size of the new nation.

See List 5.15, Events Leading up to the American Revolution.

Copyright © 2010 by Gary Robert Muschla, Judith A. Muschla, and Erin Muschla

List 5.18   Facts About the Declaration of Independence

The Declaration of Independence is among the most famous political documents ever written. It declared the American colonies to be free and independent states. It also proclaimed that all men are created equal, and that governments derive their power from the consent of the governed. Following are noteworthy facts about the Declaration of Independence.

- The first step toward the declaration was taken on June 7, 1776. Richard Henry Lee of the Virginia delegation to the Continental Congress put forth a resolution that the colonies had the right to be free, independent states. John Adams seconded the motion.
- On June 11, a committee, including Thomas Jefferson, Benjamin Franklin, John Adams, Roger Sherman, and Robert R. Livingston, was appointed to prepare a declaration based on Lee's resolution.
- Thomas Jefferson was the principal writer of the declaration.
- The first part of the declaration outlines American citizens' basic rights. The second part describes many of the grievances the colonies had against Great Britain.
- The Continental Congress adopted the Declaration of Independence on July 4, 1776.
- The declaration was adopted by a unanimous vote of the delegates of twelve colonies.
- The delegates of New York did not vote, because they had not been authorized to do so. Only July 9, the New York Provincial Congress voted to endorse the declaration.
- The document was finally signed on August 2, 1776, by fifty-three members of the Continental Congress. Three members who were absent signed later.

 Did you know? On July 8, 1776, the Liberty Bell was rung to call citizens to hear the first public reading of the Declaration of Independence.

See List 5.19, Facts About the Constitution; List 5.20, Facts About the Bill of Rights.

Copyright © 2010 by Gary Robert Muschla, Judith A. Muschla, and Erin Muschla

List 5.19   Facts About the Constitution

The Constitution sets the principles and basic laws on which the U.S. government is based. Following are facts about the writing and ratification of the American Constitution.

- In 1781, the Articles of Confederation, first proposed in 1776, were ratified by all thirteen states. The new official title of Congress was The United States in Congress Assembled.

- By 1786, it had become clear that the national government was weak and ineffective.

- In February 1787, Congress called for a Constitutional Convention to revise the Articles of Confederation.

- The Constitutional Convention met in Philadelphia on May 25, 1787.

- All states, except Rhode Island, which opposed revising the Articles of Confederation, sent delegates.

- George Washington was chosen as president of the convention.

- Many issues of government were discussed, and all major issues were eventually resolved through compromise.

- On September 12, 1787, the convention concluded the writing of the Constitution. The Constitution begins with the preamble, which states that the U.S. government was created by the people and for the benefit of the people. Seven Articles, or sections, follow:

  ○ Article I creates the legislative branch of the government. It describes the House of Representatives and the Senate, and the responsibilities and powers of each. (Together the House of Representatives and the Senate are referred to as Congress.)

  ○ Article II creates the executive branch and describes the responsibilities and powers of the president.

  ○ Article III creates the judicial branch of the government and describes the Supreme Court and the court system.

  ○ Article IV describes the rights and powers of the states.

  ○ Article V describes how amendments can be made to the Constitution.

  ○ Article VI states that the Constitution embodies the laws of the country.

  ○ Article VII explains how the Constitution would be ratified by the states.

- Thirty-nine of fifty-five of the delegates at the convention signed the Constitution.

Copyright © 2010 by Gary Robert Muschla, Judith A. Muschla, and Erin Muschla

List 5.19   continued

- Ratification took several months. Only the states of Delaware, New Jersey, and Georgia ratified the Constitution unanimously.
- Rhode Island was the last state to ratify, on May 29, 1790, by only two votes.

 Did you know? Rhode Island ratified the Constitution only after Congress threatened to regard the hold-out state as a foreign nation and impose duties on its exports to other states.

See List 5.18, Facts About the Declaration of Independence; List 5.20, Facts About the Bill of Rights; List 5.21, The Branches of the United States Government.

Copyright © 2010 by Gary Robert Muschla, Judith A. Muschla, and Erin Muschla

List 5.20   Facts About the Bill of Rights

The first ten amendments to the Constitution are known as the Bill of Rights. These amendments guarantee individual freedoms to the people. Following are facts about the Bill of Rights.

- Some people feared that the Constitution would make the national government too strong. These people were called antifederalists.
- The antifederalists wanted the Constitution to guarantee certain rights to citizens.
- The Bill of Rights includes the following amendments:
  - The First Amendment guarantees freedom of religion, freedom of speech, and freedom of the press.
  - The Second Amendment guarantees the right of the people to have firearms.
  - The Third Amendment prohibits soldiers from staying in a house without the owner's consent.
  - The Fourth Amendment prohibits the government from unreasonably searching people and their homes.
  - The Fifth Amendment provides that every person has the right to a trial. It also protects a person's rights while awaiting trial. Finally, it says that property cannot be taken without payment.
  - The Sixth Amendment says that every person has the right to a speedy, public trial.
  - The Seventh Amendment guarantees the right to a trial in different kinds of legal cases.
  - The Eighth Amendment makes "cruel and unusual punishment" illegal.
  - The Ninth Amendment says that people have rights that are not written in the Constitution.
  - The Tenth Amendment explains that any powers the Constitution does not give to the national government belong to the states and the people.
- The Bill of Rights became a part of the Constitution on December 15, 1791.

Did you know? There are a total of twenty-seven amendments to the Constitution.

See List 5.18, Facts About the Declaration of Independence; List 5.19, Facts About the Constitution.

Copyright © 2010 by Gary Robert Muschla, Judith A. Muschla, and Erin Muschla

List 5.21   The Branches of the United States Government

The federal government of the United States is divided into three branches: the executive branch, the legislative branch, and the judicial branch. The powers provided by the Constitution to each branch allow it to limit, or check, the powers of the other two branches. This is called the system of checks and balances. Following are descriptions of the branches of the federal government.

The Executive Branch

- The president is the head of the executive branch.
- The president is elected by the voters of the country.
- The president serves for a term of four years. He may run for another term, and, if elected, serve a second term.
- It is the president's responsibility to approve and carry out the laws passed by the legislative branch of the government.
- Other duties of the president include:
  - Appointing or removing cabinet members
  - Negotiating treaties
  - Serving as the commander-in-chief of the nation's military
- The executive branch of government also includes the vice president and members of the cabinet. The cabinet members are the heads of the federal government's major departments.

The Legislative Branch

- The legislative branch of the federal government is the Congress. It is made up of the House of Representatives and the Senate.
- The most important function of the legislative branch is to make laws.
- The House of Representatives contains 435 members. Each member is known as a representative. The number of representatives a state has is based on its population. States with larger populations have more representatives than states with smaller populations. Representatives are elected by the voters in their states to serve two-year terms. They are often reelected. The head of the House of Representatives is the Speaker of the House. He or she is elected by the members of the House.
- The Senate contains 100 members, two from each state. Senators are elected by the voters in their states to serve six-year terms. They are often reelected.

Copyright © 2010 by Gary Robert Muschla, Judith A. Muschla, and Erin Muschla

List 5.21   continued

The Judicial Branch

- The judicial branch of the federal government is made up of the Supreme Court and the other courts.
- The purpose of the judicial branch is to interpret the laws of the Constitution.
- The Supreme Court is the highest court in the nation. Nine judges, called Justices, currently serve on the Supreme Court. The president has the authority to nominate the Justices. The Justices must then be appointed "by and with the advice and consent of the Senate." Decisions of the Supreme Court cannot be overturned by any other court.

 Did you know? The Supreme Court can declare laws passed by Congress unconstitutional.

See List 5.19, Facts About the Constitution.

Copyright © 2010 by Gary Robert Muschla, Judith A. Muschla, and Erin Muschla

List 5.22   Famous Native Americans

Many Native Americans played significant roles in history. Following are some of the most famous.

- *Hiawatha* (Iroquois): A great leader, Hiawatha helped convince five Iroquois tribes—the Onondagas, the Senecas, the Cayugas, the Oneidas, and the Mohawks—to form the Five Nations of the Iroquois Confederacy. Henry Wadsworth Longfellow wrote "The Song of Hiawatha," which was loosely based on his life.

- *Squanto* (Wampanoag): Squanto helped the settlers of the Plymouth Colony survive by teaching them how to fish and plant corn. He also served as an interpreter between Governor William Bradford and Chief Massasoit at the Treaty of Plymouth.

- *Pocahontas* (Powhatan): Pocahontas is one of the best known Native Americans. The story that she saved the life of John Smith of the Jamestown settlement in Virginia is probably untrue. That she played a part in the relationships between the Powhatan and the English in Virginia is undisputable. She married John Rolfe, one of the original settlers.

- *Pontiac* (Ottawa): Pontiac was a chief who fought the British in the Great Lakes region. He organized a confederacy that at one time included tribes from the Great Lakes almost to the Gulf Coast.

- *Sacajawea* (Shoshone): Sacajawea married a French trapper named Toussaint Charbonneau. In 1804, she and Charbonneau accompanied Meriwether Lewis and William Clark to explore what was to become the western part of the United States. Sacajawea proved to be invaluable as a guide and interpreter.

- *Black Hawk* (Sauk): Black Hawk was a war chief. A fierce warrior, he fought settlers in Wisconsin and Illinois.

- *Sequoya* (Cherokee): Sequoya invented the Cherokee alphabet, which enabled thousands of Cherokee to learn to read and write. The sequoia tree and Sequoia National Park in California are named after him.

- *Osceola* (Creek): Osceola's mother was the daughter of a Creek chief and his father was a British trader. When he was very young, his mother took him to live in northern Florida. Eventually Osceola became a leader of the Seminoles and fought in the Second Seminole War of 1835 in Florida.

- *Tecumseh* (Shawnee): Tecumseh was a chief in the Ohio region in the early 1800s. He tried to unite native tribes to oppose white settlers.

- *Red Cloud* (Lakota): Red Cloud is remembered as being one of the most successful Native American warriors to ever confront the U.S. military. He waged what is known as Red Cloud's War in southern Montana and northern Wyoming.

- *Crazy Horse* (Lakota): Crazy Horse was a leader in the Great Sioux War in the mid-1870s. He was an opponent of the U.S. government throughout his life.

Copyright © 2010 by Gary Robert Muschla, Judith A. Muschla, and Erin Muschla

- *Geronimo* (Apache): Although not a chief, Geronimo was a great military leader. He fought the U.S. government for much of his life.
- *Sitting Bull* (Sioux): A holy man, Sitting Bull helped defeat George Custer at the Battle of Little Bighorn 1876. At one time he was a performer in Buffalo Bill's Wild West Show.
- *Cochise* (Apache): Cochise was a chief of the Chiricahua Apache in Arizona. He led the fight against white settlers.
- *Chief Joseph* (Nez Percé): A chief of his tribe, Joseph led his people in resisting white settlement in the western United States. He was known and respected for his courage and military skill.

Did you know? After marrying John Rolfe, Pocahontas traveled with him to England, where she met the king and queen.

Copyright © 2010 by Gary Robert Muschla, Judith A. Muschla, and Erin Muschla

List 5.23   Famous Figures of American Folklore

American folklore mixes fact, fantasy, and symbolism in stories that tell of the growth of the new nation. It embodies the beliefs, traditions, and customs of common people. Following are some of the most well-known characters in American folklore.

- *Paul Bunyan*: A lumberjack, Paul Bunyan never found an obstacle he could not overcome. He traveled the West with his blue-ox, Babe.
- *Febold Feboldson*: A pioneer who was said to have come from Sweden, Febold Feboldson could bust any drought on the prairie.
- *Mike Fink*: Known as the King of the Keelboaters, Mike Fink symbolized the tough men who ran keelboats up and down the Ohio and Mississippi Rivers.
- *John Henry*: John Henry was the greatest of the railroad men. Although he raced against a steam-powered hammer and won, he died soon after his victory.
- *Johnny Inkslinger*: A bookkeeper, Johnny Inkslinger used a fountain pen that was connected by a hose to a barrel of ink. It was said that he tallied the logs that Paul Bunyan cut.
- *Casey Jones*: The greatest of the railroad engineers, Casey Jones was never late.
- *Joe Magarac*: Joe Magarac was the greatest of the steelworkers. He was made of steel.
- *Old Stormalong*: Old Stormalong was one of the greatest sailors of all time. His ship was called the *Courser*.
- *Pecos Bill*: The greatest cowboy of all, one of Pecos Bill's great feats was riding a tornado.
- *Slue-Foot Sue*: As Pecos Bill's girlfriend, and, in some stories, wife, Slue-Foot Sue shared many adventures with the great cowboy.

Did you know? Many stories of folklore were first told orally and were written down only after countless tellings. This is why some stories have various versions.

Copyright © 2010 by Gary Robert Muschla, Judith A. Muschla, and Erin Muschla

List 5.24   Causes of the Civil War

The Civil War was truly an American tragedy. More American soldiers died in the Civil War than in World War I and World War II combined. Following are the major causes of the war between the states.

Slavery

- By the early 1800s, the country was becoming divided over the issue of slavery. Many people in the North opposed it, while people in the South viewed holding slaves as a right.
- As the Union grew, slave owners wanted new states to permit slavery. Northerners generally opposed this.

Economic and Social Differences Between the North and South

- The economy of the Northeast and Midwest was based on family farms and industrialization. The South had little industry and relied on growing cotton on large plantations. Slaves were vital to the South's economy.
- The population of the North was growing much faster than the population of the South. The North benefited from immigration, especially from Ireland, England, and Germany.
- Because of its slower population growth, the South was losing influence in national politics.

States Rights Versus Federal Rights

- Because a national identity had not yet fully developed, many people were more loyal to their state than the federal government. This was especially true of the South.
- Southern states believed that they had the right to ignore federal laws they viewed as unconstitutional.
- Southern states believed that they had the right to secede from the Union.

The Election of Abraham Lincoln

- The Republican Party chose Abraham Lincoln as its candidate for president in 1860.
- Because Lincoln opposed the spread of slavery, southern states thought that he would try to abolish it.
- When Lincoln won the election, the states of South Carolina, Mississippi, Florida, Alabama, Georgia, and Louisiana seceded from the Union.
- The seceding states formed a new nation—the Confederate States of America. Jefferson Davis was the new nation's president.

Copyright © 2010 by Gary Robert Muschla, Judith A. Muschla, and Erin Muschla

List 5.24   continued

- The states of Virginia, Arkansas, Tennessee, Texas, and North Carolina soon seceded and joined the Confederacy.
- War became inevitable.

 Did you know? Kentucky and Missouri were known as border states. People who supported the Union (Unionists) and those who supported secession (Secessionists) struggled for control.

See List 5.25, Great Events of the Civil War.

Copyright © 2010 by Gary Robert Muschla, Judith A. Muschla, and Erin Muschla

List 5.25   Great Events of the Civil War

The Civil War lasted four years, from 1861 to 1865. Many great and terrible events occurred during the war. The following were among the most significant.

- *Attack on Fort Sumter*, April 1861: The war begins with Confederate forces firing on Union troops at Fort Sumter, South Carolina. The troops at the fort surrender.

- *First Battle of Bull Run, Virginia*, July 1861: Southern troops gain a major victory.

- *Blockade of the South*, July 1861: The Union Navy blocks southern shipping, making it difficult for the South to import materials. To counter the Union action, the South begins building fast, small ships that can outmaneuver and outrun the larger Union vessels.

- *First naval battle between ironclad ships*, March 1862: The Confederate *Merrimac* and the Union *Monitor* fight for several hours off the Virginia coast. Although the battle ends in a draw, it signals the beginning of a new kind of naval ship. The reign of the wooden war ship was done.

- *The Battle of Shiloh, Tennessee*, April 1862: Confederate forces almost defeat Union troops, but Union reinforcements turn the battle.

- *The Second Battle of Bull Run*, August 1862: Confederate troops defeat Union troops.

- *The Emancipation Proclamation*, January 1863: On January first Lincoln issues the Emancipation Proclamation that declares all slaves in the eyes of the federal government are free.

- *The Battle of Gettysburg, Pennsylvania*, July 1863: More than 28,000 Confederate and 23,000 Union soldiers die, are wounded, or are missing in the bloodiest battle of the Civil War. It is at Gettysburg that Lincoln later delivers his "Gettysburg Address."

- *Sherman's taking of Atlanta, Georgia, and march to the sea*, August–November 1864: The Union General William T. Sherman captures and burns Atlanta. He then leads his army through Georgia to the sea, destroying everything in its path.

- *Lincoln's reelection*, November 1864: Abraham Lincoln is elected to a second term as president. Andrew Johnson is his vice president.

- *The Thirteenth Amendment to the Constitution*, January 1865: Congress passes the Thirteenth Amendment, prohibiting slavery in the United States.

- *Robert E. Lee surrenders at the Appomattox Court House in Virginia*, April 1865: With Lee's surrender to Union General Ulysses S. Grant on April 9, the war ends.

Did you know? General Grant's terms for surrender included a general pardon and allowed Lee to disband his army and send his troops home.

See List 5.24, Causes of the Civil War.

Copyright © 2010 by Gary Robert Muschla, Judith A. Muschla, and Erin Muschla

List 5.26   The Presidents

The president of the United States has often been called the world's greatest leader. Following are the individuals who have served as president.

1. **George Washington**
   Born: February 22, 1732   Died: December 14, 1799
   Political party: None
   Served as president: 1789–1797

2. **John Adams**
   Born: October 30, 1735   Died: July 4, 1826
   Political party: Federalist
   Served as president: 1797–1801

3. **Thomas Jefferson**
   Born: April 13, 1743   Died: July 4, 1826
   Political party: Democratic-Republican
   Served as president: 1801–1809

4. **James Madison**
   Born: March 16, 1751   Died: June 28, 1836
   Political party: Democratic-Republican
   Served as president: 1809–1817

5. **James Monroe**
   Born: April 28, 1758   Died: July 4, 1831
   Political party: Democratic-Republican
   Served as president: 1817–1825

6. **John Quincy Adams**
   Born: July 11, 1767   Died: February 23, 1848
   Political party: Democratic-Republican
   Served as president: 1825–1829

7. **Andrew Jackson**
   Born: March 15, 1767   Died: June 8, 1845
   Political party: Democratic
   Served as president: 1829–1837

8. **Martin Van Buren**
   Born: December 5, 1782   Died: July 24, 1862
   Political party: Democratic
   Served as president: 1837–1841

9. **William Henry Harrison**
   Born: February 9, 1773   Died: April 4, 1841
   Political party: Whig
   Served as president: 1841

Copyright © 2010 by Gary Robert Muschla, Judith A. Muschla, and Erin Muschla

10. **John Tyler**

    Born: March 29, 1790   Died: January 18, 1862

    Political party: Whig

    Served as president: 1841–1845

11. **James K. Polk**

    Born: November 2, 1795   Died: June 15, 1849

    Political party: Democratic

    Served as president: 1845–1849

12. **Zachary Taylor**

    Born: November 24, 1784   Died: July 9, 1850

    Political party: Whig

    Served as president: 1849–1850

13. **Millard Fillmore**

    Born: January 7, 1800   Died: March 8, 1874

    Political party: Whig

    Served as president: 1850–1853

14. **Franklin Pierce**

    Born: November 23, 1804   Died: October 8, 1869

    Political party: Democratic

    Served as president: 1853–1857

15. **James Buchanan**

    Born: April 23, 1791   Died: June 1, 1868

    Political party: Democratic

    Served as president: 1857–1861

16. **Abraham Lincoln**

    Born: February 12, 1809   Died: April 15, 1865

    Political party: Republican

    Served as president: 1861–1865

17. **Andrew Johnson**

    Born: December 29, 1808   Died: July 31, 1875

    Political party: Republican

    Served as president: 1865–1869

18. **Ulysses S. Grant**

    Born: April 27, 1822   Died: July 23, 1885

    Political party: Republican

    Served as president: 1869–1877

Copyright © 2010 by Gary Robert Muschla, Judith A. Muschla, and Erin Muschla

19. **Rutherford B. Hayes**

    Born: October 4, 1822   Died: January 17, 1893

    Political party: Republican

    Served as president: 1877–1881

20. **James A. Garfield**

    Born: November 19, 1831   Died: September 19, 1881

    Political party: Republican

    Served as president: 1881

21. **Chester A. Arthur**

    Born: October 5, 1829   Died: November 18, 1886

    Political party: Republican

    Served as president: 1881–1885

22. **Grover Cleveland**

    Born: March 18, 1837   Died: June 24, 1908

    Political party: Democratic

    Served as president: 1885–1889

23. **Benjamin Harrison**

    Born: August 20, 1833   Died: March 13, 1901

    Political party: Republican

    Served as president: 1889–1893

24. **Grover Cleveland**

    Born: March 18, 1837   Died: June 24, 1908

    Political party: Democratic

    Served as president: 1893–1897

25. **William McKinley**

    Born: January 29, 1843   Died: September 14, 1901

    Political party: Republican

    Served as president: 1897–1901

26. **Theodore Roosevelt**

    Born: October 27, 1858   Died: January 6, 1919

    Political party: Republican

    Served as president: 1901–1909

27. **William H. Taft**

    Born: September 15, 1857   Died: March 8, 1930

    Political party: Republican

    Served as president: 1909–1913

Copyright © 2010 by Gary Robert Muschla, Judith A. Muschla, and Erin Muschla

28. **Woodrow Wilson**

   Born: December 28, 1856   Died: February 3, 1924

   Political party: Democratic

   Served as president: 1913–1921

29. **Warren G. Harding**

   Born: November 2, 1865   Died: August 2, 1923

   Political party: Republican

   Served as president: 1921–1923

30. **Calvin Coolidge**

   Born: July 4, 1872   Died: January 5, 1933

   Political party: Republican

   Served as president: 1923–1929

31. **Herbert C. Hoover**

   Born: August 10, 1874   Died: October 20, 1964

   Political party: Republican

   Served as president: 1929–1933

32. **Franklin D. Roosevelt**

   Born: January 30, 1882   Died: April 12, 1945

   Political party: Democratic

   Served as president: 1933–1945

33. **Harry S. Truman**

   Born: May 8, 1884   Died: December 26, 1972

   Political party: Democratic

   Served as president: 1945–1953

34. **Dwight D. Eisenhower**

   Born: October 14, 1890   Died: March 28, 1969

   Political party: Republican

   Served as president: 1953–1961

35. **John F. Kennedy**

   Born: May 29, 1917   Died: November 22, 1963

   Political party: Democratic

   Served as president: 1961–1963

36. **Lyndon B. Johnson**

   Born: August 27, 1908   Died: January 22, 1973

   Political party: Democratic

   Served as president: 1963–1969

Copyright © 2010 by Gary Robert Muschla, Judith A. Muschla, and Erin Muschla

37. **Richard M. Nixon**

    Born: January 9, 1913   Died: April 22, 1994

    Political party: Republican

    Served as president: 1969–1974

38. **Gerald R. Ford**

    Born: July 14, 1913   Died: December 26, 2006

    Political party: Republican

    Served as president: 1974–1977

39. **Jimmy Carter**

    Born: October 1, 1924

    Political party: Democratic

    Served as president: 1977–1981

40. **Ronald Reagan**

    Born: February 6, 1911   Died: June 5, 2004

    Political party: Republican

    Served as president: 1981–1989

41. **George H. W. Bush**

    Born: June 12, 1924

    Political party: Republican

    Served as president: 1989–1993

42. **William J. Clinton**

    Born: August 19, 1946

    Political party: Democratic

    Served as president: 1993–2001

43. **George W. Bush**

    Born: July 6, 1946

    Political party: Republican

    Served as president: 2001–2009

44. **Barack Obama**

    Born: August 4, 1961

    Party: Democratic

    Served as president: 2009–

 Did you know? Gerald R. Ford was the only president who was not elected as either president or vice president.

See List 5.27, Presidential Trivia.

Copyright © 2010 by Gary Robert Muschla, Judith A. Muschla, and Erin Muschla

List 5.27   Presidential Trivia

Most presidents are known and remembered for their great acts. Following are some interesting but little known facts about the presidents.

- John Adams was the first president to serve in Washington, D.C.
- John Quincy Adams was the first president to be photographed. His picture was taken in 1843.
- William Henry Harrison gave the longest Inaugural Speech and served the shortest term. He died after nine months in office, probably due to complications of an illness he contracted while giving his speech on a bitterly cold day.
- Zachary Taylor's horse Whitey often grazed on the White House lawn.
- James Buchannan was the only president who was unmarried.
- Abraham Lincoln was the only president to patent an invention. He invented a device to help boats cross shallow water.
- Rutherford B. Hayes had the first telephone installed in the White House.
- Grover Cleveland was the only president to serve two nonconsecutive terms. The candy bar Baby Ruth is named after his daughter, Ruth.
- Benjamin Harrison was the only president who was the grandson of a president. His grandfather was William Henry Harrison.
- The teddy bear was named after Theodore Roosevelt.
- William H. Taft was the first president to throw the first pitch at the start of a baseball season.
- Franklin D. Roosevelt's portrait is on the dime. He was a strong supporter of the March of Dimes, an organization whose goal is to combat polio. (He was stricken with polio and spent much of his later life in a wheelchair.)
- John F. Kennedy's naval career was immortalized in the film *PT 109*.
- Gerald R. Ford was a football coach after he graduated from college.
- Richard M. Nixon was the only president to resign from office.
- Ronald Reagan starred in movies and television before he entered politics.
- George H. W. Bush was the first president to spend a holiday with the overseas troops.

 Did you know? Three presidents died on the Fourth of July: John Adams (1826), Thomas Jefferson (1826), and James Monroe (1831).

See List 5.26, The Presidents.

Copyright © 2010 by Gary Robert Muschla, Judith A. Muschla, and Erin Muschla

The Elementary Teacher's Book of Lists

List 5.28   Federal Holidays

Copyright © 2010 by Gary Robert Muschla, Judith A. Muschla, and Erin Muschla

The United States government has established ten days as federal holidays. Following are these holidays and some facts about each.

- *New Year's Day*: January 1. This holiday celebrates the ending of one year and the beginning of the next. It can be traced back to the ancient Romans.

- *Martin Luther King Jr. Day*: The third Monday in January. This day honors the birth of the civil rights leader who was born on July 15, 1929.

- *Washington's Birthday*: The third Monday in February. This day honors the birth of the first president who was born on February 22, 1732. Sometimes this holiday is called Presidents' Day to honor both George Washington and Abraham Lincoln. Lincoln was born on February 12, 1809.

- *Memorial Day*: The last Monday in May. This holiday originated in 1868 as a day for people to decorate the graves of Civil War soldiers. Now it is set aside to remember all of the war dead. Memorial Day was once called Decoration Day.

- *Independence Day*: The Fourth of July. It is the anniversary of July 4, 1776, when the thirteen colonies declared their independence from Great Britain.

- *Labor Day*: The first Monday in September. This day was first celebrated in 1882 to honor American workers.

- *Columbus Day*: The second Monday in October. This holiday marks the anniversary of Christopher Columbus's landing in the New World on October 12, 1492.

- *Veterans Day*: November 11. This holiday honors all of the veterans of the armed forces. Veterans Day was once called Armistice Day, marking the agreement that ended World War I.

- *Thanksgiving*: The fourth Thursday in November. The first Thanksgiving was observed by the Pilgrims in 1621. The Pilgrims celebrated the harvest of the Plymouth colony and gave thanks for the bountiful feast.

- *Christmas*: December 25. This holiday celebrates the anniversary of the birth of Jesus Christ.

 Did you know? Federal holidays apply to federal workers and Washington, D.C. States choose which holidays they celebrate, but most celebrate federal holidays.

See List 5.29, Other Days to Celebrate; List 5.31, Major Religious Holidays.

List 5.29   Other Days to Celebrate

Aside from federal holidays, many Americans celebrate other special days and times. Following are some of the most popular and best known.

- *Groundhog Day*: February 2. Some people believe that if a groundhog sees his shadow on this day, winter will last for six more weeks. If he does not see his shadow, winter will end in four weeks.

- *Valentine's Day*: February 14. This day is celebrated with cards, candy, and expressions of love. It is named for St. Valentine, a third-century martyr.

- *Mardi Gras*: The day before Lent begins. Also called ''Fat Tuesday,'' Mardi Gras is the time of carnivals and celebrations before Ash Wednesday, the beginning of Lent. New Orleans is famous for its Mardi Gras celebration.

- *April Fool's Day*: April 1. People play jokes on each other on this day.

- *Earth Day*: April 22. The purpose of Earth Day is to make people aware of and appreciate the environment.

- *Arbor Day*: Celebrated on different days in different states each spring. Arbor Day is a day for planting trees and recognizing the importance of the environment.

- *Mother's Day*: The second Sunday in May. This day honors mothers. Its roots can be traced to seventeenth-century England and Mothering Sunday.

- *Father's Day*: The third Sunday in June. This day honors fathers. It was first observed in 1910 in Spokane, Washington.

- *Halloween*: October 31. This day of ghosts, goblins, and jack-o-lanterns originated in ancient Britain. Druids, who were ancient priests, wore costumes and lit fires on October 31 to chase away evil spirits.

- *Kwanzaa*: December 26–January 1. This African American holiday honors African cultures and heritage.

 Did you know? One of the most famous groundhogs in the world is Punxsutawney Phil. He lives in a special habitat by the Punxsutawney Library in Pennsylvania. Each year on February 2, Phil comes out of his habitat and offers his prediction of the length of the winter.

See List 5.28, Federal Holidays; List 5.31, Major Religious Holidays.

Copyright © 2010 by Gary Robert Muschla, Judith A. Muschla, and Erin Muschla

List 5.30   Major Religions Around the World

Many people around world belong to religious groups. Following is information about the world's major religions.

Christianity

- Christianity began with Jesus Christ in the first century A.D.
- People who believe in Christianity are called Christians.
- Christians believe in one God.
- There are about two billion Christians. They are found in nearly all parts of the world.
- About one billion Christians are Roman Catholics. Other large groups are Orthodox Christians and Protestants. There are many groups of Protestants.

Islam

- Islam began with Muhammad in A.D. 610.
- People who believe in Islam are called Muslims.
- Muslims believe in one God.
- There are more than one billion Muslims. Most Muslims live in the Middle East, Northern Africa, and parts of Asia.
- About 80% of all Muslims are Sunni Muslims. Shiite Muslims are another large group.

Judaism

- Judaism began about 2000 B.C. with Abraham.
- People who believe in Judaism are called Jews.
- Jews believe in one God.
- There about fifteen million Jews around the world. Most Jews live in Israel and the United States.

Hinduism

- Hinduism began about 1500 B.C. No single individual founded Hinduism.
- People who believe in Hinduism are called Hindus.
- Hindus believe that there are many gods and goddesses.
- There are nearly one billion Hindus. Most live in India.

Buddhism

- Gautama Siddhartha began Buddhism about 525 B.C.
- People who believe in Buddhism are called Buddhists.

Copyright © 2010 by Gary Robert Muschla, Judith A. Muschla, and Erin Muschla

List 5.30   continued

- Buddhists believe that people should strive to live their lives in perfect peace. This state is called Nirvana.
- There are about 350 million Buddhists. Most live in Asia.

 Did you know? From the earliest civilizations, religion has played an important part in the lives of people.

See List 5.31, Major Religious Holidays.

List 5.31   Major Religious Holidays

Most religions have days that celebrate special events. Except for Christmas, the actual day on which major religious holidays are celebrated varies each year. Following are important holidays for Christians, Muslims, and Jews.

Christian Holidays

- *Ash Wednesday*: First day of Lent
- *Easter*: Resurrection of Jesus
- *Pentecost*: Feast of the Holy Spirit
- *Christmas Day*: Birth of Jesus

Muslim Holidays

- *Muharram*: Muslim New Year
- *Mawlid al-Nabi*: Birth of Muhammad
- *Ramadan*: Month of fasting
- *Eid al-Fitr*: End of Ramadan

Jewish Holidays

- *Passover*: Feast of unleavened bread
- *Rosh Hashanah*: Jewish New Year
- *Yom Kippur*: Day of atonement
- *Hanukkah*: Festival of lights

 Did you know? Christmas day is the only religious holiday that is also a federal holiday.

See List 5.28, Federal Holidays; List 5.30, Major Religions Around the World.

Copyright © 2010 by Gary Robert Muschla, Judith A. Muschla, and Erin Muschla

List 5.32   Famous Human-Made Structures Around the World

Throughout history, people have built impressive structures. The examples that follow are but a sampling of the many magnificent structures around the world. Although varying in design and purpose, each is proof of human beings' ingenuity and industry.

- *The Great Sphinx of Giza*: Created around 2500 B.C., the Great Sphinx is the one of the largest stone statues in the world. It is in the form of a reclining lion with the head of a man.

- *Stonehenge*: Built around 2000 B.C., Stonehenge is an arrangement of enormous stones located in southern England. Some historians believe that the arrangement is designed to measure the movement of the sun and moon.

- *The Parthenon of Greece*: Completed in 438 B.C. in Athens, the Parthenon served as a temple for the goddess Athena.

- *The Great Wall of China*: Begun in 228 B.C., the Great Wall was intended to keep barbaric tribes from attacking China.

- *The Pantheon*: Completed in the first century B.C., the Pantheon at Rome has been used as a place of worship for more than 2,000 years.

- *The Colosseum of Rome*: Officially opened in A.D. 80, the Colosseum was an enormous Roman amphitheater. Modern scholars believe it could seat at least 50,000 people.

- *The Statues of Easter Island*: Standing between ten and forty feet in height, some 900 stone statues dot Easter Island in the South Pacific Ocean, about 2,300 miles (3,700 kilometers) off the coast of Chile. The first statues were carved as early as A.D. 500. The purpose of the statues remains a mystery.

- *The Tower of London*: Begun in 1078, the central tower originally was a fortress. In time, more buildings were added and the Tower of London served as a royal residence and later as a prison.

- *Alhambra*: Built in the mid-fourteenth century, the Alhambra in Granada, Spain, is one of the greatest achievements of Muslim architecture. It was designed to be a palace and fortress of the Moorish rulers of Southern Spain.

- *The Vatican*: A number of buildings in Rome, the Vatican serves as the residence of the pope and is the center of Roman Catholicism.

- *The Taj Mahal*: Completed in 1650 at Agra, India, Shah Jahan built the Taj Mahal as a tomb for his wife. Many consider the building to be among the most beautiful in the world.

Copyright © 2010 by Gary Robert Muschla, Judith A. Muschla, and Erin Muschla

- *The Eiffel Tower*: Finished in 1889, the Eiffel Tower is one of the most well-known structures in the world. Standing 1,063 feet (324 m), it is the tallest structure in Paris.

- *Mount Rushmore*: Completed in 1941, Mount Rushmore in South Dakota contains the carved likenesses of Presidents George Washington, Thomas Jefferson, Abraham Lincoln, and Theodore Roosevelt.

- *The Statue of Liberty*: Standing on Liberty Island in New York Harbor, the statue is a symbol of freedom throughout the world.

- *The Seattle Space Needle*: Built for the 1962 Seattle World's Fair, the Space Needle rises 605 feet. An observation deck and revolving restaurant are at its top.

 Did you know? The Statue of Liberty was originally called *Liberty Enlightening the World*.

Copyright © 2010 by Gary Robert Muschla, Judith A. Muschla, and Erin Muschla

List 5.33   U.S. Landmarks

A *landmark* is a place of social, geographical, historical, or symbolic importance. Many landmarks are found throughout the United States. The following are some of the best known. There are, of course, many more.

- *The Alamo*: An old mission, the Alamo was the site of a battle between 187 Texans and 4,000 Mexican soldiers during the Texas war of independence from Mexico.

- *Arlington National Cemetery*: Arlington is a military cemetery. It covers 642 acres in Virginia on the Potomac River, opposite Washington, D.C. The Tomb of the Unknown Soldier is in Arlington.

- *Capitol Building*: The Capitol, located in Washington, D.C., is the place Congress meets and conducts business. Although the original structure was built in 1792, several modifications have been made over the years to achieve its present form.

- *Devil's Tower National Monument*: Located in Wyoming, Devil's Tower National Monument was established in 1906. It was the first national monument in the United States. A natural rock formation 1,267 feet (386 meters) tall, the monument resembles a huge petrified tree stump.

- *Empire State Building*: Built in 1931, the Empire State Building is a tourist attraction known the world over. It is 102 floors high. On a clear day, a person can see the surrounding countryside for 80 miles (129 kilometers).

- *Golden Gate Bridge*: The Golden Gate Bridge in San Francisco is among the most famous bridges in the world. Spanning the Golden Gate, the opening of San Francisco Bay to the Pacific Ocean, the bridge's total length is 8,981 feet (2,737 meters). It was completed in 1937.

- *Grand Canyon*: Located in Arizona, the Grand Canyon is an enormous valley, 277 miles (446 kilometers) long and 4 to 18 miles (6 to 29 kilometers) wide. It reaches a depth of more than 1 mile (1.6 kilometers). In 1908, a part of the Grand Canyon was established as a national monument.

- *Jefferson Memorial*: Located in Washington, D.C., the memorial honors Thomas Jefferson, the third president of the United States. Jefferson wrote the draft of the Declaration of Independence. The memorial was completed in 1943.

- *Liberty Bell*: Located in Philadelphia, the Liberty Bell was rung on July 8, 1776, at the first public reading of the Declaration of Independence.

- *Lincoln Memorial*: Located in Washington, D.C., the memorial is a tribute to Abraham Lincoln, our sixteenth president. The memorial was completed in 1922.

- *Mount Rushmore*: The likenesses of George Washington, Thomas Jefferson, Abraham Lincoln, and Theodore Roosevelt are carved into towering rock. Each likeness is between 50 and 70 feet (15 to 21 meters) high. Mount Rushmore is located in South Dakota.

Copyright © 2010 by Gary Robert Muschla, Judith A. Muschla, and Erin Muschla

- *Smithsonian Institution*: Located in Washington, D.C., the Smithsonian is a network of museums, research centers, art galleries, and the National Zoo. It includes the Museum of Natural History, the National Air and Space Museum, the African Art Museum, and the National Portrait Gallery.

- *Statue of Liberty*: The Statue of Liberty was a gift of the French people to the American people to commemorate the centennial of American independence. Located on Liberty Island at the entrance to New York Harbor, the statue has become a symbol of world freedom.

- *U.S. Holocaust Memorial:* Opened in 1993 in Washington, D.C., the museum contains material and information about the murders of more than six million Jews by Nazi Germany between 1933 and 1945.

- *Vietnam Veterans Memorial*: Located in Washington, D.C., the memorial remembers the service men and women who died during the Vietnam War.

- *Washington Monument*: Located in Washington, D.C., the memorial was built to honor George Washington, our nation's first president. It was opened to the public in 1888.

- *White House*: Located in Washington, D.C., at 1600 Pennsylvania Avenue, the White House is the official residence of the U.S. president.

 Did you know? Prior to 1956, Liberty Island was called Bedloe's Island.

See List 5.32, Famous Human-Made Structures Around the World.

Copyright © 2010 by Gary Robert Muschla, Judith A. Muschla, and Erin Muschla

List 5.34   Calendar Words and Facts

A *calendar* is a system for measuring time. It divides time into years, months, weeks, and days. Following are words and facts about calendars.

Calendar Words

- *Fall equinox*: The first day of autumn, around September 21. Day and night are about the same length.
- *Spring equinox*: The first day of spring, around March 21. Day and night are about the same length.
- *Summer solstice*: The first day of summer, around June 21. The first day of summer is the longest day of the year in the Northern Hemisphere.
- *Winter solstice*: The first day of winter, around December 21. The first day of winter is the shortest day of the year in the Northern Hemisphere.

Calendar Facts

- Throughout history, calendars have been based on the movements of the Earth, moon, and sun.
    - One day is the average time for the Earth to rotate on its axis.
    - One year is based on one revolution of the Earth around the sun.
    - In ancient times, a month was calculated on the movement of the moon around the Earth. In our modern calendar, twelve months are adjusted to fit into the solar year.
- Ancient civilizations invented calendars to keep track of time.
    - The Babylonians had a calendar based on twelve lunar months.
    - The Egyptians had a calendar based on a solar year.
    - Julius Caesar, a Roman dictator, instituted the use of a solar calendar based on 365 days with a leap year of 366 days every fourth year. Called the Julian calendar, it established the order of the months and days of the week as they are today.
- Although the Julian calendar was remarkably accurate for its time, its year was 11 minutes and 14 seconds longer than the solar year. Still, it was used throughout Europe until 1582. By then the equinoxes and solstices no longer fell on the correct dates, and some church holidays no longer occurred in the proper season. Pope Gregory XIII ordered a new calendar. This calendar, called the Gregorian calendar, was more accurate and is used throughout much of the world today.

Copyright © 2010 by Gary Robert Muschla, Judith A. Muschla, and Erin Muschla

List 5.34   **continued**

- The Gregorian calendar is not the only calendar used today. Other calendars include:
  - The Jewish calendar, which is counted from 3761 B.C.
  - The Islamic calendar, which is counted from A.D. 622
  - The Chinese calendar, which is counted from 2637 B.C.
  - The Hindu calendar (known as the Indian National calendar), which is counted from A.D. 78

 Did you know? Because of the tilt of the Earth's axis, the seasons in the Southern Hemisphere are opposite to those of the Northern Hemisphere. Thus, when it is winter north of the equator, it is summer south of the equator.

See List 3.41, Time Words.

Copyright © 2010 by Gary Robert Muschla, Judith A. Muschla, and Erin Muschla

List 5.35 Checklist for a Successful Social Studies Program

Effective social studies instruction in the primary and elementary grades provides students with the foundation for success in social studies in middle school and high school. Evaluating your social studies program according to the following criteria can help you build a program that ensures your students gain fundamental skills in a positive classroom setting.

- ☑ Social studies is never neglected; it is a vital part of your curriculum.

- ☑ Content, skills, and activities are developed around core grade-level concepts.

- ☑ Instruction meets students' individual needs and preferred learning styles.

- ☑ A broad purpose of the class is to help students understand geography and basic political, economic, and social institutions and systems.

- ☑ A consistent goal of instruction is to provide students with information and understanding of the past so that (1) they can better understand the present, and (2) they can formulate reasonable expectations for the future.

- ☑ Instruction provides students with the skills necessary for problem solving, critical thinking, and making informed decisions.

- ☑ Along with instruction designed for the whole class, activities for groups and individuals are provided.

- ☑ Communication in both written and oral form is encouraged.

- ☑ Technology is integrated with activities as much as possible. (The Internet is a powerful medium for bringing the world into the classroom.)

- ☑ Assessment focuses not only on concepts and facts but on applications of learned skills.

Did you know? Perhaps more than any other subject, social studies helps students become knowledgeable and responsible members of society.

Copyright © 2010 by Gary Robert Muschla, Judith A. Muschla, and Erin Muschla

General Reference for Elementary Teachers

Your teaching day can be filled with so many tasks and responsibilities that you may, at times, come to feel overwhelmed, stressed, and dissatisfied. The lists in this section can help make your day more manageable, less stressful, and more rewarding.

List 6.1   The Elementary Teacher's Responsibilities

Less than a generation ago, teachers were viewed as dispensers of knowledge. The teacher lectured, provided examples, and assigned work. Students learned passively, sitting at their desks, taking notes, and completing worksheets or assignments in their texts. In recent years, education has shifted from being teacher centered to student centered. Teachers are now facilitators of knowledge, and students take an active role in learning. Along with acquiring information, students learn to think critically, explore concepts, and discover insights. As the role of the student has changed, so has the role of the teacher. Following is a list of the many responsibilities of the typical elementary teacher.

- Ensures a safe classroom
- Creates a positive atmosphere that maximizes learning
- Maintains a neat and organized classroom that supports the learning efforts of students
- Establishes and maintains classroom rules and procedures
- Upholds the rules of the school
- Maintains appropriate standards for behavior
- Takes time to get to know the students in his or her class
- Is aware of the individual needs of students
- Plans lessons and activities that meet the objectives of state standards and the district's curriculum
- Designs challenging but achievable objectives and lessons based on students' readiness and prior knowledge
- Follows IEPS (Individualized Education Plans) and 504 plans
- Creates interesting lessons
- Provides differentiated instruction to meet the needs of all students and their learning styles
- Promotes the learning of study skills
- Reflects upon lessons and improves content and delivery as necessary
- Provides ongoing assessment (both formal and informal) of student work
- Utilizes various types of assessments that meet the needs of all learning styles
- Offers praise for good work
- Provides constructive criticism, support, and guidance to help students improve
- Fosters the growth of social skills in students
- Collaborates with other teachers in planning and instruction
- Organizes field trips, holiday parties, and special events
- Maintains contact with other teachers, parents, guardians, and administrators as necessary
- Establishes positive rapport with students, other staff members, and parents and guardians
- Attends faculty meetings, in-services, and workshops

Copyright © 2010 by Gary Robert Muschla, Judith A. Muschla, and Erin Muschla

List 6.1   continued

- Participates in meaningful and continuous professional development
- Becomes a valued member of his or her school community

 Did you know? Underlying all of your other responsibilities is this one: Help each student achieve more in your class than anyone would have ever thought possible.

List 6.2   Basic Materials and Supplies Your Classroom Should Have

The typical primary and elementary classrooms require a variety of materials and supplies. The following list contains the basics.

Pencils and pens	Transparencies
Erasers	Computers and printers
Markers	Calculators
Colored pencils	Maps
Chalk or dry-erase markers	Globes
Glue (sticks and bottles)	Posters
Scissors	Reference books
Rulers (metric and customary)	Novels and nonfiction books
Yardsticks and meter sticks	Rewards
Lined paper	Stickers
Notebook paper	Storage bins
Drawing paper	Storage cabinet
Graph paper	Bell
Paper trays	Timers
Construction paper (various colors and sizes)	Calendar
	Paper towels
Paper clips (assorted sizes)	Tissues
Tape	Hand sanitizer
Stapler (and staples)	Bulletin board supplies
Overhead projector	Board games for recess

 Did you know? You can never have enough boxes of tissues for your classroom.

Copyright © 2010 by Gary Robert Muschla, Judith A. Muschla, and Erin Muschla

List 6.3   How to Create a Positive Classroom Atmosphere

Whether you teach in a basement classroom in a hundred-year-old school or a classroom in a brand-new building does not matter as much as the atmosphere you create in your classroom. Students whose classrooms are neat and organized, in which routines are practical, and in which learning is valued produce better work than those whose classrooms are uninspired. The following list contains suggestions for creating a positive environment for learning in your classroom.

- Make certain that your classroom supports learning. Lighting should be adequate; lights should be bright but not harsh. The walls should be clean. Paint should be a neutral color, neither vivid nor dark. Repairs—for example, broken shades, torn rugs, or broken cabinet doors—should be done promptly.
- Arrange the furniture in your classroom to facilitate instruction and learning. Consider the following:
  - Position your desk where it will best support your teaching style. Many teachers prefer to place their desk at the front of the room; others prefer the back. Ideally, you should be able to see all of your students from your desk.
  - Place storage cabinets, carts, bookshelves, tables, and any extra chairs away from high-traffic areas but in spots that are easily accessible.
  - Arrange student desks to support instruction and activities. You might, for example, arrange desks in small groups to foster discussion. You might instead seat students in pairs so that they can work as partners. Or you may set up desks in rows for individual work. You may, of course, rearrange desks during class, depending on specific activities.
  - Make sure that all students can see the boards and screens from their seats.
  - The arrangement of furniture should allow for easy and safe movement around the classroom.
- Carefully consider seating plans. No matter how you choose to arrange the desks in your classroom, you must take into account the placement of students, for example:
  - Avoid placing talkative students near each other. If possible, they should also be out of eye sight from one another.
  - Consider placing disruptive students near your desk.
  - Avoid seating easily distracted students near areas of high traffic or interest.
  - Implement seating requirements of IEPs (Individualized Education Plans) and 504 plans.
  - Separate students who do not get along. This will reduce potential conflicts.

Copyright © 2010 by Gary Robert Muschla, Judith A. Muschla, and Erin Muschla

List 6.3   continued

- If another teacher or paraeducator works in your classroom with students, confer with her about seating. She may be able to offer helpful suggestions where a student should be placed.

- Decorate your classroom by attaching posters to walls. Posters that serve as reminders, such as for classroom rules and learning tools—for example, steps for solving word problems—are valuable additions to any classroom.

- Use bulletin boards to highlight learning concepts.

- Display the work of your students throughout the classroom.

- Place materials and supplies in easily accessible places.

- Create a safe, comfortable, and supportive environment. Show your students that you value each of them by doing the following:

  - Greet your students by name each day at your classroom door.

  - Address your students by their names throughout the day.

  - Make eye contact with all of your students when speaking to them.

  - Model positive behavior for your students.

  - Acknowledge the positive behavior of your students.

  - Use positive language; avoid using sarcasm.

  - Use positive body language. Be at ease with your students; smile often.

  - Treat all your students equally.

  - Foster an atmosphere of respect for others and acceptance of differences.

  - Get to know your students, their likes and dislikes.

- Provide opportunities for individual, paired, and group learning.

- Plan meaningful lessons and activities that relate to your students' lives.

- Provide instruction that meets the needs of diverse learning styles.

- Provide assessments that meet the needs of all learners.

- Be flexible. By coping with the surprises of each day, you are creating an environment in which your students feel safe and comfortable.

- Foster a sense of community in your classroom.

 Did you know? When you show your students your interest and excitement in learning, they will be interested and excited, too.

See List 6.4, Creating an Effective Learning Environment in an Inclusive Classroom.

Copyright © 2010 by Gary Robert Muschla, Judith A. Muschla, and Erin Muschla

List 6.4   Creating an Effective Learning Environment in an Inclusive Classroom

Although some of your special needs students may require minor, if any, modifications in the classroom, others may need special accommodations if they are to be successful in class. The following suggestions can help you to create an effective learning environment for your students.

- Make your classroom welcoming to students. Make sure it has proper lighting and its walls are clean, colorful, and visually appealing. Decorate the classroom with inspirational and interesting posters and pictures.

- Establish clear and practical classroom rules. Post procedures on the wall and remind students of the proper procedures as necessary. Enforce the rules fairly and consistently.

- Organize your classroom. Avoid clutter, which can be distracting to students. Place similar materials together. For example, placing crayons, colored pencils, markers, rulers, scissors, and tape in the same corner of the classroom makes it easy for students to obtain the materials they need. Insist that students put materials back after they are finished using them.

- Teach your students organizational skills. All of the materials of the same subjects should be kept together. Consider requiring students to use a three-ring binder for storing homework, class work, tests, quizzes, and other important papers. Make sure that students' desks are clear of unnecessary books and materials. Remind them to keep the areas around their desks clear of papers, books, sweatshirts, and so on. Once each week, provide time to clean out and organize desks.

- Require students to write down their assignments in assignment pads or agendas.

- Give shorter assignments so that students can realize success.

- Break long assignments down into smaller units. For example, divide a project into four or five parts with separate due dates for each part.

- Regularly update homework and special instructions for assignments on your school's homework hotline or Web site for students and their parents or guardians.

- Provide students with extra time when necessary to complete tasks.

- Provide time for repetition and review of ideas and facts.

- Design lessons that address diverse learning styles.

- Provide activities for the whole class, groups, and individuals.

- Use manipulatives to help make abstract ideas more concrete.

- Use technology whenever possible.

- Always speak clearly and give students time to process information. Wait for students to formulate responses to your questions.

Copyright © 2010 by Gary Robert Muschla, Judith A. Muschla, and Erin Muschla

- Keep instructions clear. Provide both verbal and written instructions one step at a time. Large print is helpful.

- Seat students where they will work best without distraction. Talkative students should be seated next to quiet ones; students with vision or hearing problems should be seated near the front of the room. There are always a few students, of course, who should be seated close to you.

- Provide tables and study carrels for students to work on specific activities.

- Provide alternate forms of assessment, including:
  - Oral tests
  - Open book tests
  - Tests without time limits
  - Portfolios
  - Creative displays and models
  - Demonstration of understanding through manipulatives
  - Projects
  - Anecdotal record of teacher's observation

- Conference with students often. Brief conferences allow your students to ask you questions, receive feedback on their work, and build confidence. Conferences allow your students to interact with you on a one-to-one basis, which is especially important for shy or quiet students.

- Become familiar with your students' strengths and weaknesses. Do not ask them to do things they are unable to do.

 Did you know? Necessary accommodations for special needs students are listed in their IEPs.

See List 6.3, How to Create a Positive Classroom Atmosphere.

Copyright © 2010 by Gary Robert Muschla, Judith A. Muschla, and Erin Muschla

List 6.5   Basic Special Education Terminology

Like most disciplines in education, special education relies on specific terminology. Teachers of inclusive classrooms, as well as other teachers whose classes include special needs students, will regularly use many of the words contained in the following list.

- *Ability grouping*: The grouping of students based on achievement in a subject or subjects
- *Advocate*: An individual who works to improve the educational program for special needs students
- *Age appropriate*: Activities and performance that fall within the norms for a student's chronological age
- *Age norms*: Ranges of performance that are based on the average performance of students in different age groups
- *Anecdotal record*: A record of observations of a student's behavior
- *Annual goals*: Yearly goals specified in a student's Individualized Education Plan (IEP)
- *Articulation*: The utterance of speech sounds
- *At risk*: A term for students who have a high probability for experiencing learning, social, or medical problems
- *Attention deficit disorder* (ADD): A classification used to describe students (or adults) who have short attention, are easily distracted, and are often impulsive
- *Attention deficit hyperactive disorder* (ADHD): A classification used to describe students (or adults) who have short attention and are easily distracted, impulsive, and hyperactive
- *Baseline measure*: The measure of behavior or performance before an instructional procedure is started and that will later be measured again
- *Behavior modification*: Procedures used to change behavior
- *Criterion-referenced tests*: Tests in which a student is evaluated according to his performance and is not compared to the performance of others
- *Declassification*: The process by which it is decided that a student no longer needs special education services
- *Deficit*: Achievement that falls short of expectations for a student
- *Developmental disorder*: A disorder that occurs at some point in a child's development which may retard progress
- *Developmental tests*: Tests that compare a student's development to others of the same age
- *Diagnosis*: A specific disorder based on evaluation
- *Disability*: A physical or mental problem that prevents a student from functioning at a normal level
- *Distractibility*: The inability to maintain attention
- *Evaluation*: A process used to determine whether a student qualifies for special education services

Copyright © 2010 by Gary Robert Muschla, Judith A. Muschla, and Erin Muschla

- *Exceptional children*: Students whose performance indicates a major gap between their ability and achievement, requiring special instruction or accommodations

- *504 plan*: A legally binding document that outlines specific classroom and instructional modifications teachers must provide for students with physical or mental disabilities but who are not in special education programs

- *Hyperactivity*: A condition in which a student is excessively active

- *Impulsivity*: Behavior characterized by actions that have little or no thought

- *Inclusive classroom*: A classroom in which a general education teacher and a special education teacher coteach general education and special education students

- *Individualized Education Plan* (IEP): A written plan developed by the special education team that states a student's goals and the methods for attaining those goals

- *Intervention*: Services designed to help a disabled student

- *Learning disability*: A disability in which students of average or above average intelligence perform well below their ability

- *Least restrictive environment* (LRE): The educational setting of special needs students who are placed where they can learn to the best of their abilities and also have contact with children without disabilities

- *Mainstreaming*: The practice of placing special needs students in regular classrooms for some or all of the school day

- *Mental age*: A student's intellectual functioning in comparison to the average for children of her age

- *Norm-referenced tests*: Tests that compare a student's performance to the performance of other students of the same age

- *Paraeducator*: An individual who assists special education teachers and general education teachers by working directly with special needs students

- *Paraprofessional*: A paraeducator

- *Placement*: The specific program to which a special needs student is assigned

- *Remediation*: A program or activity that is designed to help students overcome a weakness or disability

- *Resource room*: A room that serves a special education student's needs to learn specific skills

- *Self-contained class*: A classroom specifically for special needs students

 Did you know? When conversing with parents or guardians regarding their children, speak plainly, simply, and with consideration. Avoid labeling students based on their disabilities.

Copyright © 2010 by Gary Robert Muschla, Judith A. Muschla, and Erin Muschla

List 6.6   Basic Learning Styles

In recent years much has been written about individual learning styles. Although different authors offer different breakdowns, basic learning styles can be divided into three types: auditory, visual, and kinesthetic. Designing and presenting lessons and activities that address the learning styles of your students will maximize the benefits of your instruction. Following are some suggestions.

1. *Auditory learners* learn best through activities that rely on hearing, for example:

- Reading aloud
- Being read to
- Listening to explanations
- Class and group discussions
- Oral question and answer
- Oral review of vocabulary words
- Dramatic readings
- Oral reports
- Taking turns reading with a partner
- Retelling
- Summarizing

2. *Visual learners* learn best through activities that rely on seeing, for example:

- Silent reading
- Reading and taking notes
- Creating story boards
- Interpreting cartoons
- Photo essays
- Making a flowchart
- Writing an outline
- Studying a diagram, chart, graph, or table
- Viewing models
- Viewing maps

3. *Kinesthetic learners* learn best through hands-on activities that allow them to interact physically with materials as they complete tasks, for example:

- Working with manipulatives
- Doing experiments
- Drawing a map
- Writing answers or reports on a computer
- Using a calculator to solve math problems
- Building a model
- Playing educational games
- Acting out a scene
- Role playing
- Creating dioramas

Many activities, of course, address more than one learning style. Taking turns reading with a partner, for instance, is both auditory and visual. Writing a report on a computer is kinesthetic as well as visual.

 Did you know? Most students, despite having a preferred learning style, learn in various ways. To find more information about learning styles, visit the Web site www.learningstyles-online.com.

Copyright © 2010 by Gary Robert Muschla, Judith A. Muschla, and Erin Muschla

Assessments provide a means of determining whether your students have met specific objectives. The following list contains terms related to assessment.

- *Alternative assessment*: An assessment other than the traditional assessment provided by a test or quiz. Examples of alternative assessments include portfolios, reports, demonstrations, skits, and plays.

- *Authentic assessment*: An assessment that requires students to perform real-life tasks to show mastery of concepts.

- *Benchmark*: A description of what students are expected to know at a given time or by a specific grade. Benchmarks are often used in conjunction with standards.

- *Criterion-referenced assessment*: An assessment in which a student's performance is compared to learning objectives and to the performances of other students.

- *Critical thinking*: A thought process that requires analysis, evaluation, and reflection rather than a single-solution response. Critical thinking is also referred to as higher-order or higher-level thinking.

- *Formative assessment*: An assessment that is part of the instructional process. It provides the teacher with information about student understanding as students are learning, and allows the teacher to make adjustments in instruction in order to meet his or her objectives. Examples of formative assessment include observation, thumbs-up/thumbs-down, and student-teacher conferencing.

- *Holistic scoring*: Scoring that assigns a single overall score to an assessment, rather than scoring parts individually.

- *Inquiry*: A process in which students investigate a problem and propose a solution.

- *Norm-referenced assessment*: An assessment in which a student's performance is evaluated in relation to the performance of other students. A standardized test is an example.

- *Open-ended question*: A question in which students are required to generate a response to a problem that has no single correct answer. Sometimes open-ended questions are referred to as *open-ended tasks*.

- *Performance task*: An assessment in which students are required to apply a wide range of skills and knowledge to solve a complex problem.

- *Portfolio assessment*: An alternative assessment that is based on the evaluation of a student's work over a period of time. The focus of the assessment is on the student's developmental progress.

- *Rubrics*: Specific criteria used to evaluate students' work. A rubric describes what is being assessed, provides a scale for scoring, and helps teachers rate the work of their students.

Copyright © 2010 by Gary Robert Muschla, Judith A. Muschla, and Erin Muschla

List 6.7   continued

- *Standardized test*: An assessment that is administered and scored in the same way for all students. It is designed to measure skills and knowledge students should know at a particular time. Standardized tests are often state mandated.

- *Standards*: Statements of what students should know at a particular time.

- *Summative assessment*: An assessment that identifies what objectives students have mastered at a given point. An example of a summative assessment is a unit test.

- *Traditional assessment*: An assessment in which students respond to a variety of different kinds of questions, including multiple-choice, true/false, matching, fill-in, and short answer.

- *Validity*: An indication that an assessment measures the objective it was designed to measure.

 Did you know? Many teachers use alternative assessments to determine mastery of concepts and meet the needs of various learning styles.

See List 6.8, Alternative Assessments.

Copyright © 2010 by Gary Robert Muschla, Judith A. Muschla, and Erin Muschla

List 6.8   Alternative Assessments

Although traditional forms of assessment such as tests and quizzes remain the most common assessment tools, they do not always meet the needs of all students. Students who have poor reading skills, for example, may understand the material they are being tested on, but they may have trouble understanding the questions on the test. In recent years, various alternative assessments have become popular as a means of measuring student progress. Following are several examples.

- Checklists
- Demonstrations
- Drawings
- Interviews
- Math journals
- Models
- Online assignments
- Open book or open notebook tests
- Oral reports
- Portfolios
- Reading logs
- Reflective summaries
- Research projects
- Retellings
- Science experiments
- Self-evaluations
- Skits
- Songs
- Take-home tests

 Did you know? Alternative assessments should never entirely replace traditional tests and quizzes but be used in addition to them.

See List 6.7, Assessment Terms; List 6.9, How to Use Portfolios in Your Class.

Copyright © 2010 by Gary Robert Muschla, Judith A. Muschla, and Erin Muschla

List 6.9   How to Use Portfolios in Your Class

Portfolios are useful for displaying a student's growth over a period of time. They allow you to view each student's progress individually and allow students to become active participants in the learning process. The following tips will help you to use portfolios effectively in your classroom.

- Determine how you will use portfolios. You may use portfolios to show student progress, as an alternative form of assessment, or simply as a means for reflection on students' work.

- Decide how you will create portfolios for your students—for example, in manila folders, two-pocket folders, or binders.

- Decide where you will keep your students' portfolios—on a bookshelf, in a bin, in a cardboard box. It is generally not advisable to permit students to take their portfolios home, because students may lose them or forget to bring them back.

- Decide how often you will place work in the portfolios—once every two weeks, once each month, or once each marking period. Trying to place too many items in portfolios quickly becomes a burden; placing too few results in a portfolio that offers little insight about a student. For most teachers, one or two items every few weeks is manageable without being overwhelming.

- Determine what work will go into your students' portfolios. Depending on their age, you may allow your students to select examples of their best work. You may, of course, provide guidance by requiring students to include specific examples. The work students provide should directly relate to the purpose of the portfolio.

- Allow time for reflection. Have students periodically look through their portfolios. Their focus should be to see their progress and how they may reach future goals. You may prefer to have them answer questions such as the following:
  ○ What are the strengths of my portfolio?
  ○ What are its weaknesses?
  ○ What can I do to improve my work?
  ○ How have I improved?
  ○ Is my portfolio a good example of my work as a student? Why or why not?

 Did you know? Portfolios often provide a more comprehensive view of a student's overall achievement than traditional forms of assessment.

Copyright © 2010 by Gary Robert Muschla, Judith A. Muschla, and Erin Muschla

List 6.10   Tips for Managing Your Classroom

The establishment of practical policies and procedures is essential for effectively managing your classroom. Efficient routines offer structure, reduce confusion, and help your day run smoothly. The following tips can help you to manage your classroom with confidence and competence.

- Start each day promptly. Students should enter the classroom in an orderly manner, put their belongings away, and sit down at their desks. They should remain quiet as you take attendance, make announcements, and complete opening routines. An orderly beginning leads smoothly into the rest of the day.

- Have student volunteers distribute and collect forms and handouts.

- Always write assignments in the same place each day.

- Update your homework hotline or homework Web site daily.

- Establish a system for distributing and collecting assignments. You may have volunteers help, have students pass materials up and down rows, or have specific places where students pick up and drop off their work.

- Have additional copies of worksheets and activities available for students in case they misplace theirs. Let students know where these materials are.

- Keep separate trays on your desk (or near your desk) for homework, class work, and other papers. Either color code or clearly label the trays.

- When using manipulatives or supplies, consider pre-packing or separating materials before the lesson. This will facilitate distribution.

- Always check before a lesson that you have all the materials students will need.

- Check that any equipment you need is working before you start a lesson. Be ready in case equipment fails. For example, if you intend to use a Web site for showing your students virtual manipulatives and your school's Internet connection is down, have models on hand that you can use instead.

- Establish routines for acquiring and using materials and supplies. For example, students should take the shortest route to obtain rulers and scissors and not meander through the class. They should obtain only what they need, and always put unused materials and supplies back where they belong. They should be willing to share when necessary.

- Keep teacher materials and student materials in separate parts of the classroom. Students should not use your materials.

- Have students accept responsibility for helping you keep the classroom organized. You might have volunteers straighten bookshelves, clean and wash the boards, and make certain at the end of the day that all supplies are returned to their proper places.

- Set up procedures for moving furniture for group work. Insist that students form their groups in an orderly fashion.

Copyright © 2010 by Gary Robert Muschla, Judith A. Muschla, and Erin Muschla

The Elementary Teacher's Book of Lists

List 6.10   continued

- Establish rules for computer use, time limits, and steps for logging on and off computers.

- Establish rules for leaving class. For example, encourage students not to ask to go to the lavatory during instruction, except in the case of an emergency.

- Set up procedures for lining up to go to another class and for lunch. Students should get up from their desks and walk to the door quietly. They should proceed through the halls in an orderly manner.

- Set up routines for leaving at the end of the day. Students should check that they have written down all their assignments, packed all their books and materials, cleaned up papers around their desks, and straightened their desks. They should make sure that they got their coats, hats, gloves, and knapsacks before they line up.

 Did you know? Establishing and following practical routines enables you, and your students, to be more productive.

See List 6.11, Tips for Organizing Your Classroom; List 6.12, Tips for Managing Time.

Copyright © 2010 by Gary Robert Muschla, Judith A. Muschla, and Erin Muschla

List 6.11   Tips for Organizing Your Classroom

An organized classroom adds to a positive atmosphere and fosters learning. The following suggestions can help you organize your classroom for efficiency and practicality.

- Arrange the desks in your classroom so that all students have a clear view of you, the boards, and the screens. Whether you set up desks in rows, in pairs, or in groups, be sure there is enough room between them for students and adults to walk through the classroom easily.

- Set learning stations, computer tables, and displays in corners or at the sides of the room. They should be out of the direct line of sight of students at their desks.

- Organize your desk for productivity. Keep the top clear so that you have room to work. Keep materials neatly in the drawers. Do not allow students to sit at your desk or go into its drawers.

- Keep your keys, purse, tote bag, and other personal items in a safe place.

- Organize your file cabinet. Obtain several folders and set up files according to your needs. Consider having separate files for things such as student information, attendance records, progress reports, report card grades, seating charts, standardized test information, state standards, curriculum guides, your evaluations, and unit and lesson plans.

- Keep as many files as possible electronically. Set up folders for files on the same topic or subject. Use short, but specific names for files, for example, "Science, Unit 1." Always back up your files on flash drives or CDs.

- Utilize file cabinets, storage cabinets, and bookshelves efficiently. Avoid storing materials in boxes at the back of the room where they might eventually be forgotten or mistakenly moved and lost.

- Store similar materials and supplies together. Place the same types of materials in containers and label them. Paper should be kept in one spot; crayons, colored pencils, and markers in another; rulers, scissors, glue sticks, and tape in yet another. Choose locations that are easily accessible to your students and you.

- Store items according to the frequency of their use. Materials that are used often should be kept in the front of a storage cabinet where they can be reached easily. Those that are seldom used should be stored near the back.

- Expensive items such as calculators and batteries should be kept in locked cabinets.

- Store equipment—for example, an overhead projector—in a corner of the room, away from students so that it does not hinder classroom traffic or tempt inquisitive fingers.

Copyright © 2010 by Gary Robert Muschla, Judith A. Muschla, and Erin Muschla

List 6.11   continued

- Keep reference materials and books on the same shelves or carts.
- Allow yourself time at the end of the day to put things away so that you can start the new day without having to search for items because they are not in the right place.

 Did you know? When your students see their teacher and classroom organized, they will come to understand the value of organization.

See List 6.10, Tips for Managing Your Classroom; List 6.12, Tips for Managing Time.

Copyright © 2010 by Gary Robert Muschla, Judith A. Muschla, and Erin Muschla

List 6.12   Tips for Managing Time

No teacher ever has enough time to complete all she has to do each day. The following tips can help you mange your time in school efficiently.

- Before leaving for school, check that you have everything you will need for the day—tote bag or briefcase, lunch, transparencies you made at home last night, and the social studies tests you corrected. Arriving at school and remembering that you left an important item home is not the way to start the day.

- Obtain a calendar or planner and record dates, events, and tasks you must complete each day. Calendars and planners come in many forms, both paper and electronic, and you should select the one that works best for you. Be diligent in recording events and activities, and update your schedule regularly. Being well planned is one of the most important ways you can manage time.

- Prioritize and list the tasks you must do each day.

- Attend to memos and announcements as soon as you receive them.

- Correct and return students' work promptly. Avoid allowing papers to pile up.

- Try to handle each set of papers once. Record grades as soon as you are done correcting papers.

- Stagger tests, projects, and major activities so that you are not burdened with having too many papers to correct at the same time.

- Encourage students to make up missed work promptly.

- Keep your desk and all of your files, both paper and electronic, in order.

- Schedule your tasks for efficiency. For example, if you arrive early at school each day, do your planning before school starts. If you prefer to do your planning at home, use your time at school to complete other tasks, such as grading papers. If you have a late afternoon prep period, use that time to photocopy materials for the next day.

- Try to complete tasks in one sitting. Avoid starting, stopping, and continuing. For example, do not start planning a lesson, put the lesson aside to correct a few quizzes, then return to planning. You will lose focus and waste time.

- Use free time effectively. Even if you have only a few minutes, you can check e-mail, call a parent, or review a Web site you are considering using for an activity.

- Answer e-mails and respond to phone calls promptly. Have all the materials and information you need before responding. For instance, if a parent or guardian leaves a phone message questioning a test score, have the test and your grade book on hand when you call. This will allow you to provide accurate answers to any questions.

Copyright © 2010 by Gary Robert Muschla, Judith A. Muschla, and Erin Muschla

List 6.12   continued

- Set up practical classroom procedures. Remind students to follow the procedures.
- Enlist the aid of student helpers whenever possible. Students can help you distribute and collect papers, straighten books on shelves, and change bulletin boards.
- Address problems promptly to keep students concentrated on their work and not waste time.
- Begin meetings on time and keep focused on their purpose. Certainly some polite small talk is acceptable, but it should not lengthen the meeting or disrupt its agenda.

 Did you know? Managing time effectively will help you to get the most out of each day.

See List 6.10, Tips for Managing Your Classroom; List 6.11, Tips for Organizing Your Classroom.

Copyright © 2010 by Gary Robert Muschla, Judith A. Muschla, and Erin Muschla

List 6.13   Reward Options for Students

While keeping in mind that positive behavior is expected of students and should be understood by students as the proper way to conduct themselves, giving students rewards for appropriate behavior can be a powerful motivational tool. Following are some ways you can reward students for exemplarily actions.

- Go to lunch a few minutes early
- Be first in line
- Stay at recess a few minutes longer
- Play an educational computer game
- Choose his or her seat for a day
- Receive fun stickers
- Receive pencils or pens
- Receive a homework pass
- Choose a game at recess
- Be the teacher's helper for a day
- Receive certificates for a job well done
- Be a helper at the office
- Receive free time at the end of the day
- Have lunch with the teacher or principal
- Have lunch with a friend from another class
- Visit another class for indoor recess
- Choose a class job for a week
- Choose a book for the teacher to read to the class
- Go to another class and help younger children
- Keep a stuffed animal on his or her desk for a day
- Be a leader or captain in a class game
- Go first in a class game
- Choose fun worksheets
- Take care of the class animals for a day
- Take care of the class plants for a day

 Did you know? Limit the rewards you give, for rewards can quickly get out of hand if used too much. Reserve rewards for specific behaviors you wish to encourage.

Copyright © 2010 by Gary Robert Muschla, Judith A. Muschla, and Erin Muschla

List 6.14   Conducting Effective Conferences with Students

Conferencing with students can provide valuable insight into their progress, allow you to reinforce or reteach specific skills, and give students a chance to ask you questions that they may be reluctant to ask during a whole-class or group activity. Conferences with students need not be long to be effective. Three to five minutes is usually enough time to address specific problems or issues. A table at the back of the room or two desks pushed together in a corner are sufficient for meeting. The following tips will help you to use conferencing to enhance student learning.

- Determine the purpose of the conference. Will it be to check progress, allow time for student questions, or address a particular skill? A clear purpose helps ensure a productive conference.

- Inform students what they need to bring to the conference. This might be homework or class work, a rough draft, directions for a project, and so on.

- Provide work for the rest of the class during conferences. This should be something that students can complete independently so that they do not need to ask you questions when you are conferencing.

- Students should sit next to you or at an angle so that you can review work together. Sitting opposite you can be intimidating to some students.

- Be prepared for the conference and have notes regarding points you would like to address. For example, if you are meeting with a student about her rough draft of a story, read the story prior to the conference so that you can use the conference most effectively.

- Start the conference by noting positive points about the student's work or behavior.

- Address only one or two specific skills or issues during the conference. Trying to discuss too many items will likely be frustrating for the student, and he or she may leave the conference feeling overwhelmed.

- Ask guided questions that relate to the purpose of the conference, such as:
  - What have you done so far?
  - In what other ways might you . . . ?
  - What is going well?
  - What you are having trouble with?
  - What questions do you have?

- Be helpful and specific with your suggestions, avoid negative comments, and offer genuine praise. Instead of "You forgot to use a comma here," say "A comma is necessary before a conjunction that connects two short sentences." Instead of "You have to try harder," say "I'm confident you can do better." Instead of "Good effort," say "I can see that you put a lot of time and thought into making this project outstanding."

- Close the conference by summarizing the main points and what the student should do to continue his or her progress.

 Did you know? Conferences provide you with a wonderful opportunity to get to know your students, as well as helping them with their work.

See List 6.15, Conducting Effective Conferences with Parents and Guardians.

Copyright © 2010 by Gary Robert Muschla, Judith A. Muschla, and Erin Muschla

List 6.15   Conducting Effective Conferences with Parents and Guardians

Conferences provide a chance for teachers and parents and guardians to discuss students' progress and work together in support of learning. The following tips will help you conduct positive conferences with the parents and guardians of your students.

- Decide where you will hold your conferences. A table at the back of the room or two desks pushed together is fine. Avoid sitting behind your desk with the parent or guardian sitting in front of you, for this will make you seem aloof and distant.

- Set up a waiting area outside your classroom. Place a few chairs, and hang examples of students' work on the wall or a bulletin board.

- Check your schedule so that you have an idea of who is coming, but remember that some parents or guardians may simply show up. Try to fit them in. If you are unable to meet with them because of a full schedule, set up a conference (or a phone conference) with them for another day.

- Have a goal for the each conference. Maybe the student needs to study more for tests; perhaps she needs to complete homework consistently; or she might need to pay better attention in class.

- Be sure that files, portfolios, and grades are up to date for each student. Review information and gather examples of work. Write notes about individual students and questions you want to ask parents or guardians. Storing information for each student in a separate folder can help keep you organized.

- Anticipate questions and concerns that parents and guardians might have. For example, they may be worried that the new reading program your school has implemented is not challenging enough for their child, or, conversely, too demanding. Considering answers to such questions in advance will help prevent you from being taken off guard.

- Greet parents and guardians at the door, introduce yourself, and welcome them into your classroom. Thank them for coming.

- Provide paper and pens should parents or guardians wish to take notes. Of course, you should have a pen and paper handy to write notes of your own.

- Begin the conference with some positive comments about the student's strengths.

- During the conference, focus on the student's progress and how she might continue her good work or work to improve her achievement. Discuss any behavior problems and any other issues of concern. Always back up your statements with examples of the student's work or actions.

- Remain professional. If a parent or guardian becomes upset or defensive, calmly remind her that both of you must work together for the benefit of her child.

Copyright © 2010 by Gary Robert Muschla, Judith A. Muschla, and Erin Muschla

List 6.15   continued

- Remember to keep the conference focused on the particular student. Some parents and guardians will ask about other students, teachers, or administrators. Avoid discussing others. Refer to others only in specific circumstances that directly involve the student, and even then be careful not to say anything that might be misconstrued.

- Answer any questions parents or guardians have. If you are unable to provide an answer, say that you do not have that information and that you will check and call them tomorrow.

- Establish a plan for resolving any problems the student is confronting. Clearly explain what you will do, and offer suggestions how the parents or guardians can help their child at home.

- Summarize the main points of the conference and restate any actions that you and they have agreed to do.

- Conclude with a thank-you, and remind them to contact you with any questions or concerns they may have.

- Be sure to follow up with any actions you said you would take.

 Did you know? Parents and guardians are children's first teachers. Involving them in their children's formal education will be a big boost to their children's achievement.

See List 6.14, Conducting Effective Conferences with Students.

Copyright © 2010 by Gary Robert Muschla, Judith A. Muschla, and Erin Muschla

List 6.16   Tips for Communicating with Parents and Guardians

Not only do the best teachers know how to communicate effectively with students, they know how to communicate effectively with parents and guardians as well. The following list contains suggestions for positive communication with parents and guardians.

- Always be professional.
- Be friendly and positive.
- Be respectful and patient.
- Speak clearly.
- Listen to what the parent or guardian is saying. Remember that effective communication involves both speaking and listening.
- Avoid using educational jargon with which parents and guardians may be unfamiliar. Use layman's terms instead.
- Do not compare a student to a sibling or other student in the classroom.
- Do not talk about other students, other parents or guardians, teachers, administrators, or other school personnel.
- Avoid gossip.
- Keep a record of the times that you contact a parent or guardian.
- Before you phone or e-mail a parent or guardian, make sure you know his or her correct last name. (A student's last name may be different from that of his parents or guardians.) Make notes to organize your thoughts about the reason for your call. If you are calling about a problem, have a plan in mind to solve it. Have paper and a pen handy to write notes.
- When you speak with a parent or guardian by phone, identify yourself as his child's teacher. Refer to your notes as you speak. Listen to the parent's or guardian's response. She may be able to offer insight and have some suggestions how a problem might be solved. Write down the outcome of the conversation and any follow-up that is needed. Thank the parent or guardian for her time. Follow up as you agreed.
- When you call a parent or guardian and must leave a message, identify yourself as the student's teacher and give a very brief message about why you are calling. Do not provide specifics in case someone else listens to the message. Leave a time and phone number where you can be reached. Make a note of the time you called and the reason for the call. If you left the message with someone, note with whom.
- Avoid sending lengthy e-mails to parents or guardians about their children. Overly long messages will probably be only skimmed and important information will be overlooked. Short e-mails are useful for brief updates and great for positive messages.
- If a parent or guardian phones or e-mails you with a question about her child, respond promptly. Have any necessary information with you so that you can answer her questions thoroughly.

Copyright © 2010 by Gary Robert Muschla, Judith A. Muschla, and Erin Muschla

List 6.16   continued

- Use your discretion when you write or respond to e-mail. Do not write anything that would make you feel uncomfortable if it were read by someone else. Comments in e-mail can easily be taken out of context. If there is a problem you need to discuss with a parent or guardian, it is usually better to call or request a conference.

 Did you know? A small positive note to a parent or guardian makes a greater impression than several negative conversations.

See List 6.18, Maintaining Positive Relationships with Your Students' Parents and Guardians.

Copyright © 2010 by Gary Robert Muschla, Judith A. Muschla, and Erin Muschla

List 6.17   Suggestions for a Successful Back-to-School Night

Back-to-school night may be the first opportunity you have to meet the parents and guardians of your students. It is a time when you can introduce yourself, and explain your curriculum, policies, and expectations for the class. To make the most of your back-to-school night, consider the suggestions below.

Preparation

- Know the amount of time you will have for your presentation. This will enable you to design a presentation that will not be too short or too long.
- Plan what you will say. Include topics such as the following:
  - A basic introduction to the class
  - Your curriculum and goals
  - Class rules, procedures, and expectations
  - Class work, homework, and assessments
  - Major projects, activities, and events
  - The use of technology in your classroom
  - Grading policy
- Prepare a handout containing important information such as your school e-mail and phone number. (Do not provide your personal e-mail, phone, or home address.)
- Create a "Parent or Guardian Sign-in Sheet."
- Make sure that your classroom is neat and visually appealing. Hang up examples of students' work, set posters on walls, and display examples of texts, workbooks, and other materials students will use throughout the year.
- Practice your presentation. Make sure that its length fits your allotted time. Be sure to leave a few minutes at the end for questions.

Implementation

- Dress professionally for back-to-school night. Choose comfortable clothing.
- Arrive at school early to make sure everything is ready. Check that any equipment you will be using is working properly.
- Write your name on the board at the front of the room or outside your classroom door.
- Greet parents and guardians at your classroom's door and introduce yourself. Distributing any handouts at the door saves time during the presentation.
- Ask parents and guardians to sign-in. Have the "Parent or Guardian Sign-in Sheet," along with a pen, on a table or desk near the door (but not at the doorway). This saves time and reduces the chance that a line will form at the door.

Copyright © 2010 by Gary Robert Muschla, Judith A. Muschla, and Erin Muschla

- Begin your presentation promptly. (Do not restart for people who arrive late. Pause a moment for them to get settled, give them any handouts, and continue.)

- Speak clearly and enthusiastically. Stand straight, be confident, and make eye contact.

- Avoid speaking with any parent or guardian about her child. If necessary, tell her that you will call tomorrow to discuss any individual concerns she may have. Set up a time to call and be sure to follow through.

- Close by thanking everyone for coming and mention that you are looking forward to working with them during the year. Encourage them to contact you if a problem arises or if they have any questions or concerns.

Did you know? A PowerPoint presentation can help you make your back-to-school night a great success. Not only can you easily highlight important points, but you can print out information and give it to parents and guardians to take home.

Copyright © 2010 by Gary Robert Muschla, Judith A. Muschla, and Erin Muschla

List 6.18   Maintaining Positive Relationships with Your Students' Parents and Guardians

The support of parents and guardians for you and your program will significantly influence their child's attitude about learning. Children who see their parents or guardians and teacher working together are more likely to do well in school than children who see little cooperation between their teacher and parents or guardians. Here are some tips how you can involve parents and guardians in your program.

- Open lines of communication by doing things such as the following:
  - Always be considerate of the concerns of parents and guardians. By far most are interested in the well-being of their children.
  - Address parents and guardians by name.
  - Keep parents and guardians informed of their children's progress. E-mails, phone calls, and progress reports allow you to contact them easily.
  - Be proactive. Inform parents and guardians at the first sign of problems.
  - Encourage parents and guardians to come to back-to-school night, conferences, and special events at school.
  - Offer suggestions how they can help their children do well in school. For example, parents and guardians should check their children's assignment pads or agendas each evening.
  - Give clear directions for assignments so that parents and guardians can understand what their child is expected to do.
  - Let parents and guardians know how and when you can be contacted.
  - Respond to questions in an efficient manner.
  - Be willing to listen to the cares and worries of parents and guardians.
  - Be upbeat and positive and offer to help in whatever way you can.
- Share information by doing things such as the following:
  - Explain your policies in person at back-to-school night, on handouts for students to give to parents and guardians, or on the Web site of your school or classroom. (Knowing a policy prevents a parent or guardian from assuming you are treating his child unfairly.)
  - Inform parents and guardians of your classroom rules, school rules that directly apply to students, grading policy, homework policy, and how to make up work. Especially note when you are available to provide extra help.
  - Encourage parents and guardians to check homework hotlines or homework Web sites regularly.
  - Inform them of any special school days such as back-to-school night, conferences, or concerts.
  - Create a class newsletter or Web site and inform parents and guardians of classroom activities and events.

Copyright © 2010 by Gary Robert Muschla, Judith A. Muschla, and Erin Muschla

- With the permission of your principal, invite parents and guardians to visit your classroom to observe, and, if appropriate, take part in special events.

- Always act in a professional manner by doing things such as the following:
  - Know the standards for the grade level you teach.
  - Dress appropriately.
  - Follow school policies.
  - Treat each child fairly.
  - Avoid sarcasm.
  - Do not lose your temper.
  - Do not gossip.
  - Never talk about other students or other student's parents or guardians.

- Establish a presence outside the classroom, for example:
  - Attend PTA meetings and support their functions.
  - Go to school programs such as concerts, drama productions, or games that involve your students.
  - Consider helping with after-school activities such as being an advisor of a club, being a coach, or being a chaperone.

Did you know? Nurturing positive relationships with your students' parents and guardians requires effort, patience, and understanding.

See List 6.16, Tips for Communicating with Parents and Guardians; List 6.19, Helping Parents and Guardians Help Their Children.

Copyright © 2010 by Gary Robert Muschla, Judith A. Muschla, and Erin Muschla

List 6.19   Helping Parents and Guardians Help Their Children

Most parents and guardians want to help their children succeed in school, but they may not know how. They may have had poor experiences in school when they were growing up; they may not speak English well; or they may simply not feel confident to help their children with schoolwork. These parents and guardians will welcome your guidance. Offer them the following suggestions for helping their children in school.

- Attend back-to-school night and conferences. These events will help keep you informed of your child's programs, activities, and achievement in school.
- Attend PTA meetings and become involved with activities for parents and guardians.
- Obtain the necessary materials and supplies your child will need for school, for example, a three-ring binder, assignment pad, pencils and pens.
- Provide a quiet place at home for your child to do schoolwork. This place should contain a desk or table and adequate lighting.
- Organize school supplies. Have pencils, pens, paper, crayons, markers, a stapler and other supplies handy.
- Make it clear that you expect your child to complete his or her schoolwork. If necessary check his or her assignment pads or agenda, the school's homework hotline, or class Web site for assignments. Do not hesitate to contact the teacher by e-mail or phone in order to ensure that your child is completing his or her work.
- Set rules at home. For example, homework is to be done right after dinner, projects are to be started well in advance of due dates, and book bags and knapsacks are to be packed right after homework is finished. Rules may include limits on watching TV and time spent on the computer. Enforce the rules consistently and fairly for all your children.
- For older students, check their homework after they complete it. For younger students, check their work periodically as they complete it.
- Read to your child and encourage him or her to read to you. Read a variety of materials—novels, nonfiction books, newspaper and magazine articles, and information on Web sites. Discuss what you read. Ask questions that recall details and questions that stimulate higher-level thinking, such as:
  - Who is the main character? (detail)
  - What happened next? (detail)
  - What else might the character have done to solve the problem? (higher-level thinking)
  - What might have been the character's reason for doing that? (higher-level)
- Talk with your child about his or her school day, especially about assignments.

Copyright © 2010 by Gary Robert Muschla, Judith A. Muschla, and Erin Muschla

List 6.19   continued

- Provide opportunities for your child to write at home, for example, journal entries, grocery lists, and thank-you notes for gifts. Even e-mail can be a writing opportunity, provided the message is written with correct grammar and punctuation.

- Provide opportunities to do math. When shopping, ask your child to estimate the total cost of purchases. Counting change is a necessary skill and one you can ask your child to do whenever he or she pays for something. Recipes often rely on fractions and are an excellent means of showing the practicality of understanding fractions.

- Talk with your child about what is happening in his or her world and the world at large. Most children are like sponges; they absorb facts and ideas from simple conversation.

 Did you know? Excellent information for parents and guardians who wish to help their children in school can be found at www.internet4classrooms.com/parents.htm.

See List 6.18, Maintaining Positive Relationships with Your Students' Parents and Guardians.

Copyright © 2010 by Gary Robert Muschla, Judith A. Muschla, and Erin Muschla

Your classroom is the home of you and your students for the school day. Bulletin boards can enhance your room's appearance, as well as promote student learning. Following are some tips for planning outstanding bulletin boards.

- Provide a background. The background might be construction paper, rolled paper, or wrapping paper. Select a color that coordinates well with the room's color and that will augment the theme of the bulletin board. For example, a light brown background might be a good choice for a bulletin board about autumn. Avoid making a background too busy, which will be distracting.

- Make a border. A border will frame the board, making it more attractive.

- Designate one bulletin board, or a section of a large board, for the lunch menu, announcements, and school-related activities. Include a calendar. A calendar helps young students learn the months and days of the week, and is particularly useful for highlighting special days.

- Display the work of your students on bulletin boards. Students take pride in seeing their work displayed, but also enjoy seeing the work of others. Examples of outstanding work can inspire others to try harder.

- Display posters on your bulletin boards. Posters come in a variety of types, such as:

  - Motivational: "Success comes form hard work."

  - Procedural: "Steps for Problem Solving"

  - Informational: "Parts of a Computer"

- Change and update your bulletin boards regularly.

Did you know? You can find ideas for bulletin boards sorted by month, subject, and theme at The Teacher's Corner, www.theteacherscorner.net/bulletinboards/index.htm.

Copyright © 2010 by Gary Robert Muschla, Judith A. Muschla, and Erin Muschla

List 6.21   Tips for Planning Field Trips

Field trips are a great way to supplement your curriculum and engage students with interesting activities outside the classroom. While there are many places you can take your students—for example, a supermarket, science center, park, museum, or fire house—any field trip should relate directly to your curriculum so that optimal learning occurs. Like all other activities you plan for your students, preparation is the key. Following are suggestions for planning a successful field trip.

- If you will be going with other teachers, set up a meeting to discuss the field trip.

- Select a place for your field trip that will satisfy your educational goals and that will be interesting for your students.

- Do preliminary research. Contact the site of your field trip and find out about their hours, admissions, and any special rules. Ask about group rates or student prices.

- Check with your principal or supervisor for initial approval of your field trip.

- Contact bus companies (and any other companies that will provide transportation) to determine your travel costs.

- Check your school calendar to make sure that the day you select does not conflict with any other major school event. (Inadvertently scheduling your trip on the day of the spring concert at your school will cause problems.)

- Find out what, if any, funds are available for your trip. If funds are lacking, you will need to collect money from students for the costs. Calculate your total costs—transportation, admissions, lunch (if necessary), and any other requirements. Divide the total costs by the number of students you anticipate going, keeping in mind that some students will probably not go. You must make allowance for these students and estimate your costs accordingly.

- Obtain final approval from your principal or supervisor. Be sure to submit any necessary paperwork.

- Book the trip. Arrange for transportation and reserve your destination. Obtain letters of confirmation for each reservation you place. Put all information regarding the trip in a folder in your filing cabinet (or another safe place) from which you can easily access it if necessary.

- Ask your school's librarian to set up a display of books that relate to your upcoming field trip. This will make it easy for students to find information.

- Check with your school's nurse about any students who might have allergies or medical issues of which you need to be aware. Also, check if the nurse needs to accompany you on your field trip.

- Consider parent and guardian chaperones. Ideally, you would like individuals who are reliable and who can manage a group of students. You may prefer to contact these people individually and ask them if they will chaperone your trip.

Copyright © 2010 by Gary Robert Muschla, Judith A. Muschla, and Erin Muschla

- Write a letter to parents, announcing your upcoming field trip. Include information such as:
  - Destination
  - Purpose and goals
  - Costs
  - Dress code
  - Required items to bring, for example, a bagged lunch and snack
  - Items not to bring, for example, video games, junk foods, or beverages in glass bottles
  - Departure and return times
  - Your school e-mail address or phone number
  - Permission slip to be signed by the parent or guardian and returned to you. (*Note:* The permission slip you send home should be consistent with your school's policies. Most schools have standard permission forms.)

- One week before your trip, confirm all reservations for transportation and for your destination.

- If you are going with other teachers, meet and establish general rules for students. The rules should be consistent for each class. Also decide on activities, if any, that students will be required to complete.

- Discuss the trip with your students, including any activities. Talk about rules and behavior for the trip, and emphasize that students are to listen to the instructions of their chaperones.

- Prepare an emergency kit, including tissues, sanitary wipes, and bandages for skinned knees. (Check your school's policies regarding how much, if any, first aid you can administer should the need arise. If your school nurse is accompanying you, she will likely bring a first-aid kit and handle emergencies.)

- Ask your chaperones to come to school a little early on the day of the trip so that you can meet with them prior to the start of school. Explain their duties and provide them with an overview of the day. Also provide them with an itinerary and a list of students who will be in their groups. Depending on your school's policies, you might want to exchange cell phone numbers should someone get lost or separated.

- Before leaving the classroom, organize your students into groups with their chaperones. Make sure that all students are accounted for.

- Enjoy the trip. At its conclusion, be sure to thank your chaperones and any teachers who helped.

Did you know? Most students enjoy field trips so much that they do not realize they are learning.

Copyright © 2010 by Gary Robert Muschla, Judith A. Muschla, and Erin Muschla

List 6.22 How to Become an Expert in All the Subjects You Teach

Effective teaching begins with a thorough understanding of subject matter. The best teachers are recognized as experts in their field. They are the ones other teachers go to when they have a question about a topic. The following suggestions can help you become an expert in your class.

- Know the state standards for the subjects you teach. You can find your state standards on the Web site of your state department of education, or at www.educationworld.com.standards/state. Knowing the standards enables you to plan lessons and activities that will help your students learn the concepts and acquire the skills necessary for success at their grade level.

- Know your curriculum and its objectives for each subject. Your curriculum provides a framework for the content of that subject.

- Know the subject matter you are teaching. For example, when your school adopts new textbooks, be sure to review material before presenting it to your students. Make certain that you fully understand the material. If necessary, consult other sources for background information.

- Attend in-services, workshops, seminars, and conferences about teaching and the subjects you teach. Attending such events can help keep you current with subject matter and inspire you with new ideas, activities, and teaching methods.

- Advance your own education by enrolling in graduate courses at local or on-line universities and colleges.

- Observe other great teachers. Seeing how your colleagues manage their classrooms, plan lessons, and deliver instruction can help you improve your own skills. (Before observing another teacher, always request her permission. Although some people feel uncomfortable being observed, others will be happy to have you watch them teach.)

- Join professional organizations that can keep you informed of current issues, support your work in the classroom, and allow you the opportunity to network with other teachers. Most organizations provide journals as part of their membership. Some organizations you might consider include:

  ○ American Federation of Teachers, www.aft.org

  ○ International Reading Association, www.reading.org

  ○ National Council for Geographic Education, www.ncge.org

  ○ National Council of Teachers of English, www.ncte.org

  ○ National Council of Teachers of Mathematics, www.nctm.org

  ○ National Education Association, www.nea.org

  ○ National Science Teachers Association, www.nsta.org

- Build a professional library of books and resources that support your teaching. Along with reference books on specific subjects, include a dictionary, thesaurus, atlas, almanac, and encyclopedia.

- Remain curious and enthusiastic about learning.

 Did you know? Being an expert includes being able to admit when you do not know an answer. When a student asks you a question that stumps you, say that you are not sure of the answer but will check and tell the student tomorrow. Even better, invite the student to help you look up the answer to his question.

Copyright © 2010 by Gary Robert Muschla, Judith A. Muschla, and Erin Muschla

List 6.23   Suggestions for Managing Discipline

Like every other teacher, you are responsible for maintaining a classroom atmosphere that is conducive to learning. This requires that you manage instances of inappropriate behavior promptly and effectively. You must establish classroom rules for behavior, based on your school's policies, and enforce the rules consistently. Following are suggestions for managing common examples of misbehavior.

Tardiness

- Repeated tardiness becomes a serious problem. Not only does a late-arriving student disrupt your class, but if the tardiness is permitted to continue without consequence, other students may come to feel that they, too, can be late.

- When a student comes to your class late, instruct him or her to sit down and begin work. Give the student any materials he or she needs and ask the student to follow along. If necessary, briefly explain what the student is to do.

- Avoid detailed explanations that will extend the interruption and may lose the attention of the other students.

- Do not stop your lesson to discuss with the student his or her reason for being late, or why it is important that he or she comes to class on time.

- After you have finished the lesson, or after school, talk with the student. Ask the student why he or she was late, and emphasize that being late undermines his or her learning and interrupts the learning of others. Take steps to resolve the problem. For example, if a student is habitually tardy because her mother is late in driving her to school, contact the student's mother to discuss the importance of her daughter arriving at school on time.

Not Completing Work

- If students are to reach their greatest achievement in your class, they must complete their work.

- Establish clear rules for the completion of student work and equally clear consequences for incomplete work.

- When a student does not finish his or her work, speak to the student about the importance of completing all assignments. Explain that the skills he or she learns today are necessary for learning the skills of tomorrow. When the student does not complete today's work, he or she makes learning new material harder.

- Remind the student to stay on task during class.

- At the end of each day, check that the student has written down his or her assignments in his or her assignment pad or agenda.

- Provide the student (and his or her parents or guardians, if necessary) with strategies for completing work at home. The student should start his or her assignments after school or after dinner, and work on them until they are finished. He or she should begin long-term assignments well in advance of the due date.

Copyright © 2010 by Gary Robert Muschla, Judith A. Muschla, and Erin Muschla

- If your school has an after-school homework club, recommend that the student join.
- Ask the student's parents or guardians to check that he or she completes his or her homework each night.

Not Paying Attention in Class

- Students may not pay attention in class for a variety of reasons. They may be bored with the lesson, concerned with other things, or simply daydreaming. Regardless of the reason, their inattentiveness hampers learning.
- Monitor the student closely and keep him or her on task. When you realize that the student's attention is drifting, remind him or her to focus on the topic at hand. You might ask the student a question that regains his or her attention.
- Position the student's desk near the front of the room, closer to yours so that you can monitor him or her more easily.
- When you circulate around the classroom, stop at the student's desk to make sure he or she is focused on work. Offer praise when appropriate.
- When organizing groups, place this student with enthusiastic students who will draw him or her into the activity.
- Design instruction to appeal to this student's learning preferences. For example, if he or she is a kinesthetic learner, a hands-on activity is likely to hold his or her interest.
- If the student continues to be inattentive in class, contact his or her parents or guardians to discuss the problem.

Talking Excessively

- Most students like to talk. Some, however, talk excessively and can disturb other students.
- Do not tolerate excessive talking in your classroom, especially when you are teaching.
- When necessary, remind students to stay on task by saying, "Excuse me, we need to concentrate on our work." Simple reminders like this can refocus a student's attention.
- Place the seats of the excessive talkers in your class close to your desk where you can monitor their behavior. Avoid seating them near students who may serve as an audience.
- When organizing groups, place the talkers with students who will remain focused on their assignment and not take part in unnecessary conversation.
- If necessary, speak with your talkers after school. Discuss how their talking disturbs others and disrupts learning for themselves as well as the students who listen to them.
- For extreme cases, contact parents or guardians to discuss the problem.

Copyright © 2010 by Gary Robert Muschla, Judith A. Muschla, and Erin Muschla

Talking Out of Turn

- Unlike the excessive talker who engages in random, off-task conversation, the student who talks out of turn is often on-task but prone to interrupt you or other students.

- Although these students may be quite enthusiastic, they can easily dominate and disrupt discussions. You must rein them in.

- Have clear rules about speaking in turn, for example, raising one's hand and being called on before speaking. Explain the rules and make certain that students understand them.

- When a student interrupts you or other students, remind him or her of the classroom's rules for talking in turn. For some students, you will need to remind them of this frequently.

- Be sure to call on this student during discussions and activities; however, be careful not to call on him or her so much that you are ignoring others.

Asking to Leave the Class Frequently

- If permitted, some students would spend more time out of class at the water fountain, the lavatory, or simply walking the halls than they would spend in class. While you should never deny a request of a student to go the lavatory for an emergency, you must control the number of times students leave class.

- Establish clear rules for leaving class, based on your school's policies.

- Consider using a class "Sign-Out Sheet." A sign-out sheet is useful for recording times and places students go. Periodically review the sheet to find if any students are leaving class too often.

- When students request to leave class often, speak with them about the importance of not missing class time.

- Do not excuse students from work because they were out of class.

- Consult the school nurse about any students who ask to use the lavatory excessively; the student may have a health issue. If there is no disorder, speak to the student about his or her frequent requests to use the lavatory.

- If necessary, speak to the student's parents or guardians.

Note Passing

- Students who are writing and passing notes are not paying attention to their work. Their learning, as well as the learning of others, is undermined.

- Confiscate any notes students are passing. Avoid opening or reading them, however. Not only are they technically the student's property, but they may contain embarrassing information that you will then have to address.

- As you circulate around the room, watch for note passing and closely monitor students you suspect of passing notes. Students are less likely to try to pass notes when you are nearby.

Copyright © 2010 by Gary Robert Muschla, Judith A. Muschla, and Erin Muschla

Copyright © 2010 by Gary Robert Muschla, Judith A. Muschla, and Erin Muschla

List 6.23   continued

- Speak with habitual note passers after school. Explain that passing notes interferes with their learning, as well as the learning of the receivers of the notes.
- For serious instances of note passing, contact the student's parents or guardians and discuss the problem.

Seeking Attention

- Some students seek attention. They may feel ignored at home and act in a manner that will gain your notice and the notice of their classmates. They may speak out of turn, ask irrelevant questions, sharpen a pencil during a lesson, or make sounds or jokes. They want to be noticed.
- Do not tolerate disruptive behavior, for this will embolden the attention seeker.
- Respond to the behavior promptly, and enforce your class rules.
- Do not discuss the behavior during class, as not only will you be giving the student your attention, but the other students will give him their attention as well.
- Speak to the student after school about his behavior. Explain that it undermines learning, both for him or her and other students.
- Provide opportunities for the student to be noticed—for example, being the spokesperson for a group, handing out flyers for home, or collecting materials.
- Praise the student when he or she demonstrates appropriate behavior.

Not Following Directions

- There are many ways a student may not follow directions. The student may not write down his or her assignments; he or she may not put materials back in their proper places when finished with them; the student may simply ignore your request to do what you ask. For your class to run smoothly, students must follow your directions.
- When you give oral directions, speak slowly and clearly to give students time to process the information. Written directions must also be clear. When writing on the board, avoid making your letters too small or squeezing words together. Highlight important points with colored chalk or markers.
- Encourage your students to ask you if they do not understand something.
- When students fail to follow directions, simply remind them to complete what you asked them to do. If necessary, explain the directions again to make sure they understand what is expected of them.

Gum Chewing, Eating, or Drinking in Class

- Many students enjoy chewing gum, eating candy, or sipping water or fruit juices in class. If you have a snack period and students keep their snacks in their desks, the temptation for snacking before snack time can be great. Chewing gum, eating, or drinking in class, however, can be distracting and messy.

- Establish clear rules regarding food in your classroom. For example, do not allow your students to chew gum, which inevitably winds up on the floor, stuck to desks, and waiting on someone's chair. Also do not allow your students to drink or eat candy or other junk foods. Enforce the rules consistently.

- If your class has a snack time, emphasize to your students that snacks can only be eaten during snack time. (The exception is the child who is permitted to eat food because of a medical condition.) Snack time should last only a few minutes.

- Set rules for eating and drinking during snack time in accordance with your school's policies. Send a letter home to parents and guardians explaining your requirements for snack time. Consider the following examples:
  - Students should bring healthy snacks to school (no junk food).
  - Beverages should be juice or water. (Students should not bring glass bottles.)
  - Students should bring napkins (although you should have extras on hand).
  - Students should not eat their snacks near computers, printers, or other equipment.
  - Students must clean up after themselves, putting all bags, wrappers, napkins, and so on in the trash. Plastic bottles should be recycled.

Using Technology Inappropriately

- Even young students today are familiar with technology such as computers, printers, and calculators. They should be expected to use technology in class properly.

- Establish rules for using technology in your classroom, based on the technology policies of your school.

- Provide clear instructions for using technology in class. For example, computers should be turned on and off correctly and should be used only for class activities. Students should not visit unauthorized Web sites or check e-mail.

- Circulate around the room when students use technology. Monitor their use of equipment and offer guidance as necessary.

- In cases where students misuse technology, correct them and explain what they did wrong.

- In the case of malfunctioning equipment, instruct students to tell you immediately. This allows you to check the problem, which might be easy to fix, or arrange for the tech person in your school to correct the problem.

Sleeping in School

- Sometimes students may fall asleep in class. They may not feel well, they may be taking doctor-prescribed medicine, or they may be staying up too late at night. Whatever the cause, these students are not learning and are a distraction to others.

Copyright © 2010 by Gary Robert Muschla, Judith A. Muschla, and Erin Muschla

Copyright © 2010 by Gary Robert Muschla, Judith A. Muschla, and Erin Muschla

List 6.23   continued

- Never allow a student to sleep in class. Gently wake the student and send him or her to the nurse. Do not ask another student to wake him or her, for this will only cause amusement and greater disruption.

- Try to find out why the student was sleeping in class. If he or she is taking medication, it is likely that the school nurse will contact his or her parents or guardians. Perhaps the dosage needs to be adjusted. If the student is tired because he or she stayed up too late, speak to the student about the importance of his or her school work and encourage him or her to go to sleep earlier.

- Contact the student's parents or guardians to discuss the problem and enlist their support.

Saying Inappropriate Words and Comments

- Students sometimes say inappropriate words and make inappropriate comments in school. They may speak with profanities, hurl racial slurs, or make sexual references. Such words are offensive, disturbing, and hurtful.

- Never accept profanity or distasteful comments in your classroom.

- Respond calmly to inappropriate words and comments. Explain to the student that what he or she said was offensive. It is disrespectful to you and others. Be clear: Such language is unacceptable.

- Be attuned to the feelings of other students, particularly those at whom the remarks were aimed. Do not allow any student to verbally ridicule or harass others.

- If necessary, contact the student's parents or guardians to discuss the problem. In extreme cases, refer the student to an administrator.

Talking Back

- You should not permit any student to talk back to you. Students must recognize your authority in the classroom and treat you with respect.

- In the case of a student talking back to you, remain calm and say: "I must have heard you incorrectly." A comment such as this allows the student to think about his or her initial response and back away from a potential major conflict with you.

- Never argue with a student. If a student attempts to argue with you, take him or her into the hall where you can speak privately. (Keep in mind, however, that you are legally responsible for your other students, and you should position yourself so that you can continue monitoring the class.)

- Speak to the student after school and explain that you cannot allow him or her to disobey you or disturb the class. Tell the student that you are willing to listen to him or her, but that he or she must speak to you in a respectful manner.

- Contact the parents or guardians of students who continue to talk back. If necessary, refer the student to an administrator.

Using Cell Phones

- Although very young students may not have cell phones, many elementary students do. Cell phones can be a distraction in class as students quietly send text messages to each other, access games, or surf the Internet.

- Since it is likely your school has a strict policy regarding cell phones, be sure to explain the rules to your students. In many districts, students are not allowed to have cell phones in school. For others, if students have a cell phone (some parents or guardians may insist that their children be allowed to have phones in case of an emergency), they must keep the phones in their knapsacks or book bags. Policy may require you to confiscate the cell phones of students who use them in class.

- Explain your school's cell phone policy to parents and guardians at back-to-school night. Emphasize that you are required to enforce the school's polices.

- If you must confiscate a student's cell phone, keep it safe and give it to an administrator as soon as possible. Complete any paperwork regarding the phone.

- Avoid using your cell phone in front of your students. They will surely question why you can use yours but they cannot use theirs.

Cheating

- Cheating is a dishonest act. Other students become resentful of cheaters, who they recognize are receiving credit for work that was not done and earning grades that were not deserved. They know that cheating is wrong, yet the cheater seems to benefit.

- Follow and enforce your school's policies on cheating. Explain the policy to your students.

- Emphasize that cheating is dishonest, on the part of the cheater and any person who allows him or her to copy work or answers.

- Never accuse a student of cheating unless you have solid proof. Even then, avoid accusing a student in front of the class, which will likely result in a strong denial. Speak to the student after school and show him or her your proof. Confronted with proof in this manner, it is hard for a cheater to deny his or her actions.

- To discourage cheating, monitor your students closely, particularly during tests and quizzes. Circulate around the room, and pause near the desks of students you suspect might be cheating. Consider changing a few problems and handing out slightly different tests to alternate rows of students. For homework and class work, always require students to write answers in complete sentences, and show their work for math problems. Such requirements make copying more difficult.

Stealing

- Stealing is a serious matter in any school. It is often easier to take steps to prevent stealing than to deal with theft once it has been committed.

Copyright © 2010 by Gary Robert Muschla, Judith A. Muschla, and Erin Muschla

- Encourage your students to keep track of their possessions. They should not leave valuable items on their desks or around the classroom.

- Never leave your personal belongings, such as your purse, keys, flash drive, or grade book, in open view unattended.

- Place any money you collect in a locked drawer or cabinet; hand the money in to the office as soon as possible.

- Do not allow students to go into your desk drawers.

- Always lock your classroom when you leave.

- If a student tells you that an item was stolen, first make certain that it has not simply been misplaced. Suggest that the student check his or her backpack, desk, coat, and so on. Most things thought to be stolen are found after a thorough search.

- If an item is stolen, announce to the class that the item is missing. Do not say it was stolen. Ask if anyone might have borrowed it without asking, or picked it up by mistake. Often, someone will just happen to find the item. If the item remains missing, explain that if anyone finds and returns it later, you will appreciate their efforts at finding it and not ask any questions.

- Valuable items that are not returned require the involvement of an administrator. Contact your administrator and, if possible, do not allow students to leave the room until he or she arrives, at which point the administrator will assume management of the problem.

- Should you catch a student stealing, follow your school's policy, which most likely will require you to refer the incident directly to an administrator.

Fighting

- Anger and extreme frustration on the parts of students can sometimes lead to fighting. To prevent students from injuring each other, you must act quickly.

- Call the office or send a student for an administrator or another teacher for assistance immediately.

- Attempt to calm the students who are fighting.

- Tell the other students to keep safely out of the way of the fight.

- Be sure to follow your school's policy regarding fighting. In many school districts, teachers are discouraged from trying to physically stop a fight between students. In the case of a student being hurt because of your actions—even if you stop him from hurting another student—you can be held liable. Moreover, you yourself may be injured.

- Call or send for the school nurse if students are injured.

- Be sure to complete any required forms or reports about the fight.

Did you know? Preventing as much inappropriate behavior as possible and addressing instances of inappropriate behavior promptly, effectively, and fairly are critical factors in managing discipline in your classroom.

Copyright © 2010 by Gary Robert Muschla, Judith A. Muschla, and Erin Muschla

List 6.24   Useful Web Sites for Teachers

The Internet is a vast, almost limitless source of information. In the following list, we have included some Web sites that we have no doubt you will find helpful to your program. *Note*: Many of these sites provide links to other useful sites.

Language Arts

- Bookhive, http://www.plcm.org/bookhive (information about children's books and authors; book reviews)
- I Love Language, www.ilovelanguage.com (language translator)
- International Reading Association, www.reading.org (provides support for reading teachers)
- National Council of Teachers of English (NCTE), www.ncte.org (organization devoted to the support of teaching and learning of language arts)
- Web English Teacher, http://webenglishteacher.com (information, activities, and lesson plans for reading and language arts teachers)
- Yahoo!'s Babel Fish, http://babelfish.yahoo.com (language translator)

Math

- About Mathematics, www.math.about.com (information, lesson plans, and resources for math teachers)
- Convert Me, www.convert-me.com (measurement conversions)
- Figure This!, www.figurethis.org/teacher_corner.htm (various materials, resources, and handouts, including family activities)
- Math.com, www.math.com (lesson plans, resources, and activities)
- National Council of Teachers of Mathematics (NCTM), www.nctm.org (organization devoted to the teaching and learning of mathematics)
- National Library of Virtual Manipulatives, www.nlvm.usu.edu (virtual manipulatives for all grade levels)
- The Math Forum, www.mathforum.org (professional development, problems of the week, math questions and answers, and more)

Science

- Cool Science for Curious Kids, http://www.hhmi.org/coolscience (information and activities about plants and animals)
- Discovery Channel School, http://school.discovery.com/index.html (multimedia, interactive options for the classroom, with content linked to the programming of the Discovery Channel and the Learning Channel)
- Electronic Zoo, http://netvet.wustl.edu/ssi.htm (resources and links useful for studying animals)
- National Science Teachers Association, www.nsta.org (provides support for science teachers)

Copyright © 2010 by Gary Robert Muschla, Judith A. Muschla, and Erin Muschla

Copyright © 2010 by Gary Robert Muschla, Judith A. Muschla, and Erin Muschla

List 6.24   continued

- NASA Observatorium, http://observe.ivv.nasa.gov (excellent site for the study of space, geared to young students)
- NASA's Planetary Photojournal, http://photojournal.jpl.nasa.gov (over one thousand images of space)
- On Line Coloring Book for Endangered Species, http://biology.usgs.gov/features/kidscorner/index.html (coloring pages for many endangered animals)
- Volcano World, http://volcano.oregonstate.edu/education/index.html (information on volcanoes)

Social Studies

- Color Landform Atlas of the United States, http://fermi.jhuapl.edu/states.html (information and maps of the fifty states)
- Flags, http://www.flags.net (flags and information about the countries of the world)
- National Council for Geographic Education, www.ncge.org (provides support for geography teachers)
- National Geographic Kids, http://www.nationalgeographic.com/kids (engaging site for students, based on the content of National Geographic)
- Smithsonian's History Explorer, http://historyexplorer.americanhistory.si.edu/index.asp (comprehensive site with vast resources, information, and activities)

Of Special Interest to Teachers

- Best Web Quests, www.bestwebquests.com (Web quests on numerous topics)
- Class Notes Online, www.classnotesonline.com (information for creating and posting a classroom Web page)
- Education World, www.educationworld.com (extensive information, including standards for subjects and grades by state)
- Grade Book Wizard, www.gradebookwizard.com (electronic grade book)
- Internet 4 Classrooms, www.internet4classrooms.com (information and help for teachers in various subjects)
- Learning-Styles-Online, www.learningstyles-online.com (comprehensive information on the learning styles of students)

List 6.24   continued

- Kathy Schrock's Guide for Education, http://school.discovery.com/schrockguide (vast guide for information and links in various subject areas)
- My Grade Book, www.mygradebook.com (electronic grade book)
- School Notes, www.schoolnotes.com (information for creating and posting a classroom Web page)
- Sites for Teachers, www.sitesforteachers.com (extensive links on information, activities, and links to sites on numerous subjects)
- Teachnology, www.teach-nology.com (contains information, lesson plans, and activities for numerous subjects and topics)
- U.S. Department of Education, www.ed.gov (comprehensive site containing information on various topics in education)

Did you know? Many Web sites update their content regularly, and you should visit them often.

Copyright © 2010 by Gary Robert Muschla, Judith A. Muschla, and Erin Muschla

At the end of the school year, you should complete a self-appraisal, focusing on your skills in carrying out your overall responsibilities as a teacher, managing your classroom, planning effective lessons, and delivering instruction to your students. Answering the questions that follow can help you grow in all areas of teaching, and help you make your class interesting, productive, and rewarding for your students. If you answer "No" to any of the questions, ask yourself how you can improve this area for next year.

- Did I create a safe, positive, and appealing environment for learning?
- Did I establish and consistently and fairly enforce practical classroom rules and procedures?
- Did I maintain appropriate standards for behavior?
- While being demanding in my expectations, was I also considerate of the individual needs of my students?
- Did I design lessons to meet the academic standards at my grade level?
- Did I satisfy the objectives of my curriculum in each subject?
- Did I plan interesting lessons and provide instruction that satisfied the needs of different learning styles?
- Did I encourage my students to assume responsibility for learning and help them become independent learners?
- Did I provide activities for the whole class, groups, and individuals?
- Did I encourage and respond to students' questions?
- Did I provide activities that require critical thinking?
- Were my methods of evaluation and assessment fair and consistent?
- Did I satisfy the requirements of the IEPs and 504 plans of my students?
- Did I foster the development of social skills in my students?
- Did I continue to grow professionally by attending faculty meetings, in-services, and workshops?
- Did I build on my strengths as a teacher and work to improve my weaknesses?
- Did I maintain positive relationships with colleagues and administrators?
- Did I nurture and maintain positive relationships with parents and guardians?
- Did I encourage parents and guardians to support their children's learning by offering them suggestions and guidance?
- Did I support my school's PTA and assume a positive rule in my school community?

 Did you know? Honest self-appraisal is the first step toward self-improvement.

Copyright © 2010 by Gary Robert Muschla, Judith A. Muschla, and Erin Muschla